CHURCH
IN THE
BARRIO

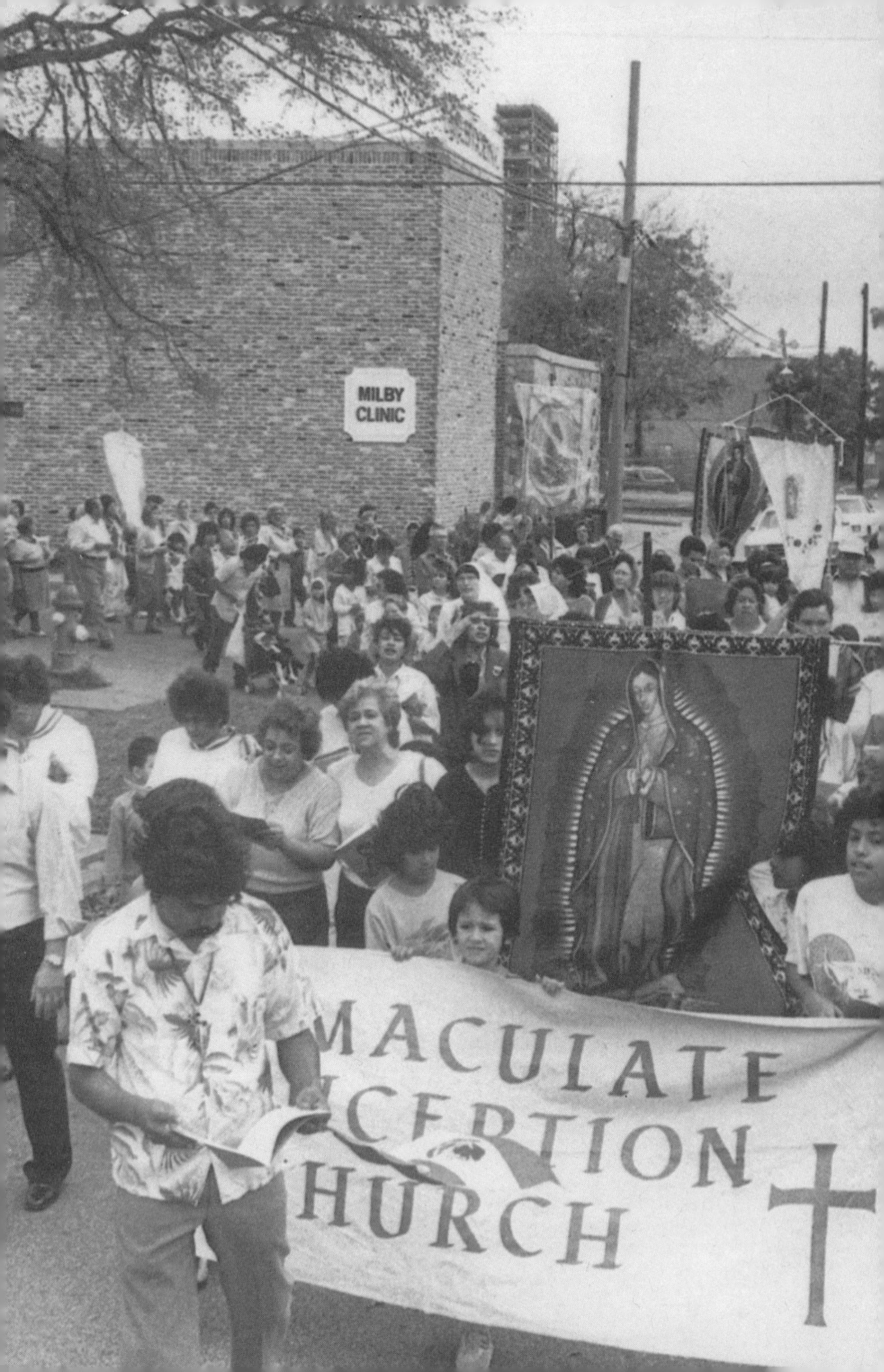
MILBY
CLINIC
MACULATE
NCERTION
HURCH

THE CHURCH IN THE BARRIO

Mexican American
Ethno-Catholicism
in Houston

Roberto R. Treviño

THE UNIVERSITY OF
NORTH CAROLINA PRESS
CHAPEL HILL

Designed by Rebecca M. Giménez
Set in Monotype Dante
by Keystone Typesetting, Inc.

The paper in this book meets the guidelines for permanence and
durability of the Committee on Production Guidelines for Book
Longevity of the Council on Library Resources.

Library of Congress Cataloging-in-Publication Data
Treviño, Roberto R.
The church in the barrio : Mexican American ethno-Catholicism
in Houston / Roberto R. Treviño.
p. cm.
Includes bibliographical references and index.
ISBN-13: 978-0-8078-2996-7 (cloth: alk. paper)
ISBN-10: 0-8078-2996-x (cloth: alk. paper)
ISBN-13: 978-0-8078-5667-3 (pbk.: alk. paper)
ISBN-10: 0-8078-5667-3 (pbk.: alk. paper)
1. Church work with Mexican Americans—Texas—Houston.
2. Catholic Church—Texas—Houston—History. 3. Houston (Tex.)—
Church history. I. Title.
BV4468.2.M48T74   2006
282'.7641411'08968—dc22   2005022338

cloth   10 09 08 07 06   5 4 3 2 1
paper   10 09 08 07 06   5 4 3 2 1

Portions of this work have appeared, in somewhat different form,
in Roberto R. Treviño, "Facing Jim Crow: Catholic Sisters and the
'Mexican Problem' in Texas," *Western Historical Quarterly* 34, no. 2
(Summer 2003): 139–64 (© Western History Association; reprinted by
permission); and "In Their Own Way: Parish Funding and Mexican-
American Ethnicity in Catholic Houston, 1911–1972," *Latino Studies
Journal* 5 (September 1994): 87–107 (reprinted by permission).

Para mis padres,

GERÓNIMO R. TREVIÑO (1920–1995)

and

HILARIA R. TREVIÑO,

mis primeros y mejores maestros

CONTENTS

Illustrations

PREFACE

I grew up in a very Catholic culture, even though I am not Catholic. I spent my early childhood in Mathis, a speck on the rural landscape of the South Texas Gulf Coast, where almost everyone was Mexican and Catholic. My Presbyterian parents' home was next door to my Catholic grandparents, within walking distance of several aunts, uncles, and cousins—all Catholic—and almost literally surrounded by Mexican American Catholic friends and acquaintances. Six days of every week I lived and played in a largely Catholic world; alongside my brothers, my Catholic cousins were my best friends and constant companions, my Catholic grandparents, aunts, and uncles a source of knowledge, emotional succor, delicious food, and entertainment. But on Sundays we went our separate ways. They went to Mass (however infrequently, I noted jealously) and we unfailingly attended services either at the local Menonite Church or at our *Iglesia Presbiteriana Mexicana* in what seemed to be faraway Beeville, some thirty miles down the highway. Later, in Houston, Mexican American Catholicism would also permeate much of my social and professional life. Indeed it still does.

Growing up as a minority within a minority, I compared myself and my mother's Protestant side of our family to my father's Catholic side, and wondered about that familiar yet foreign world that enveloped me. As a child I never entered a Catholic church but I distinctly recall wondering what it would be like to go inside. My Catholic family's religious world remained mysterious to me despite the familiarity it came to have for me through all I experienced of it as a child—the flickering votive candles casting a warm glow on pictures of relatives and saints; the ever-present *Guadalupana* gracing calendars year after year; and the occasional gentle teasing that reminded us we were the *aleluyas* (Protestants) of the Treviño clan. None of this difference and mystery mattered much to me as a child—we were all family and friends, all simply *mexicanos*. But as an adult I became increasingly intrigued by Catholicism's pervasiveness and potency in my people's history and culture. I sensed that this religiosity that had always been everywhere around and so close to me was at the core of the Mexican American experience; I wanted to know how this could be. This book is the result of those long-gestating ruminations. Reflecting on how I have tried to understand my family and my people through their religious history, I realize that I have been working on this book for a very long time.

Many people helped me write this book. The project began as a doctoral dissertation at Stanford University, where a Mellon Fellowship in the Humanities, a Ford Dissertation Fellowship, and the Department of History's Fellows Program generously funded six years of graduate study. I also benefited greatly from two postdoctoral opportunities, the Pew Program in Religion and American History at Yale University and the Young Scholars in American Religion Program at Indiana University–Purdue University at Indianapolis. I am grateful to these organizations for helping me become a historian.

The professionalism and patience of many archivists, librarians, and women and men of the Catholic Church greatly facilitated my research. At the Archives of the Oblate Fathers of Mary Immaculate in San Antonio, the late Father William Watson and his assistants, Gladys Novak and Gloria Pantoja, led me to a wealth of information. Sister Mary Paul Valdez and the late Sister Theresa Joseph Powers provided many useful documents and oral history leads at the Archives of the Congregation of the Sisters of Divine Providence, San Antonio. Brother Michael Grace likewise made useful suggestions and pointed me to important materials during my visit to the Archives of Loyola University of Chicago. I am grateful to Bishop Joseph A. Fiorenza for access to the Archives of the Diocese of Galveston-Houston, to Monsignor Daniel Scheel, who facilitated my research at the Galveston-Houston Chancery and in various parishes in Houston, and to Mary Acosta, Marion Zientek, Bob Giles, and Lisa May, who made my research in Houston very fruitful. I greatly appreciate Bishop John McCarthy's graciousness during my research at the Catholic Archives of Texas in Austin, his contagious enthusiasm for church history and politics, and his interest in my research. In Austin, archivists Michael Zilligen and the late Kinga Perzynska gave me invaluable help. The staff at the Stanford University libraries gave me crucial support, and I am particularly indebted to Sonia Moss. In Houston, Louis Marchiafava and his staff at the Houston Metropolitan Research Center were ever forthcoming and helpful, and I am especially grateful to my friend and respected colleague Dr. Thomas H. Kreneck, who opened many doors for me in the Bayou City and beyond and gave me generous and expert guidance. I am also greatly indebted to the parishioners who graciously opened their homes and hearts to me and taught me much about the Mexican American Catholic experience in Houston; without them this book would be much poorer.

Additionally, I have been blessed with the friendship and tutelage of outstanding individuals who have shaped my intellectual development and the writing of this book. My fellow Tejanos, Tatcho Mindiola, Arnoldo De León, and Tom Kreneck, have long been sources of encouragement and good counsel. Similarly, I was also helped along the way by such exemplars as Anne Butler, Clyde Milner, Neil Foley, Ramón Gutiérrez, James Kirby Martin, George Fredrickson, Renato Rosaldo, Jon Butler, Harry Stout, Philip Gleason, and my former colleagues in the Department of History at the University of Colorado at Colorado Springs, particularly Harlow Sheidley. At the University of Texas at Arlington my history department colleagues have been ever supportive, as have my colleagues at the Center for Mexican American Studies. I am especially thankful for those individuals who took time from their busy lives to comment on all or parts of the manuscript. Timothy M. Matovina's close and repeated readings of the entire manuscript provided challenging questions that significantly improved my work. Others, including Rudy Busto, John McGreevy, Arnoldo De León, Gilberto Hinojosa, Jay P. Dolan, and Christian Zlolniski, also generously shared their time and wisdom to help me strengthen this book. For his steadying influence early in my career and unfailing support over the years I am grateful to my friend and mentor, Professor Albert M. Camarillo. My sincere thanks also go to senior editor Charles Grench and his fine staff. I will be ever grateful for Chuck's crucial encouragement and guidance, and for the skill and professionalism shown by the individuals at UNC Press who helped bring this work to fruition.

Most of all it is my anchor in life, *mi familia*, that deserves much of the credit for this book. I thank my brothers and sisters for their encouragement, and my sons, Robert André and Samuel Benjamin, for their special inspiration. My wife, Barbara, sustained me throughout the peaks and valleys of this work with constant good humor and enthusiasm; her role in writing this book was immensurable. My most profound thanks, of course, are reserved for my first and most important teachers, *mis padres*, Hilaria and Gerónimo Treviño, for a lifetime of unconditional love.

The Church in the Barrio

Map 1. The Vicinity of Houston, 1929

Introduction

ith nervous anticipation, nineteen-year-old Angie García and two friends drove toward the city of Harlingen in the Rio Grande Valley of South Texas. They were on their way to enroll in a technical training course, betting it would bring exciting new adventures into their young lives. Yet even as important as it was to arrive on time at their appointment, the threesome just *had* to make one stop along the way—at the town of San Juan, Texas. San Juan is home to the famous Shrine of the Virgin of San Juan del Valle, a popular pilgrimage site for Mexican American Catholics modeled after the seventeenth-century shrine of the Virgen de San Juan de los Lagos located in Jalisco, Mexico. "As surely as they must breathe air to live," a newspaper reported, "they must first pray and ask the help of the Virgin Mary as they take a new step in their lives."[1]

On the same page of that newspaper, another article described a common scene at the older shrine in Jalisco, Mexico. There "thousands—sometimes tens of thousands of people—crawl, pray, weep and hold infants aloft . . . in the suffocating heat," as they "work their way inch-by-inch up the aisles and, at long last, kneel reverently before the image of the Virgin Mary." Marveling at the sight of the faithful in Jalisco, a cleric remarked, "Everyone who sees this can, at the very least, begin to understand faith."[2]

Understanding Mexican American Ethno-Catholicism

But how are we to understand this faith? How can we begin to appreciate its importance to Mexican Americans today—people like Angie

García and her friends in South Texas, for example? How do we fathom its meaning among the legions of Mexican faithful who, year after year, trek to the seventeenth-century shrine in Jalisco? And how can we understand the mystical bond that connects Mexican and Mexican American Catholics in different places and times? In short, how can we understand the role of Catholicism in Mexican American history? These are timely questions when we consider that today Latinos comprise more than one-third of that faith tradition and very soon roughly half of all U.S. Catholics will be Latinos. "The U.S. Catholic Church is being inexorably transformed into a Latino church," a prominent cleric recently observed. "That presents an interesting challenge to the historically Anglo-dominated church in the United States, which does not respond to another style of Catholicism that is more graphic and expressive."[3] For many Americans, Mexicans evoke images of fervent Catholicism. Indeed, many people automatically associate "Mexican American" with "Catholic" and would readily agree that Catholicism has played an important role in Mexican American history, as the conventional wisdom has long assumed. But precisely *how* has that importance revealed itself in the Mexican American experience? That is the driving question behind this book. *The Church in the Barrio* offers some answers to that question. Based on the history of Mexican American Catholics in Houston, it examines some of the ways this faith has shaped Chicano history.[4]

Throughout this book I use the term "ethno-Catholicism" to refer to the Mexican American way of being Catholic. As a result of Spain's encounter with the New World, pre-Reformation Spanish Christianity blended with Mexican Indian worldviews to produce a unique Mexican Catholic identity and way of life. Mexican Americans in Texas and the Southwest carried on this ethnoreligion that, in the spirit of its medieval and Indian roots, made room for faith healing and other practices deemed superstitious by clergy; favored saint veneration, home altar worship, and community-centered religious celebration that blurred the line between the sacred and the secular; and tended simultaneously to selectively participate in the institutional Catholic

Church yet hold it at arm's length. Ethno-Catholicism was essentially countercultural, as it represented an "organic, holistic worldview . . . at odds with post-Enlightenment notions of time and space, of the material and the spiritual, and of the person's place within time and space, within the material and spiritual dimensions of reality."[5]

The Church in the Barrio refutes the notion that this so-called popular Catholicism was (is) an inferior expression of spirituality. Despite the fact that I show how clergy often denigrated Mexicans' way of being Catholic and how Mexicans doggedly clung to it, I do not rigidly juxtapose the institution's religion against the people's. Framing religious experience as dichotomies—"elite versus popular" or "folk versus formal" religion—may indeed reveal struggles between the powerful and the less powerful in a society, but it also distorts historical reality.[6] Such neat categories simply do not convey the complexities of the *interaction* that has characterized the relationship between the faithful and religious institutions. While tensions have certainly existed between Mexicans and the U.S. Catholic Church, historical evidence also suggests that this social distance has not been totally unbridgeable nor completely antagonistic; ethno-Catholicism is not the polar opposite of institutional Catholicism.[7] Rather, Mexicans in the United States have had an *interactive* relationship with the institutional church, one that at different historical moments has been characterized by varying degrees of resistance and accommodation.

I found a sensible framework for understanding the role of Catholicism in Mexican American history in cultural resistance theory and historical studies that explore the centrality of religion among African Americans and other "outsiders." Those familiar with the works of James C. Scott, Lawrence W. Levine, Eugene D. Genovese, Albert J. Raboteau, and R. Laurence Moore will see their influence in this book. In different ways, each of these scholars has cogently shown how people have relied on their faith traditions to resist oppression, define themselves, build communities, and thrive in hostile environments. The ideas of two anthropologists, Deborah Reed-Danahay's notion of French subalterns "making do" and Margaret A. Gibson's portrayal of "accommodation without assimilation" among Sikh immigrant students, also helped me understand how Mexican Catholics coped with pressures of social and religious assimilation in Houston.[8] As Reed-Danahay and Gibson have shown, it is important to distinguish between resistance and accommodation. Marginalized peoples who face pressures to assimilate choose from a range of responses when they confront threats to their identity and way of life. Some of their responses clearly are forms of outright resistance. However, ethno-religious minorities historically have also adopted other strategies, including cultural change or compromise, a mix of resistance and compromise, or various degrees of compliance. In other words, they have found ways of "making do" and have chosen "accommodation without assimilation" in addition to clear-cut resistance.[9]

Houston's Mexican and Mexican American Catholics, like other folks in history, responded in a variety of ways to the assimilation pressures exerted by U.S. society and the Catholic Church—and their faith was central to those responses. Catholic theologians are increasingly recognizing the importance of this aspect of Latino Catholicism. Historian and theologian Timothy Matovina observes that in the "continuing struggle with prejudice and cultural rejection, ethno-religious celebrations . . . reinforce group identity, engender a sense of belonging, and express a collective protest and resistance against the assimilatory demands of the dominant culture."[10] As Matovina's work has capably shown for the nineteenth century and as my book illustrates for the twentieth, Catholicism has long been a shaping force in the spiritual and material lives of Mexican Americans.

It is important to read this book as a social history. I did not set out to write a theological treatise on Mexican American Catholicism or to advance new theoretical frameworks with which to reconceptualize the study of Chicano history. Rather, the book is intended to show how a particular faith tradition, Mexican American ethno-Catholicism, historically has played an important role in the social arena. The Mexican American way of being Catholic is layered with historical meaning. Understanding this faith tradition not only allows us to appreciate those things usually associated with religion—devotional practices, attitudes toward the sacraments, patterns of church attendance, and so on—but, equally important, it also gives us insight into other aspects of Mexican American history. That is the main purpose of the book. I hope to show that by understanding ethno-Catholicism we can more fully understand the construction of ethnic identity, the formation of communities, the sources and processes of social change, the ways people find their place in a society, and some of the implications of gender relations—subjects that too often are studied without much attention given to the role of religion. Scholars in other disciplines may find *The Church in the Barrio* useful for their own purposes, but those seeking new models with which to understand Mexican American Catholicism per se should consult the writings of Virgilio Elizondo, Orlando Espín, Roberto Goizueta, and other such insightful theologians for epistemologically and methodologically distinct interpretations.[11]

But why study Houston? Part of the answer, of course, is that I wanted to know more about the place where I came of age and spent much of my life. Beyond that, though, I have long been struck by the inattention historians have shown to "new" Chicano communities, communities that are rooted in the twentieth century, not in the Spanish colonial and Mexican eras. Of course, we can never know enough about communities that were planted during the Spanish / Mexican past, and historians should continue to study them. But years ago when a friend asked with exasperation, "Do we really need another study of Chicanos in Los Angeles?" he was making an important point. For some time now a number of cities—Houston, Dallas, Denver, Phoenix, and others—have had numerically significant and culturally vibrant Mexican communities that developed during the twentieth century, but their history remains largely unknown to us. In particular, places like Houston and Dallas—situated as they are in the East Texas borderlands between South and West—invite comparison between the two, as well as with the more familiar communities located deeper in the Southwest from which we derive much of our current understanding about Mexican American history.

Houston's early Mexican immigrants truly encountered *terra incognita* upon arriving in the Bayou City. Very little looked or sounded familiar to them. Unlike San Antonio, Los Angeles, or Albuquerque, Houston had no Spanish or Mexican past—no missions, no familiar place names or village padres, no gentle reminders of home that could help ease the new residents' transition into a bewildering new environment. Established Mexican American communities offered advantages that life in Houston lacked, such as the comfort and security of fellow Mexicans in large numbers and the social and religious networks and institutions that came with them. For Mexicans who immigrated to Houston in the early twentieth century, life was complicated by the absence of an established Mexican presence that required them to transplant and develop anew—not simply reconnect with—the cultural underpinnings of their lives. Surely this would have been more difficult to do in Houston than in the more familiar and supportive surroundings of long-established Mexican communities. In these circumstances, some aspects of religious life took on added significance, especially the kinds of customs I examine in this book that were equally social and religious and promoted a sense of community and security. In a place like Houston, the lived religion of the people of necessity cemented faith, family, identity, and community in ways that were more conscious than in the familiar atmosphere of a deeply rooted Mexican community. This is not to devalue Catholicism in older places. We know, for example, that in San Antonio, home of the Alamo, Tejanos countered inequality partly by claiming legitimacy in the region on religious grounds.[12] Rather, it is simply to remind us that the Chicano experience has not been monolithic, either in terms of region or religion, and that we should be alert to the nuances the interaction of these two factors may produce. How the relative importance of ethno-Catholicism in older versus newer Mexican American communities will be borne out awaits the findings of historians willing to use religion as a vantage point from which to examine Chicano history. For certainly our vision of the past will remain skewed without studying those new Chicano communities and their religious history.

The Church in the Barrio unfolds during the years 1911–72. I focus on this time frame because it forms a discrete part of the history of Houston's Mexican American community in at least two ways. In the social and political history of the community, these years encompass its immigrant beginnings to its maturation as a predominately native-born population at the height of the Chicano movement. That era would then be followed by a new phase as the liberal politics of the civil rights era gave way to conservatism, and immigration from other parts of Latin America raised the profile of non-Mexican Latinos in the city beginning in the early 1970s. The years 1911–72 also bracket a distinct phase of the *religious* history of Mexican Americans in Houston. The year 1911 marks the beginning of a Roman Catholic institutional presence in Houston's barrios with the arrival of the Oblates of Mary Immaculate, the missionary priests brought to the city by the Galveston Diocese (renamed the Galveston-Houston Diocese in 1959) to minister specifically to the growing Mexican population. At the other end of this time frame, the year 1972 signals the participation of lay and church leaders from Houston in the Encuentro Hispano de Pastoral (Pastoral Congress for the Spanish-speaking). That national event stands as a watershed in the religious history of Mexican American Catholics in Houston and the United States and is a logical ending point for the story of *The Church in the Barrio*.

In trying to understand some of the ways Catholicism molded the Mexican American experience in Houston, I was guided by two interrelated questions: What has been the nature of the relationship between Mexican Americans and the Catholic Church in the United States? And what role did Catholicism play in Mexican Americans' everyday lives? These broad questions raised others. How did representatives of the Catholic Church view Mexican people, and what effects did their perceptions and attitudes have on the spiritual and material life of Mexican Catholics? Part of this study analyzes how priests' and nuns' attitudes toward Mexicans affected the church's relationship with the Mexican American community. I also explore how Mexicans themselves viewed institutional requirements and the women and men who represented the Roman Catholic Church. In this regard, I show how generation, class, culture, and gender differences influenced the parishioners' religious expression and their association with the church. I was also interested in shedding light on how Catholicism was (is) related to the formation of Mexican American ethnicity, to community-building, and to notions of social justice. To reveal some of those relationships I examine, for example, *altarcitos* (home altars), *quinceañeras* (fifteen-year-olds' rite of passage), and other traditions that were both religious and social, customs that helped to mold identity and propagate strong communities. I also show how Mexicans pressed the church not only to minister to their spiritual lives but also to support their struggles for equality and a better material life.

I use both chronological and topical chapters to tell the story of *The Church in the Barrio*. Chapter 1 sketches the evolution of Mexican Catholicism from Spanish colonial times to the early twentieth century. Given their isolation and the weak institutional presence of the Roman Catholic Church in the Southwest, Spanish and Mexican Catholics in Texas developed an ethnoreligious identity rooted in home- and community-based religious practices. That ethno-Catholic way of life kept the faith alive while it celebrated their cultural heritage and helped them endure a harsh frontier existence and the social and political changes that buffeted their lives. This brand of Catholicism defined itself against (and often found itself in conflict with) the Euro-American Catholicism that accompanied the American takeover of Mexican Texas in the nineteenth century. The rest of this chapter completes the historical backdrop for the book by tracing the development of Houston's Mexican *colonias* (communities) from the nineteenth century to the early 1970s. In a city predicated on a Southern Protestant ethos, Mexican Catholics competed for cultural space not only with the Anglo majority, which included various groups of white Catholics, but also with a large black population and a Mexican Protestant presence as well.

Chapter 2 dissects the concept of ethno-Catholicism in order to illustrate its central place in this Catholic community history. A blend of the religious worldviews and practices of Old World Spanish Christians and New World Indians, Mexican ethno-Catholicism combined selective participation in formal church activities with a vibrant lived religion that prized family- and community-centered traditions. A religious style that blurred the line between the sacred and the secular and gave singular expression to the people's identity, this ethnoreligion reflected and sustained the cultural independence of Mexican American Catholics and their resistance to social inequality. Within the institutional framework, they participated in the sacraments of the Roman Catholic Church and in its organizations, but they often did so on their own terms. Similarly, keeping alive popular traditions frowned upon by church representatives allowed Mexican Catholics to assert their personal worth, confront inequality, and maintain viable families and communities.

Chapter 3 examines church representatives' perceptions of Texas Mexicans, how and why these changed over time, and the implications these shifting attitudes had for Mexican American communities. Relations between Mexicans and the church in Houston during most of the twentieth century were distant, reflecting both deeply rooted negative views held by many Catholic officials about Texas Mexicans and the parishioners' traditional ambivalence toward the institution. Nonetheless, the relationship improved over time partly because of positive attitudinal changes that developed among Catholic officials but more so because of pressures exerted by Mexicans and Mexican Americans. Their burgeoning presence and increasing political activity captured the church's attention. From the 1910s to the early 1970s, representatives of the Galveston-Houston Diocese gradually but unevenly gained a deeper understanding of Mexican-origin people and their style of Catholicism, thus paving the way for a more effective pastoral and social ministry.

Chapter 4 examines religious institutional development in two ways. First, I document the spread of parishes in Houston's barrios, arguing that while the church provided more Spanish-speaking personnel and financial support to Mexican communities over time, it was the parishioners' own initiatives that laid the groundwork for actually establishing, maintaining, and expanding Catholic churches and schools in the barrios. The rest of this chapter discusses two types of parishes, territorial and national (the former bases membership on residence within defined boundaries, the latter on a common language or ethnicity).[13] Membership in one type of parish or the other revealed social distinctions among parishioners that reflected their varying notions about ethnic identity and found expression particularly in the degree of Spanish, English, or bilingual church services used and in the names given to the parishes themselves. Houston's inner-city parishes tended to be home to people who earned less money and had closer ties generationally to Mexico, while native-born Mexican Americans who could afford to move out of the barrios often formed their own parishes in predominately white or mixed neighborhoods, or integrated themselves into existing ones.

In a different way, Chapter 5 also deals with religious institutional growth. Here I focus on parish fund-raising in order to show its links to faith, identity, and community among Mexican American Catholics. Essentially, I argue that fund-raising was both a product and a process of ethno-Catholicism. In other words, the strategies used to generate money for the parishes not only drove institutional development but also promoted a sense of ethnic and religious identity and solidarity that preserved the Mexican American way of being Catholic. In order to illustrate the strong connection between fund-raising and ethno-Catholic identity, I present a case study I call the St. Joseph–St. Stephen controversy. Reacting to the forced merger of their *iglesia mexicana* (Mexican church) with an Anglo church as a threat to their identity and way of life, parishioners at St. Stephen Parish resisted the diocesan leadership until it restored their former status as an independent Mexican national parish.

Chapter 6 traces the changing nature of the church's social ministry among Mexican parishioners between the years 1911 and 1965, emphasizing both the Mexican community's traditional self-reliance and the church's shift from ad hoc relief to more systematic material aid for its parishioners. This chapter shows how individuals within the Catholic Church had concerned themselves early on with the material needs of Mexican parishioners while, at the same time, the Mexican community had its own self-help tradition to alleviate crises and combat persistent poverty in the barrios. Over the course of the twentieth century, however, the church's social ministry gradually expanded beyond ad hoc charity. Beginning in the 1940s, Catholic social ministry slowly became more systematic even as the charitable works by nuns, priests, and other compassionate individuals continued.

Chapter 7 carries the story of social ministry from the mid-1960s to the early 1970s by focusing on the role of the Catholic Church in the Chicano movement in Houston. I argue that the church's involvement in the Chicano movement, however tentative and cautious, was significant nonetheless and that it resulted from the convergence of changing clerical attitudes and internal and external pressures exerted by Chicanas and Chicanos. The Galveston-Houston Diocese responded to the Chicano movement on two levels, individual and institutional, and with various strategies, some of which were traditional and others new. While individual Chicana nuns and Chicano priests led struggles for social equality, the church as an institution avoided fully joining in the fray of secular politics directly, trying instead to nurture rather than initiate solutions to social problems through lay rather than clerical leadership. Eventually the pressures for change culminated in 1972 in an institutional response called the *encuentros*, a series of forums to air the grievances of Latino Catholics throughout the nation.

The Church in the Barrio argues that ethno-Catholicism was a nurturing way of life for Mexican Americans in Houston, one that sustained their sense of ethnic identity and provided ways of coping with their marginality in the Catholic Church and American society. Long considered second-class Americans and often treated as social pariahs, Texas Mexicans found in ethno-Catholicism the wherewithal to overcome the stigma associated with their ethnic and religious outsider status. Their faith helped mold and preserve the people's identity; it structured their family and community relationships and institutions; it provided them both spiritual and material sustenance; and it girded them in their long quest for social justice. Ethno-Catholicism played a central role in the ongoing Mexican American pilgrimage toward greater inclusion in the religious and civic life of the Bayou City.

THE BIG PICTURE: LATINOS AND U.S. CATHOLIC HISTORY

In 1970 a group of scholars decried the scarcity of literature about Chicanos and religion, claiming that "*no* literature exists on the role of the church among the Mexican American population."[14] That claim was somewhat overstated, but not by much. More puzzling, however, is the fact that more than three decades later the religious history of Mexican Americans remains understudied despite their long association with Catholicism and their growing importance in the American Catholic Church today. The recent flourishing of U.S. religious history and the growth of Chicano history notwithstanding, scholars remind us that we know relatively little about religion as a historical force in the Mexican American experience. There have been numerous important studies about Euro-American religion in recent years, but similar attention has yet to be given to Mexicans in the United States, even by historians of the Chicano experience.[15] Fortunately, in the mid-1990s two publications, *Mexican Americans and the Catholic Church, 1900–1965* and *Tejano Religion and Ethnicity: San Antonio, 1821–1860*, began to address the lack of in-depth historical studies about Mexican Americans and religion.[16] My study resonates with both of these pioneering works, particularly with Timothy Matovina's focus on the links between Catholicism and ethnic identity and community-building in *Tejano Religion and Ethnicity*. More recently some important studies, mostly in essay form, have added to the developing historical literature on Mexican American Catholicism.[17] *The Church in the Barrio*, however, is the first book-length treatment of the role of Catholicism in the history of a twentieth-century urban Mexican American community.

Scattered observations about Mexican American Catholicism reveal that the experiences of Latino Catholics outside of Texas have both mirrored and contrasted with those of Mexican Houstonians. The style of Mexican Catholicism that evolved in Texas developed in much the same way in Mexican communities throughout the American Southwest and Midwest, its main traits evidenced in its home- and community-centeredness, its mix of institutional marginality and fervent "popular" expression, and in the faith's centrality to the people's identity.[18] Puerto Rican and Cuban Catholics in the United States also shared commonalities with Mexican Americans as they, too, followed essentially a medieval Christianity modified by New World conditions.[19] However, alongside these similarities there were some differences, the most obvious and important of which was the African influence in Puerto Rican and Cuban society. *Mulataje*, the racial and cultural mixing of African and Iberian peoples, was much more pronounced in the Caribbean than in Mexico and the Southwest, where *mestizaje*, or Spanish and Indian mixing, predominated. This basic difference explains the historical presence of the African-derived religion, *Santería*, among Cuban Americans rather than Mexican Americans, as well as Puerto Rican devotion to Our Lady of Monserrate, the Black Madonna, in contrast to Mexican American fealty to Our Lady of Guadalupe, *la morenita*, or the brown (Indian) Virgin.[20] *Mulataje* figured prominently in the history of Puerto Ricans and Cubans within the American Church, as did *mestizaje* in the Mexican American experience. While Mexican-origin Catholics were saddled with a "pagan" Indian image, the largely negative perception of Puerto Ricans in the Northeast reflected the racism and color-consciousness that infected both the American church and society in general.

Racial prejudice was also an important, though not the only, reason behind the intensive Americanization efforts aimed at Latino Catholics.[21] Of course, Latinos held no special claim in this regard; the U.S. Church subjected numerous other Catholic groups—Germans, Poles, French-Canadians, and many others—to its Americanizing zeal before Latinos had their turn. Then, too, some aspects of Americanization had a positive side, particularly nationality parishes that were meant to be way stations to Americanization. Many European immigrants preferred their own segregated and relatively underfunded national parishes where they and "their kind" worshipped in Old World familiarity. Having successfully transplanted not only their beliefs but also important tangibles such as clergy, schools, and other resources to these ethnic islands, European newcomers to America made their national parishes havens of cultural continuity, sources of emotional strength, and, equally important, training grounds and springboards for upward social mobility.[22]

But here lies a fundamental difference between the European and Latino immigrant experiences. Mexican and Puerto Rican immigration was *not* accompanied by a large-scale transplantation of their own clergy and religious structures and resources. They thus lacked the kinds of support that most European immigrants used to soften incorporation into a new society.[23] In contrast, Cuban immigrants brought with them many clergy, and they transplanted a number of important religious schools and other organizations to Miami in their post-1959 migrations, much like European immigrants had done. Like Puerto Ricans, however, Cubans continued to see themselves as temporary sojourners in the United States, and they also clung to their religious identity and Cuban roots.[24]

Aside from the more obvious differences between Latino and Euro-American immigration experiences—that is, the nearness of Latin America and its ongoing immigration versus the distance of Europe and its subsiding immigration—two factors clearly set Latinos apart from most Euro-American Catholics: their mix of pre-Reformation Christianity and indigenous African and Indian religions, and their status as people of color in a race-sensitive society. Here, too, there is one important exception to note. As we shall see, Mexican ethno-Catholicism offers striking parallels with the Catholicism of southern Italian immigrants who arrived in the late nineteenth and early twentieth centuries. U.S. Church leaders generally saw and treated southern Italians much the same way they did Mexican Americans, ridiculing and chastising their infrequent church attendance, their devotional practices that centered on shrines, pilgrimages, holy cards, and other sacramentals, and their "deficient" understanding of doctrine. But this is an exception that proves the rule: southern Italian Catholics received treatment similar to Mexicans because both groups shared an ambiguous racial status and a style of Catholicism considered suspect.

Ironically, the significant differences between most Euro-American and Latino Catholics made the latter's historical trajectory in some ways more akin to that of African American Protestants. As historian Jay P. Dolan aptly recognized, Latinos "have fashioned a Church within a Church" and recent developments in Latino Catholicism are "very similar to what has happened in the African-American Protestant Church over the course of the twentieth century."[25] Over time, both groups have created a distinct style and character within the larger frameworks of their U.S. churches, complete with unique liturgies and theologies. However, with regard to a social ministry, the black Protestant experience has differed significantly from that of Latinos. As Albert Raboteau and others have shown, African American Protestantism historically has significantly nourished not only its people's spiritual needs but also their social, economic, and political aspirations. Obviously, that has not been the case with Latinos and the Catholic Church, although the twentieth century saw some movement in that direction. The basic difference has been that African Americans historically have owned their churches and Latinos have not. Since the 1960s, Latinos have become an ever-larger part of the lay membership of the U.S. Catholic Church, but they remain a tiny portion of the clergy and episcopacy that controls it.[26]

Although the Mexican American Catholic experience in Houston has much in common with other peoples' struggles to find a place in the United States, it is more than just another chapter of American church history or simply another piece of the American cultural mosaic. By probing this religion-as-a-way-of-life, *The Church in the Barrio* goes beyond what traditional denominational history can teach us, allowing us to better understand the complicated relationship between the U.S. Catholic Church and Mexican Americans, as well as how religion permeated and influenced many other aspects of their lives. Moreover, by illuminating some of the ways Catholicism and culture interact, this book helps explain Mexican American cultural perseverance in the United States, and it challenges us to resist easy generalizations about the complex roles religions play in shaping the broader national experience.

In 1964 historian Henry May noted that a "recovery" of American religious history was under way. Subsequent decades saw the emergence of a "new religious history" as historians and other scholars rejuvenated the study of religion and its impact in the American experience.[27] This book is offered as part of that ongoing work and in the hope of enlisting others in a task too long ignored and still in its infancy—the recovery of Chicano religious history.

ONE

They started gathering at four in the morning at the rail depot where the nuns were supposed to depart. There were about 300 of them by nine o'clock, 300 angry Mexicans. They were furious at their bishop for not letting some refugee Sisters of Charity from Mexico stay and minister to their community in Brownsville. The nuns were badly needed, and the parishioners, though impoverished, were willing to help feed and house them. But the bishop refused, and he ordered the nuns to move along quickly. Incensed, the protesters' numbers and passions quickly swelled. Three thousand strong, they made fiery speeches and unhitched and pulled away the rail car the sisters were going to board. *¡Que se vaya el obispo!* yelled the crowd— Make the bishop go! *¡Fuera el obispo!* they cried—Out with the bishop! The police were unable to control them. Desperate, the mayor appealed to the bishop to calm the crowd, but the bishop refused. He declined to face his parishioners—the "half-civilized Mexican greasers," as he was wont to call them.[1]

This telling incident in Brownsville, Texas, in 1875 reveals important elements that helped shape the lives of Mexican Catholics in Texas and the Southwest. In the nineteenth century and well into the twentieth, most Mexican Americans were both socially and religiously marginalized; they were, in the eyes of many Americans, a pariah community. The same was true in early twentieth-century Houston. There, parishioners considered themselves *muy católicos*, very Catholic, yet churchmen and Anglo society often held them in contempt. Over time, however, Mexican and Mexican American Catholics in the Bayou City shed much of their status as social outcasts and made strides toward greater participation in the city's religious and civic life. How can we explain this? The answer to that question is the central story of this book, and to begin to answer it we must first understand the historical context in which that gradual transformation took place.

This chapter traces the history of Tejano Catholicism and the development of Houston's Mexican community. It introduces the concept of Mexican American ethno-Catholicism: a home- and community-based faith that melded Spanish medieval Christianity and New World indigenous religion into a style of Roman Catholicism ambivalently tied to the formal church but inextricably fused with the people's ethnic identity. This chapter, then, forms the backdrop for the remainder of the book, mapping the religious and historical landscape across which Mexican Catholics journeyed to forge a place for themselves in the Bayou City.

Católicos in a Changing Society

The antecedents of Tejano Catholicism and Houston's Mexican community reach back to 1519, when Spanish explorers claimed the territory that later became Texas as part of Spain's empire in the Americas. Spain never paid much attention to Texas because it lacked the glitter of the Aztec empire in central Mexico. Consequently, the scattered outposts of hardy soldiers, priests, and colonists who represented Spain's tenuous claim to frontier Texas remained isolated from Spanish culture and institutions, separated by vast distances from the hub of colonial society in Mexico City and imbued with a spirit of independence.[2] By the time Mexico broke from Spain in 1821, the Gulf Coast winds had long since swept away any trace of El Orcoquísac, a fort and mission complex that once stood some thirty-five miles east of present-day Houston. Spain lost Texas to Mexico but laid the foundation of Mexican and Mexican American Catholicism.[3] In turn, Mexico lost Texas when a flood of illegal immigrants from the United States set the stage for the war of Texas independence, a revolution that the Texans won at the battle of San Jacinto in April 1836—in the swampy land that eventually developed into suburbs of the soon-to-be city of Houston.[4]

Seeking to protect its flock in the predominately Protestant Republic of Texas, the Vatican began paying more attention to this region by transferring administrative control of it from the northern Mexican Diocese of Linares to the Diocese of New Orleans in 1840. In 1847 Rome established the Diocese of Galveston, and in 1849 Bishop John M. Odin imported a small group of French missionaries, the Oblate Fathers of Mary Immaculate, to work among the Mexican population in Texas. The Oblates faced huge difficulties, given the enormity of the Galveston Diocese (which then comprised all of present-day Texas and some neighboring territories), their widely scattered parishioners, and a perennial shortage of clergy.[5] Class differences, cultural animosities, and racism compounded these problems. Clerics steeped in European values and traditions directed the church's work well into the twentieth century. Mostly French initially, some of these churchmen denigrated Mexicans and their brand of Catholicism. In deep South Texas, for instance, two highly placed clerics, Father Florent Vandenberghe and Father Dominic Manucy, dreaded having to work with destitute Mexican parishioners, preferring instead "civilized" people, that is, Americans and European immigrants—their racial and cultural cousins who gave them greater financial support.[6] Clearly, the Catholic Church in Texas mirrored the racial hierarchies and social relations of the time, and, consequently, some of its policies helped propagate the social inequality that marked the lives of Mexicans and other people of color.

In the face of prejudice and neglect, Texas Mexicans developed an ambivalent relationship with the institutional church, alternately accepting and rejecting its requirements and ultimately interpreting and practicing their faith in ways that met their own needs. They had an unbounded reverence for Our Lady of Guadalupe and other saints and often expressed great respect for the priesthood. Mexicans followed the basic tenets of Roman Catholicism and faithfully observed traditional holy days, but they also ignored some requirements, such as marrying within the church. And they clung to unsanctioned traditions such as home altar worship, a custom that bypassed the institutional church by personally invoking the intercession of saints. In the eyes of most churchmen, Mexicans were not good mass-and-sacraments Catholics; clergymen often criticized their sporadic church attendance and chafed at their "indifference" toward the sacraments. On the other hand, priests noted how scrupulously Mexicans attended to *particular* rituals, especially baptism and confirmation. Tejanas and Tejanos were ignorant about doctrine, reports claimed, but they displayed great reverence for certain aspects of the faith; they saw themselves as "good" Catholics, while church leaders often viewed them as "bad" ones.[7]

Ethnic animosity and class and cultural barriers partly explain these polar views, but they also stemmed from the distinct histories of Latin American and U.S. Catholicism. The Catholicism Spain brought to the Americas in 1492 was actually medieval Christianity, the religion shared by western Europeans before Martin Luther's Reformation split them into warring factions of Protestants and Catholics in 1517. In what is now central Mexico, conquered indigenous peoples syncretized the old Spanish medieval Christianity with their own religions, giving rise to a distinct "Mexican" Catholicism. Somewhat later in Europe—after the Columbian voyages and the Protestant Reformation—a new form of Catholicism began to develop as a result of the Council of Trent (1545–63). Often called the Counter-Reformation, the Catholic reform and revitalization movement that began at Trent led to the rise of "Tridentine" Catholicism (derived from *Tridentum*, Latin for the city of Trent, Italy). This new style of Roman Catholicism—a modernized and intellectualized version of the old medieval Christianity—spread throughout northern and western Europe. Later it came with the British to

North America, where eventually it would confront the old medieval Christianity—or "pre-Tridentine" Catholicism—the Spanish had brought earlier.

These two Catholic traditions differed in important ways. Tridentine Catholicism emphasized doctrinal knowledge and decorum over emotional display; required strict church attendance and adherence to church-approved practices; and tended to separate the sacred from the secular and "real" religion from superstition or other popular religious customs that the church hierarchy regarded as inferior "folk" Catholicism. In contrast, Catholicism in New Spain (Mexico) remained essentially pre-Tridentine, flavored by the Mesoamerican religious worldview with which it blended during the initial Spanish conquest and evangelization. This way of being Catholic embraced the permeability of the spiritual and material realms—religion, superstition, and magic all overlapped in daily life. Pre-Tridentine Catholics worried little about the nuances of theology or the issue of decorum in worship, finding in pilgrimages, saint veneration, and feasts ample outlets for their fervent religious expression and celebration. This outlook typified fifteenth- and sixteenth-century European Christians, most of whom "were still viewing life through a Medieval prism, possessing a worldview that knew no separation between religion and society. . . . The two realms were interwoven in such a way that it was unthinkable to distinguish the sacred from the secular, to separate religion from the activities of daily life."[8]

Over time this pre-Tridentine way of being Catholic spread northward from central Mexico to the Spanish northern provinces (present-day Texas and the Southwest). There, during centuries of frontier isolation, it became the Spanish/Mexican cultural core, permeating and integrating all aspects of Tejano life and becoming intimately tied to the people's very identity—it became Tejano ethno-Catholicism. This was the religious and cultural world of Texas Mexicans when, after the Mexican-American War of 1846–48, they suddenly found themselves under the critical eye of a more modernized Roman Catholic Church of the United States.

Anxious to find its niche in a Protestant nation, the Catholic Church supported the U.S. takeover of the Southwest and portrayed the Mexican Catholicism it encountered there as an embarrassing anachronism. All of this did not augur well for Texas Mexicans, a mestizo (mixed-race) people who followed a religious tradition loathed by their conquerors.[9] Nonetheless, nineteenth-century Mexican American Catholics made sense of their lives through their ethnoreligion:

> By taking those beliefs and practices from Catholicism that fit into their life as poor and oppressed folk, Tejanos continued syncretizing old religious world views. While seemingly backward and superstitious at times, their religion rejected the lessons of passivity and resignation historically inculcated into dependent classes by institutional Catholicism. . . . Instead, their religion . . . gave them a vital insight into life, one which . . . played a crucial role in perpetuating the conditions of normalcy in Tejano homes. It was what permitted them to go on searching for an improved economic, social, and political life.[10]

Texas Mexicans held tenaciously to their own brand of Catholicism because it suited their particular spiritual needs and helped them deal with their social subordination. "By taking refuge in this religious world . . . [Mexican Catholics] were also preserving one of the most important roots of their cultural identity." Catholic lay societies also reinforced a sense of peoplehood. By creating and controlling these institutions themselves, Mexicans expressed their independence from the clergy and strengthened their communities.[11] A form of cultural resistance, ethno-Catholicism gave Tejanos the self-respect and confidence with which to cope with material deprivation and social marginality; it served them well despite the disdain with which much of the modern Catholic leadership and society viewed it in the nineteenth century.

As the twentieth century dawned, Spanish priests increasingly replaced the French missionaries who had predominated in the work among Texas Mexicans.[12] But, although they could at least communicate with their parishioners, Spaniards often proved to be as condescending toward Mexicans as their predecessors, and an icy gap separated them from their charges.[13] Nuns and priests fleeing the dislocations of the Mexican Revolution of 1910 augmented the work of the Spanish clergy in Texas during the early twentieth century. The church set up "Mexican" churches, clinics, and other facilities so as not to offend Anglos accustomed to separation of the races.[14] Thus both immigrant and native-born Mexicans had long been social and religious outsiders in the eyes of many Americans when Houston's *colonia* (community) began to form.

MEXICANS IN THE BAYOU CITY: BEGINNINGS, 1836–1930

In August 1836, John and Augustus Allen mapped and began selling land in a speculative town they named Houston, in honor of the hero of Texas independence, General Sam Houston. The creation of the Allen brothers' masterful boosterism, the new town began inauspiciously on the mosquito- and snake-infested banks of Buffalo Bayou, only twenty miles from the site where Texas independence had been won scarcely four months before.[15] There was a Mexican presence in Houston from the city's very beginning, albeit involuntary. Alongside slaves, Mexican prisoners of war cleared and drained the swampy land on which Houston was built, and local officials parceled out some 100 prisoners as servants in the city between 1836 and 1839.[16]

Apparently, few Mexicans lived in Houston during most of the nineteenth century. Mexican immigrants were not drawn as much to the East Texas region around Houston as they were to El Paso, San Antonio, and the Rio Grande Valley, places with large and long-established Mexican populations. East Texas Anglo communities steeped in Deep South traditions preferred white and Negro sharecroppers; they made it clear that Mexicans were not welcome.[17] Consequently, Mexicans were almost invisible in Houston during most of the nineteenth century. Census counts listed only six to eighteen individuals in the city at various times between 1850 and 1880.[18]

Meanwhile, in the last three decades of the nineteenth century, far-reaching changes unfolded in Mexico and the American Southwest that would steadily draw more Mexicans and Mexican Americans into Houston. The 1870s saw the beginning of intensive industrialization in Texas and the Southwest, as well as in Mexico under the dictatorship of President Porfirio Díaz, in ways that complemented both regions. In the headlong rush to modernization, the expansion of railroads throughout the Southwest and into northern and central Mexico proved pivotal by interlocking the regions' economies and people. The completion of a transnational railroad network in 1890 (see Map 2) fed a voracious appetite for labor in Texas and the Southwest, as well as farther east into Louisiana, and was essential to the export-oriented Mexican economy.[19] The railroads provided Mexicans an escape from the hardships of Porfirian modernization and jobs in *el norte* (the United States). For Mexican Americans, the railroads opened up new jobs in their native land. With time, more Mexicans and Mexican Americans passed through Houston on the expanding iron web, some bound for Louisiana's sugar cane and cotton fields, others imported temporarily as strikebreakers.[20] In the late 1800s and early 1900s, Mexican immigrants and Mexican Americans who filtered in and out of Houston began to stay, often earning a living as food vendors and unskilled workers in the growing city. By 1900 nearly 500 Mexican-origin people lived in Houston. By 1910 the haphazard trickle had become a steady influx as some 2,000, mostly native-born Mexican Americans, made the Bayou City their home.[21]

The transformation of Houston's economy in the early twentieth century triggered dramatic growth in the city's Mexican community and firmly established its foundation. During the nineteenth century, Houston had grown into an important commercial center by improving its port and rail facilities to serve the agricultural production of southeast Texas. The city's economy had been built around the marketing of cotton, grain, and lumber and on plentiful black labor. But in the first decades of the twentieth century, oil and gas became in-

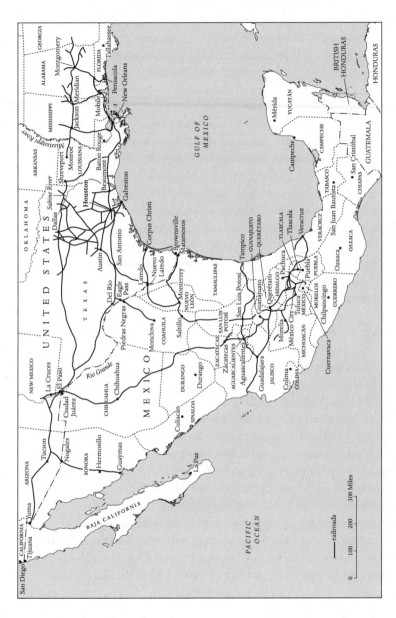

Map 2. U.S.-Mexico Railroad Connections, 1910

creasingly important to Houston's economy, as did a preference for Mexican labor.[22] Early in the twentieth century, Houston employers used Mexican Houstonians as *enganchadores* (labor agents) to recruit Mexican workers.[23] Swelling numbers of Mexican immigrants, as well as native-born Tejanos, responded to the calls for workers. They streamed into Houston during the 1910s and 1920s for several reasons. For one thing, Mexico's brutal drive to modernize culminated in the bloody Revolution of 1910, which drove large numbers of Mexicans into Texas. Meanwhile, the rise of commercial agriculture in Texas increasingly displaced rural Mexican Americans into urban employment. At about the same time, discoveries of oil near Houston gave rise to a booming petroleum industry centered in Houston and its well-developed financial and transportation infrastructure. Thus "the city where seventeen railroads meet the sea" became a magnet that attracted thousands of Mexican and Mexican American workers, offering jobs, as well as the means to reach them. World War I's labor shortages and the immigration restrictions of the 1920s (which were waived for Mexicans) also attracted workers to the Bayou City. As a result, Houston's Mexican-origin population expanded from 2,000 in 1910 to 6,000 in 1920, and then leaped to about 15,000 by 1930.[24]

Some Mexicans entered the city by way of the East Texas lumber mills owned by Houston entrepreneur John Kirby, or from places farther east. For instance, the family of Mary Villagómez worked briefly in the East Texas sawmill town of Saratoga before settling in Magnolia Park on Houston's east side in the late 1910s while Juan Rodríguez came to the city's Fifth Ward with his family from Louisiana, where his father had worked for the Southern Pacific Railroad.[25] Increasingly in the 1910s and 1920s, however, Mexicans found jobs in the new oil and gas sector of the economy and its related ship channel and railroad industries. In reality, they took jobs wherever they could. Mrs. Petra Guillén recalled, for example, that many men worked in the oil refineries and railroads while women worked as seamstresses or in food-packing plants and burlap bag companies, or they picked strawberries in the surrounding rural areas. With time, Mexican barbers, tailors, cooks, and other service workers also found a niche in the city's growing economy.[26]

These workers were part of a polyglot scene in early-twentieth-century Houston. In the 1910s and 1920s Mexican immigrants and native-born Mexican Americans jostled for jobs, housing, and cultural space in the Bayou City alongside a large black population and a smattering of various European immigrants. Blacks historically have been numerous in Houston, forming, for example, almost 40 percent of its population from the 1870s to the 1890s; between 1910 and 1970 they comprised from 21 percent to 32.7 percent of the city's inhabitants. As for its white population, Houston, like other southern cities, received some of the overflow of the "new" immigration of southern and eastern Europeans that flooded the eastern seaboard and parts of the Midwest in the late nineteenth and early twentieth centuries. In 1910 the roughly 2,000 Mexicans and Mexican Americans in Houston lived among much smaller pockets of Italians, Russians, Austro-Hungarians, Greeks, and a number of other European immigrants (plus thirty Asians—twenty Japanese, and ten Chinese). By 1930 there were almost twice as many Mexicans in the city—about 15,000—than all first- and second-generation eastern and southern Europeans combined, which totaled 8,339. Despite the diversity of the city's "new" immigrants, Houston remained numerically dominated by the northern and western European–heritage groups who founded the city, particularly Germans and British. In fact, Germans historically played a central role in Houston, far outnumbering other whites such as the British, Irish, Canadians, French, Czechs, Poles, and Scandinavian groups who historically have comprised a smaller part of the city's ethnic mosaic (see Figure 1).[27]

Thus Houston's Mexican communities took root in a society that historically had been black and white but one that increasingly became tri-ethnic—black, white, *and* brown (see Table A.1). In a city that considered them nonwhite, Mexicans stood out even though their numbers were much smaller than those in such places as San Antonio or Los Angeles. Aside from blacks, Mexicans in Houston were the only

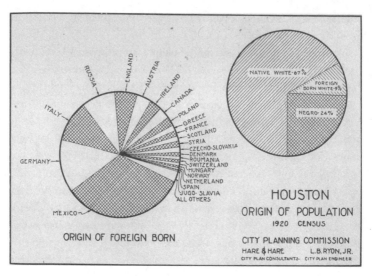

Fig. 1. Houston, Origin of Population, 1929

racial "other" present in significant and growing numbers in the early twentieth century.

In 1910 Houston's Mexicans were scattered around the margins of downtown. Most of them first congregated in what became known as El Segundo Barrio (Second Ward Neighborhood), an area just east of downtown. An enclave soon formed some two miles east of El Segundo within the Anglo suburb of Magnolia Park, sparked by the need for workers to enlarge the Houston Ship Channel between 1912 and 1914. Two smaller pockets also began to take shape during these years on the fringes of downtown, one on the north side (Fifth Ward) and another on the west side (First and Sixth Wards). These barrios became home to a steadily increasing stream of Mexican immigrants, who were joined by a small number of native-born Tejanos and Tejanas also seeking better opportunities. Most arrivals to these neighborhoods gravitated to the numerous railroad yards where jobs and cheap housing—often just railroad boxcars converted into crude shelters—were plentiful.[28]

Many Americans recoiled as thousands of Mexicans flooded Texas and the Southwest. Eventually a fierce debate embroiled the nation over the so-called Mexican problem, the dilemma of needing the Mexicans' labor but resenting their economic competition and supposed unassimilable nature.[29] In the face of hostility, this unprecedented Mexican migration to the United States in the early twentieth century clearly stamped its imprint on the Bayou City's budding *colonia*. The earlier arrivals came from Mexico's northeastern states bordering on Texas—Coahuila, Nuevo León, and Tamaulipas. The even larger flow of the 1920s streamed in from Mexico's Central Plateau, from the states of San Luis Potosí, Zacatecas, Aguascalientes, Guanajuato, Jalisco, and Michoacán. This was clearly an immigrant community, tightly knit and Mexico oriented but one in which even the Texas-born residents still identified strongly with *la patria querida* (beloved Mexico). Most important, white Houstonians, including clergy, rarely distinguished between immigrant Mexicans and native-born Mexican Americans; to most people they were all simply "Mexicans," that is, outsiders.[30] The few who tried to pass as whites drew derisive names, such as *catrines* (dandies) and *abolillados* (gringoized), in a community that tightly clung to its Mexicanness.[31]

The neighborhoods "used to be like families," a longtime resident of Second Ward recalled; close ties, reciprocity, and frequent socialization marked barrio life. Indeed, many of the residents were actually relatives, as extended families were often linked through chain migration, the practice of sequentially resettling family members by finding them jobs and housing through immigrant networks.[32] Mrs. Petra Guillén's family, for example, came to El Segundo Barrio with the help of an uncle who had preceded them. Similarly, Mary Villagómez arrived in the Magnolia barrio as part of an eleven-member extended family migration. Furthermore, the important Mexican custom of *compadrazgo* (godparentage) reinforced the neighborhood's familylike environment. Traditionally, godparents were close friends honored by parents to sponsor their child's baptism or some other important life-cycle ritual or celebration. The sponsors pledged to care for the child's spiritual and material life in the absence of the natural parents, thus becoming *comadre* and *compadre* ("coparents") to the mother and father and *madrina* and *padrino* (godmother and godfather) to the child. Through this form of kinship "by sentiment," godparents became members of the Mexican American extended family and couples created lifelong ties of mutual affection and support, something that contributed to the cohesiveness of Mexican communities. Thus, an "ethic of mutuality" suffused Houston's Mexican settlements and sustained them in an often hostile environment.[33]

In the early twentieth century, community activities and institutions also reflected an emergent *colonia*. As early as 1907, a *junta patriótica* (cultural committee) organized the traditional Mexican Independence Day celebrations, the *dieciséis de septiembre* festivities, and there was at least one mutual aid society formed by 1908.[34] Yet an important institution was lacking. In 1910 Houston's Mexican Catholics had no churches of their own. Some endured icy receptions at Anglo churches and were commonly segregated in the back of the sanctuary or forced to stand throughout the services even when some pews remained empty; many were kept out altogether.[35] Rejection was not new, but neither was the Mexicans' response of using their religion to mediate this hostility. They did this by nurturing their socioreligious traditions that were an integral part of daily life: Mexican families worshipped at their *altarcitos* (home altars) and carried on traditional Catholic devotions and celebrations in their own homes and in festive neighborhood gatherings. Soon after arriving in the city, Mexican and Mexican American Catholics launched money-raising projects to build their own places of worship, beginning with their mother church, Our Lady of Guadalupe, in 1912.[36]

Of course, Houston's *colonias* were embedded in a complex religious matrix. Virtually all the city's many ethnic groups, along with their religious institutions, could be found in any part of the Bayou

City, especially in the early decades of the twentieth century. When Mexicans first began congregating in Houston's Second Ward in the early 1910s, for instance, about half of the area residents were Jewish, almost 31 percent were black, and a mix of German and Irish immigrants, as well as native-born whites and Mexicans, made up the rest of the ward's population. As barrios formed in Houston's other five wards in the 1920s and 1930s, ethnic dispersal and the religious variety that went with it remained the pattern. Consequently, Mexicans shared a religious landscape that by 1941 included 4 synagogues, about 250 white and 268 black Protestant churches, as well as several white and 3 black Catholic churches. Baptists were the most numerous among both blacks and whites in this religious smorgasbord of twenty-two denominations and fifty-two nondenominational groups. As for Catholics, separate nationality parishes existed for the various European immigrant groups as a rule, but if they lacked churches of their own, European ethnics could attend any white Catholic church, unlike Mexicans and blacks. By the end of the 1930s, Houston's black Catholics belonged to either St. Nicholas, founded in 1887 in Third Ward; Our Mother of Mercy, established in 1929 in Frenchtown, the community of French-speaking Creoles from Louisiana who settled in the Fifth Ward in the 1920s; or Our Mother of Mercy's offshoot, St. Anne de Beaupre, started in 1937 in Houston Heights, a suburb on the city's northern fringe.[37]

Rounding out Houston's religious array were the *aleluyas*, as Mexican Protestants were commonly known. At roughly the same time that Catholic missionaries arrived in the city, various Anglo Protestant churches began taking notice of the growing Mexican population and started proselytizing in the barrios. As early as 1910, for instance, the Methodist Women's Board of City Missions pledged it would "establish a church for the Mexican people." Then came the Presbyterian missionaries, beginning in 1919, followed by Baptists in the early 1920s.[38] Thus, as Houston's Mexican ethno-Catholic communities formed, they did so alongside a sprinkling of *aleluya* neighbors and conscious of, if not socially integrated with, the Bayou City's diversity of ethnic peoples and faith traditions.

Clearly, ethnicity and religion set Mexicans apart from white and black Houstonians and, to some degree, from each other. The local press dubbed the *colonia* "A city within a city." Houston's "little Mexico" flourished as racial animosity mounted and the Great Depression loomed.[39]

CRISES AND GROWTH: 1930S–1950S

Unlike many cities, Houston weathered the Great Depression relatively well. But it was not without its problems; business stagnated at least temporarily, and joblessness afflicted many workers.[40] Mexicans and Mexican Americans in particular suffered greatly during *la crisis* (the Depression). Hundreds were unemployed, and many families lived on the edge of starvation during the 1930s, as employers often laid off Mexican workers first and government officials systematically denied them relief.[41]

In addition, Mexicans and Mexican Americans in Houston, as elsewhere, were subject to deportation. Immigration officials routinely raided construction job sites to round up Mexican nationals for repatriation, while other government agencies used various tactics to induce Mexicans to leave the United States. As the Great Depression worsened, the Mexican consul and even local Mexican organizations encouraged the departure of indigent families with promises of help from the Mexican government and by providing transportation to the border. Faced with poor prospects and nativism, at least some 2,000 Mexicans left the Houston area for Mexico during the 1930s.[42] Despite these tribulations, however, the Mexican community not only survived but grew during the 1930s, increasing from 15,000 in 1930 to 20,000 in 1940. Some of the increase came from outlying farms, as Mexican families abandoned rural life and migrated to the city. The growth of the 1930s was not dramatic, but it proved the community's viability and permanence.[43]

Moreover, continued growth also brought a shifting ethnic consciousness and increased political activism. The Depression virtually

ended Mexican immigration for a time, and it engendered more antagonism toward Mexican-origin people. In this context, a "Mexican
American" ethnicity began to displace the "Mexican" orientation that
had characterized southwestern *colonias* in the preceding decades.[44]

In Houston, this changing ethnicity prompted the rise of numerous
civic groups, primarily among the growing middle class. These organizations were active in social, political, and welfare activities for the better-
ment of the Mexican community. Some were explicitly political organizations that held rallies and endorsed candidates; others, like the League
of United Latin American Citizens (LULAC), were officially nonpartisan
but vocal in their advocacy for Mexican Americans.[45] With its emphasis
on political involvement, education, and the mastery of English, LULAC
epitomized the emerging Mexican American mentality that saw civic
responsibility as the key to accommodation to mainstream society. Similarly, a women's cultural society, the Club Chapultepec, emphasized
equally its members' American citizenship and responsibilities, as well as
their Mexican cultural heritage. The organization tried to smooth the
way for Mexican Houstonians by educating the community at large
about Mexican culture and promoting American patriotism, but it also
protested the mistreatment of Mexicans in Houston.[46] Mexican Americans thus began to project a more visible profile and a changing ethnicity
through these and other organizations in the 1930s.

Mexican American organizations continued to advocate for the
colonia when better economic times returned in the 1940s. World War
II created an economic bonanza for Houston as its ship channel industries contributed to the war effort through the production of aviation
fuel, synthetic rubber, and war vessels.[47] Mexican workers, however,
often were barred from the higher-paying jobs and relegated to menial
employment in the oil, petrochemical, and ship-building industries.
Organizations like LULAC protested employment discrimination and
inequities in the educational and judicial systems, thereby focusing
more attention on the maturing Mexican community.[48] The potential
strength of their growing numbers was an important part of the Mexican American urbanizing experience of the post–World War II years.

Like the United States in general in the later 1940s and the 1950s, Texas Mexicans became increasingly urbanized. Before World War II, most of them lived in small towns and agricultural areas, but by 1960 they were predominately an urban population. In fact, between 1940 and 1960, Mexican Americans were the most rapidly urbanizing group in the Southwest.[49] Houston's Mexican community reflected this trend. The Mexican-origin population grew from 20,000 in 1940 to 40,000 in 1950, and, by 1960, some 75,000 Mexican Americans and Mexicans lived in Houston, the great majority of whom had migrated to the city from the rural areas and small towns of Texas.[50]

An increasing social and economic stratification also characterized the expanding postwar Mexican American community. Compared to the early twentieth century, the *colonia* of the 1940s and 1950s as a whole was much more acculturated; it was a bicultural community more so than a "little Mexico." Its demographic profile reflected its changing character. By 1950, the Spanish-speaking population of the Houston area was overwhelmingly native-born, with less than 9 percent born in Mexico. In 1960, despite the near doubling of the decennial population, only 13 percent were foreign-born. In terms of economic status, however, most of Houston's Mexican-origin people ranked among the working-class poor. The poverty that had plagued many barrios since the early twentieth century attenuated only slightly in the post–World War II years. Between 1945 and 1960, many Mexicans and Mexican Americans in Houston still contended with deplorable housing, educational inequality, disease, and other social maladies. Nonetheless, working-class families and communities remained viable and continued to manifest the coping skills and endurance they had shown historically.[51]

A small middle class had also developed. These Mexican Americans were more mobile residentially than the vast majority of their counterparts; they were most likely more acculturated than other Mexican Americans as well. Home buying reflected a degree of socioeconomic improvement among the middle class as more Mexican Americans bought homes outside Houston's traditional Mexican neighborhoods.

Even though most Mexican-origin people continued to live in the old barrios in 1960, growing numbers had also moved into other parts of the city, as population expansion and a modicum of social mobility produced both a greater density of the established barrios and a dispersal of Mexicans into every part of the city in the post–World War II years. Catholic officials noted that "the Mexican population [is] moving into new subdivisions as our cities grow."[52]

The *colonia* underwent substantial changes from the 1930s through the 1950s. As their numbers grew steadily, Mexican Americans in Houston revealed their class, cultural, and generational differences and they increasingly claimed their rights as American citizens. These developments were a harbinger of greater ferment to come.

SURGE: THE 1960S AND EARLY 1970S

The 1960s and 1970s were a period of upheaval and change in America as many groups struggled to achieve social equality. Black Americans protested segregation, poverty, unemployment, and other long-standing forms of discrimination. Acting in a political climate ripe for change, other groups mounted campaigns to gain equality and self-determination: women fought to free themselves from the yoke of gender oppression; many disaffected youth sought freer lifestyles and, together with other Americans, an end to the Vietnam War; many Native American peoples demanded recognition of broken treaty promises and greater self-determination; Asian Americans forged pan-ethnic alliances to empower their communities; and Chicanos and Chicanas battled discrimination in voting, education, employment, and other areas.[53]

More than a century of struggle preceded the rise of the Chicano movement in the mid-1960s. Mexicans and Mexican Americans had resisted subjugation ever since Texas and the Southwest were wrenched from Mexico in the nineteenth century.[54] Rooted in a long tradition of resistance, *el movimiento*, as the Chicano movement came to be known, actually represented a multiplicity of efforts to redress long-standing problems stemming from social discrimination and exploitation. *El movimiento* was an explosion of different submovements that often had distinct agendas but were held together loosely by a strong undercurrent of cultural nationalism, or Chicanismo.[55]

The activities of César Chávez and Reies López Tijerina set the stage for the rise of the Chicano movement. At about the same time in the early 1960s, Chávez and Tijerina formed grassroots organizations that challenged the historical grievances of two different Mexican American constituencies. In 1962, Chávez began to organize the National Farm Workers Association to gain better working and living conditions for agricultural workers in California. In 1963, Tijerina incorporated La Alianza Federal de Mercedes (Federal Alliance of Land Grants) as a vehicle to regain the lost lands of Hispanos in New Mexico and southern Colorado. By the mid-1960s, the Gandhian persistence of Chávez and the fiery rhetoric and confrontational style of *el tigre* (as Tijerina became known) riveted national attention on Mexicans in the United States. Chávez and Tijerina catalyzed other struggles for social, political, and economic justice. In Denver, Rodolfo "Corky" Gonzales organized the Crusade for Justice to take community control of schools and foster pride among Mexican people; in Texas, José Ángel Gutiérrez became the guiding force behind La Raza Unida Party (LRUP) and its bid to harness Chicano political power; and elsewhere throughout the nation Chicanas and Chicanos spearheaded innumerable drives for social equality.[56]

As the shock waves of *el movimiento* reverberated throughout the United States, Mexican Americans used their unprecedented population expansion and political activism to demand social justice. "Mexican Americans themselves," historian Arnoldo De León noted, "used that visibility and turned to their numerical strength to attempt change in their historical condition." In Houston, the Mexican presence became ever more apparent as their number skyrocketed from 75,000 in 1960 to more than 150,000 in 1970.[57] In addition, the class, cultural, and generational differences perceptible among them in the post–World War II years became patently obvious in the 1960s and

1970s. Generally, the majority society recognized the class and cultural diversity that had developed among Mexican Houstonians, as well as their rising economic and political importance. In short, mainstream society stopped seeing Mexican Americans as exotic outsiders and "came to accept [them] as part of the city's own diverse cultural makeup."[58]

The Mexican community reflected its heterogeneity in numerous ways. On the one hand, the predominance of a bicultural way of life was evident in the proliferation of English-language and bilingual community newspapers, the abundance of English names given to "Spanish-speaking" organizations, and the prevalence of bilingualism and English-language dominance among Mexican Americans. Residential mobility continued and resulted in the formation of new Mexican American neighborhoods, mostly of the blue-collar type, outside the traditional barrios. There was also a sprinkling of Mexican American professionals in previously all-white middle-class suburbs. On the other hand, working-class Mexican Americans and a constant influx of Mexican immigrants continued to populate the old barrios; there, a few of the pre–World War II Mexicanist organizations still functioned and immigrant culture thrived.[59]

In part, the Mexican community's explosive growth in the 1960s and 1970s reflected the boom Houston experienced in its march to becoming the nation's fifth largest city and an international oil center. During this time Houston's rapidly growing oil and petrochemical industries fueled an unprecedented expansion in other sectors of the city's economy, bringing new jobs, higher wages, and a prosperity unmatched by most of the nation's urban centers.[60] But not all residents of "the oil capital of the world" shared its prosperity. Many working-class Mexican Americans still suffered chronic unemployment or were locked in low-paying dead-end jobs, despite the fact that Houston outpaced the nation in employment growth rates and showed impressive gains in per capita income during its boom years. Well-paid jobs and high-status occupations still eluded even the growing Mexican American middle class, whose members typically earned significantly less than their Anglo professional counterparts. Mexican Americans had made some gains in the 1950s, but the persistence of low incomes, poor housing, low educational levels, and other signs of marginality still marked them in the 1960s and 1970s.[61] Houston's boomtown glitz contrasted sharply with Mexican Americans' inequality, exposing the cost of their ethnicity and propelling them into social activism.

In Houston, civil rights struggles reflected the city's ethnic and religious pluralism, engaging in the tumult black, brown, and white, laity and clergy, Catholic and Protestant. The well-documented role of churches and clergy in the black civil rights struggle held true in Houston. Like their counterparts in other cities, black pastors in Houston, such as the Reverends L. H. Simpson, Earl Allen, William "Bill" Lawson, and others, exerted significant political influence from their pulpits and through their involvement in local chapters of the National Association for the Advancement of Colored People, the Southern Christian Leadership Conference, and smaller civil rights organizations.[62] Meanwhile, mostly younger Chicana and Chicano lay activists, Catholics as well as Protestants, organized outside the churches, establishing, for instance, chapters of LRUP and the Mexican American Youth Organization (MAYO), new vehicles that used confrontational tactics to challenge the older middle-class male leadership and press for social change in the Bayou City. The later 1960s and early 1970s saw Mexican Houstonians become increasingly politicized through such forums as the National Chicana Conference and by the political activism of MAYO and LRUP, and through their participation in such protests as the Texas Farm Workers' strike and the local *huelga* (strike) schools. The contagion of activism, of course, spread among Mexican American priests and sisters, as well as the city's Mexican American Protestant clergy. Leaders and organizations arose, such as Father Patricio Flores, who helped found Padres Asociados para Derechos Religiosos, Educativos y Sociales (Priests Associated for Religious, Educational and Social Rights, or PADRES); Sisters Gloria Gallardo and Gregoria Ortega, who formed Las Hermanas (Sisters), a group of militant nuns;

the Methodist pastor Rev. Arturo Fernández and other Mexican American Protestant ministers who organized the Mexican American Clergymen Association of Houston; and local Protestant attorney Benjamín Canales, assistant director of the Hispanic American Institute, a Mexican American Presbyterian advocacy organization based in Austin, Texas. And behind the scenes, highly placed white liberals in the Catholic hierarchy, such as Bishop John L. Morkovsky, Father John E. McCarthy, and Father Emile J. Farge, carried on low-profile but important activities in support of the Chicano movement.[63]

To what degree, if any, black, brown, and white Catholics made common cause for civil rights is an issue that awaits study. But, clearly, the whirlwind of protest swept up the Galveston-Houston Diocese—sometimes as an ally but often as a target of protest—as we shall see in the coming chapters. In the Bayou City, ethno-Catholicism helped sustain viable Mexican communities as they grew apace with the city but were largely shut off from its economic prosperity. It is the nature of that ethnoreligious way of life among Houston's Mexican and Mexican American Catholics to which we turn next.

TWO

ETHNO-CATHOLICISM:

EMPOWERMENT AND

WAY OF LIFE

When the Revolution of 1910 made it impossible for Ramón Villa-gómez to make a living in Mexico, he decided to head north, to the United States. "*Fina, me voy al norte* [I'm going north]," he announced to his wife. But his wife quickly deflated his plans, along with his ego: "*Mira, Ramón, tú no te vas a ir al norte* [*You're* not going north]; *nos vamos a ir* [*we* are]," she countered. "You're not going to leave me behind with the family; *we're* going up there [together]!" In this family matter the wife prevailed.[1] In another time and place a bone-weary and homesick migrant farmworker, Marcos Rodríguez, sent a letter home to Houston: "When we go to church we see a garden with many flowers that the priest tends," he wrote to his sister, "and we remember that back in Houston we have a garden of flowers named Carmelitas, Rocitas, Margaritas and Lolitas," referring to his absent siblings; "that garden is cared for by *la Virgen del Rosario*."[2]

These mundane episodes illustrate two important aspects of ethno-religiosity among Mexican Catholics in Houston: its empowering nature and its inextricability with everyday life. This chapter will show how ethno-Catholicism played a pivotal role in sustaining generations of Mexicans and Mexican Americans by giving them a sense of cultural identity and independence, community integrity and hope in the face of adversity. In their ethno-Catholicism, people like Josefina Villagómez and Marcos Rodríguez found the strength to confront life's many travails. Moreover, their Catholicism was so thoroughly enmeshed in their lives that it was more than a set of religious beliefs and practices; indeed, it defined them. Ethno-Catholicism was a part of their very being, of how they understood themselves, related to others, and found meaning in life, as well as the means to deal with life and all it offered—the welcomed, the feared, and everything in-between. In short, Mexican ethno-Catholicism was a way of life, a "lived religion."[3]

At the heart of ethno-Catholicism were the Mexicans' deep devotion to Our Lady of Guadalupe and such vibrant community traditions as the Christmastime barrio celebrations, the *quinceañera* rite of passage, and the *altarcito* practice of home altar worship. Underpinned by a worldview in which the spiritual and the material intermingled naturally in daily life, these and other home- and community-centered faith expressions coexisted with a selective participation in the formal requirements of the church. Together all of this made up the Mexican American ethno-Catholic way of life. This chapter presents a general picture of that way of life, understanding, of course, that it had variations. As some of the following chapters will show, generational, class, and other factors influenced the way Mexicans and Mexican Americans actually lived their ethno-Catholicism.

GUADALUPE, *POSADAS,* AND *PASTORELAS*

Veneration of Our Lady of Guadalupe (or *la Guadalupana*) formed the core of Mexican Catholicism. Belief in her apparition[4] profoundly affected Mexico's religious history, resulting in the conversion of millions of indigenous and mestizo (Spanish and Indian parentage) people. Guadalupe's veneration as *la Virgen Morena* (the brown Virgin) and *la Morenita* (a typically Mexican term of endearment) underscores her ethnic connection to Mexican-origin people and helps to explain why *la Guadalupana* quickly became the central figure of the people's faith. The Roman Catholic Church recognized the fervent devotion among the masses and Guadalupe's religious and cultural centrality to the nation in naming her patron saint of Mexico. In the words of one writer, Our Lady of Guadalupe was "the greatest single influence (next to God himself) on the Mexican people."[5]

La Guadalupana offered Mexicans the solace and counsel that helped them endure their tragic and turbulent history, an Oblate explained:

> Their lot has always been one of hardship, poverty, and oppression; their beloved land has been practically under continual misrule; self-centered politicians have exploited her riches and resources; their Faith . . . has been persecuted and their clergy hounded and martyred. And through all this they have come with their faith in God and their love for His Mother undimmed. In poverty, oppression, persecution, and disease . . . Guadalupe has been their Comfort and guiding Star. She has been their Mother and their Queen, their Patroness and Protectress.[6]

Deeply stamped in the Mexican psyche, Our Lady of Guadalupe became a unifying symbol for Mexican and Mexican American Catholics everywhere. Since colonial times, followers have marched under her banner not only to express their devotion and identity but also to fight for their social and political rights. In Mexico, leaders invoked Guadalupe's help in the great revolutionary movements of 1810 and 1910; in the United States during the 1960s, César Chávez and his farmworkers struggled for economic justice under her protective gaze, as did Texas farmworkers who marched on the state capital. A militant Chicano newspaper in Houston revered *la Guadalupana* as the "Mother of the Mexican Revolution" and the "Patron of the Liberation of Aztlán [the Chicano homeland]."[7]

Not surprisingly, the barrios of Houston exploded in joyous celebration every year on the Virgin's feast day. The custom dated back to the early twentieth century. The first Fiesta Guadalupana was held on December 12, 1911, at a white parish, Annunciation, where the great mass of Mexicans amazed the pastor. "Never before had such a large gathering of Mexican Catholics been seen in Houston," a parish jour-

The main altar in the sanctuary of Our Lady of Guadalupe Church in El Segundo Barrio depicts the patron saint of Mexico and the Americas. Courtesy Houston Metropolitan Research Center, Houston Public Library.

nal revealed, noting the "great enthusiasm and fervor" the Mexicans showed on that special day commemorating the appearance of the Mother of God to one of their own.[8] Throughout the years that devotion never flagged. Our Lady of Guadalupe Parish even held two services in a futile effort to accommodate the overflow crowds every December 12. Members of different parishes fondly recalled "how important" the celebrations were to all Mexicans. But participation was a devotion, not an obligation, parishioner Mary Villagómez emphasized. Thousands of faithful turned out yearly because the event touched them deeply; it was something "very meaningful to the people."[9]

But meaningful how? On a symbolic level, la Guadalupana inspired public displays of devotion because she was the Mother of all Mexican Catholics. Although Mexican culture generally associated piety with womanliness, men, too, could openly express devotion to Guadalupe because she was their "mother" and the culture demanded men's reverence for motherhood. In other circumstances, a reinterpreted Guadalupe transgressed her ascribed religious (that is, "womanly") role and took on a political one—she became María Insurgente (Mary the Revolutionary), leading bloody wars of liberation and protest movements in rural fields and city streets. In various ways, men and women found inspiration and sustenance in la Virgen Morena.

The twelfth of December climaxed a nine-day devotional period (a novena) that involved great numbers of parishioners. In 1945 St. Patrick's pastor wrote that the parishioners "worked hard for the preparation for the feast of Our Lady of Guadalupe . . . [which] was celebrated with a solemn high mass and all the ceremonies for this great day."[10] The eight days preceding the main celebration often featured nightly preaching by guest pastors. Meanwhile, some parishioners practiced the reenactment of the apparition, others prepared food, decorated floats, or readied costumes, banners, and the church altar, while still others practiced las mañanitas, the song tribute honoring the Virgin every year just before daybreak on December 12, her feast day.[11] Typically, parishioners celebrated Our Lady of Guadalupe Day with morning and evening services. The day began with a procession around the church grounds during which the faithful honored the Virgin by singing *las mañanitas* in the crisp air of the early dawn. An early morning Mass followed, and then everyone enjoyed the traditional hot chocolate and *pan dulce* (Mexican pastry), perhaps along with a schoolchildren's play about the apparition, in the social hall.[12] In 1969 the Catholic press explained, "According to tradition the people arise early in the morning on special days such as birthdays to sing praise to the honored person, in this case Our Lady of Guadalupe."[13]

The celebrations grew in size and importance over the years. By the early 1970s an increasingly elaborate Fiesta Guadalupana instituted by the diocese supplemented events at the individual parishes. These larger affairs, initially hosted by Guadalupe Parish, included huge processions and popular mariachi masses celebrated by a bishop. A procession began in midafternoon from Blessed Sacrament Church, where 2,000 or more people gathered under the prominent image of the Virgin and made a mile-and-a-half pilgrimage through the barrio to Guadalupe Church. Decorated floats, religious banners, Mexican and American flags, and placards of barrio groups created a festive air.[14]

The celebration in 1971 was especially poignant. The Chicano press hyped the coming event weeks in advance. Parishioners read that Mexican actress and recording star Queta Jiménez and an international cast of performers were scheduled to honor the Virgin by "singing the typical Mexican *mañanitas* in a local church."[15] The faithful inundated Guadalupe Church.[16] The duet of Queta Jiménez and Adolfo Garza provided the highlight of the day with a "prayer-made-song" that moved the audience to tears. "The devotees of *la Virgen Morena*," the newspaper reported, "were delighted to see the warmth with which our compatriots honored the Queen of Mexicans."[17] The event reflected the Virgin's central place in Mexican Catholicism and revealed as well the power of a popular devotion to unite a people in celebration of their shared ethnoreligious identity.

In similar fashion, the reenactment of *las posadas*, the dramatization of Mary and Joseph seeking lodging at an inn (*posada*) on their way to

Children at Our Lady of Guadalupe Parish in the 1950s reenact the Apparition of the Virgin Mary to Juan Diego as part of the annual Virgin's Feast Day celebrations. Courtesy Houston Metropolitan Research Center, Houston Public Library.

Bethlehem for the birth of Christ, also evoked ethnic solidarity. "My mother and many of these Mexican people brought customs from Mexico," Mary Villagómez explained. "They were used to having *posadas* at Christmastime. So they would have their *posadas* in the house and they would sing and pray and carry the statues of Joseph and Mary, looking for shelter and all that." People looked forward to these festive gatherings with their neighbors. "I remember distinctly," stated Villagómez, "that we would work up to that, like a big thing was coming, you know—a *posada*! We're going to have a *posada*!"[18] Parishioners in different neighborhoods staged the event at churches or in private homes in basically the same way over the years. Like other important celebrations, the *posada* involved a novena and the drama was played out on nine consecutive nights, beginning on December 16 and ending on Christmas Eve. Groups of people carrying lanterns and statues of Mary and Joseph (or led by a costumed couple) went house to house asking for a place to rest overnight. The pilgrims sang the request for shelter, were refused, and then moved on until they were finally admitted into someone's home. Inside, parishioners prayed and sang hymns. But solemnity melded with cheer. It was a real "party atmosphere," Mrs. Hope Jiménez fondly recalled. Children squealed hysterically as they smashed a piñata, showering everyone with candy and coins and raising a roar of laughter among their parents. Late into the night a jovial buzz pulsated in barrio homes as folks feasted on steamy tamales or spicy chicken *mole* and the ubiquitous hot chocolate and *pan dulce*.[19] Some *posadas* were held at churches, merging community tradition and formal worship, but the *posadas* in the barrios predated the presence of the institutional church.[20] They were clearly an expression of community solidarity that Mexicans controlled in their own homes and communities.

Mexican and Mexican American Catholics also staged *pastorelas* during the Christmas season. These nativity plays recalled the pilgrimage by shepherds (*pastores*) to visit the infant Jesus. Amateur and semiprofessional actors performed *pastorelas* throughout Texas and the Southwest. Often the same family held the honor of representing a particular character over generations. People's backyards became barrio theaters as troupes presented a *pastorela* as a "Christmas gift to the community."[21] Guadalupe parishioner Mrs. Petra Guillén remembered that residents of Second Ward requested performances and "they would do the *pastorela* in your yard." "My uncle used to be one of the *pastores*," she recalled, "so we had to follow him wherever he went on the *pastorela*."[22] These events were not simply entertainment; they represented a sacralization of barrio space and activity. As Robert

Orsi has shown, "Religious solidarity, communion within the various expressions of popular religiosity, can precede social or communal solidarity in poor communities."[23]

Thus the *pastorelas* carried a message of resistance. In the context of Mexican American marginality, "the performance of a traditional Mexican *pastorela*—in Spanish, in the backyard of a barrio home, by a close-knit company of working-class actors—assumes a real social and political significance that extends beyond the devotional," a scholar noted. The performance of a *pastorela* was "a labor of love and devotion, in denial of the dominant notion of work as wage labor." The performers were "not 'paid' for their labor here, so much as reciprocated in gratitude (in the form of tamales, drinks, dollar bills, and so forth)."[24] Participation in a *pastorela* allowed Mexicans to express their preference for their values over those of the majority society by giving them a chance to overturn the capitalist notions of labor that pervaded their lives and to "control" their own labor, however fleetingly. This symbolic inversion of control of their labor fortified their sense of self-worth and community solidarity, and it provided a psychological victory over everyday realities of ethnic tensions and class subordination. Like the *posada*, the *pastorela* was another way that Mexican ethnoreligiosity helped to build community; by celebrating in settings of their own choosing, parishioners affirmed their Mexicanness, their style of Catholicism, and their human dignity.

Quinceañeras and Altarcitos

The year 1970 was an unforgettable one for young María Quiroz. When she turned fifteen that spring, her family, friends, and community honored her with a *quinceañera*, a ceremony as elaborate as a wedding. The *quinceañera* began with a religious service, as tradition dictated. Carrying a beautiful spray of red roses, María entered St. Patrick Church dressed in a beautiful white gown, veil, and satin slippers. Her parents, godparents, eleven attendants, a page, and a flower girl accompanied her. The priest celebrated Mass and gave his blessing, and María received Communion and renewed her baptismal vows. A photo session followed the church service, and, later, a dinner and dance complete with champagne and orchestra capped the memorable day.[25]

Although laypeople and clergy alike have long disputed the *quinceañera's* origins, meanings, and form, there is no doubt that the tradition was a great event in a young woman's life, a treasured experience often noted in local newspapers.[26] The celebration was, on one level, a gift to the fifteen-year-old from her parents and relatives. The cost was often substantial, and priests and parishioners alike complained about the "extravagance." For example, Father Patricio Flores, who became the first Mexican American bishop in the U.S. Church, worried that the *quinceañeras* had "gotten out of control" and "become too commercial." Similarly, a former pastor of St. Patrick Church warned that the tradition had "developed into a social affair with the danger of the religious aspect being forgotten."[27] Even María Quiroz's mother agreed about the expense, stating, "It's a very pretty thing, an unforgettable event, but very expensive."[28]

But several families usually bore the cost, and almost everyone involved in the ceremony shared in paying the expenses, especially the godparents, as the *Houston Chronicle* reported:

> Padrinos or godparents and relatives . . . paid for the use of the Church, split the cost of the reception dinner, paid for María's hairdo, photographs, photo albums, guest books, birthday cake, champagne for the cumpleaños participants, champagne glasses, invitations, satin pillow for the tiara and gave such gifts as the tiara, the prayer book, rosary, mantilla, religious medallion, María's bouquet, charm bracelet, ring, earrings and gloves.
>
> Attendants' dresses, shoes and headdresses totaled about $35 per girl while their escorts were responsible for renting their tuxedoes, buying their partner-attendant's bouquet and chipping in to pay for the dance.[29]

Clearly, by the 1970s celebrating a *quinceañera* was often an expensive undertaking. "Frankly," Mrs. Quiroz admitted, "if we didn't have relatives who agreed to share the expense, we couldn't do it."[30] Nonetheless, the celebration of a *quinceañera* strengthened communities by nurturing family relationships and reinvigorating the old ties of *compadrazgo*.

On another level, however, the *quinceañera* tradition was double-edged. On the one hand, the custom entailed a commitment to community service. A young woman could pledge to serve her community, for example, by finishing her education. In that way she contributed to her own material well-being, as well as that of her family and her community. She could also make a commitment to help teach catechism in her parish, thereby contributing to the spiritual life of the community.[31] The custom thus had important implications for individuals, families, and communities because it promoted family and community loyalties by cementing kinship ties and eliciting commitments from succeeding generations. On the other hand, even though the *quinceañera* promoted ethnoreligious solidarity and reflected a woman's importance in her family and culture, it also perpetuated the notion of women's inequality and constrained roles in life as primarily mothers and caretakers—the guardians of home and faith. After all, the custom marked a woman's passage into a clearly patriarchal institution, the Catholic Church, which historically tried to inculcate values of women's submissiveness and proscribed role expectations, sacralizing them through the tradition of the *quinceañera*.[32]

Nonetheless, women found ways to challenge patriarchy, one of them being through the custom of keeping private home altars, *altarcitos*. This was perhaps the most characteristic and revealing tradition among Mexican Catholics:

> The house is silent and dark. In the far corner of the living room, the flickering lights of several tall votive candles illuminate a colorful assembly of plaster saints and religious lithographs, a Spanish Bible and an arrangement of family photographs. Kneeling before this rudimentary altar, a woman prays silently over her glass rosary beads. Her eyes, wet with tears in supplication, are fixed upon an

image of Our Lady of Guadalupe. Once she has finished the rosary, she addresses herself to the saints represented by the images on her altar, petitioning or thanking each of them. She asks . . . Our Lady of St. John to intercede on behalf of her sister, who has a heart condition. In return for this favor, she makes a vow to travel to the Virgin's shrine. She requests of . . . St. Jude, patron of impossible causes, that he help her son-in-law find a job with better working hours. She invokes the Sacred Heart of Jesus and prays for . . . a recently deceased neighbor. She asks San Martín de Porres, patron saint of the poor, to look after the destitute of the world. Her last prayer . . . thanks . . . Guadalupe for her husband's improved health and for the safe delivery of her newest great-granddaughter. She closes by reminding the Virgin that, in fulfillment of her vow, the baby was given the name Guadalupe as one of her middle names.[33]

This scene was commonplace in Houston barrios. Mrs. Petra Guillén, who visited many homes during her years as a missionary catechist, remembered that most homes had an *altarcito*. Other parishioners likewise recalled that altars were a "very normal" part of home life.[34]

The normality of the *altarcito* tradition belied its profound importance in the lives of Mexican Catholic women. More than any other aspect of women's religiosity, home altar worship defined, sustained, and empowered them. This was a woman's space; it was sacred and it was hers. In this holy arena, women brought together the sacred and the here-and-now, visiting, cajoling, bargaining with, and thanking their heavenly family in the pictured presence of husbands, children, and other earthly relatives. Here women spoke first and most to *la Guadalupana*—the holiest of women and the one who best understood them *as* women. They brought to *la Virgen* and the saints all their sorrows and joys, and, bathed in the balm of a sacred presence, they emerged relieved, rejuvenated, and confident.

Parishioners disagreed about the origins of the *altarcitos*, but they were united in their attachment to them. For some, home altar worship paralleled worship in the parish church. "[W]e always kneel

Home altars, such as this one belonging to Mrs. Eloisa Garza, typically featured both heavenly and earthly family members along with religious objects. Photo from *Interiores: Aspectos Seculares de la Religión* (Houston, Tex.: Houston Public Library, 1982). Photo by Guillermo Pulido.

in front of the altar in church," Immaculate Heart parishioner Mrs. Teresa Zavala reasoned, "so we sort of carry it [the practice] into the home I guess." Others speculated that *altarcitos* evolved from the scarcity of churches; thus, having a private altar, former nun Mary Villagómez explained, was "like we're in church." Another Immaculate Heart member, Mrs. Hope Jiménez, added that the images focused a person's mind on religious matters.[35] Home altars reminded one parishioner of her upbringing, and another valued them because she felt they were part of her identity as a *"mexicana."* An integral part of daily life, *altarcitos* were taken for granted and "just enjoy[ed]."[36] The tradition of saint veneration was so entwined with Mexican American ethno-Catholicism that when priests in Houston spoke against the practice in the 1960s, parishioners felt culturally threatened and resentful.[37] But they were not about to abandon their *altarcitos*. This unbroken tradition is a clear-cut example of Mexican American resistance to religious and social assimilation pressures. Parishioners offered different explanations about the meaning and endurance of *altarcitos*, but ultimately the importance of the tradition lay in how it integrated daily life and the sacred, concretizing and voicing Mexican Catholics' understanding of their religious cosmos in an intimate, familial way. *Altarcitos* particularly empowered women, giving them access to the divine and helping them to negotiate crucial family and community relationships and to deal with gender inequality and other problems life presented.

The *altarcito* tradition revealed the vital role of women and the central place of family in Mexican American culture. The home altar tradition was, first and foremost, a family custom carried on primarily by women; women kept the tradition alive and handed it down over the years.[38] "Yes, my mother had a little altar," Eloisa Garza stated, as did her daughter and her sisters. *Altarcitos* were accepted "as something we [women] just have," Luz Vara pointed out.[39] Women believed the *altarcitos* brought the divine into the home and that the religious images of the altar represented a home's "spiritual family."[40] "[M]y grandmother used to say that the first thing that a house should have is an altar," Mrs. Janie Tijerina recalled. "That was the only way you could be in the grace of God. If God is not in the family, you're not a family," she insisted.[41]

Hence, women used home altars to invoke spiritual help as caretakers of the family. Women counted on the saints like they would earthly kin; they sought guidance, consolation, strength, protection, and other favors from the sacred persons represented in the *altarcitos*.

For instance, World War II and the Vietnam War saw many soldiers' pictures on altars, invoking a favored saint's protection.[42] Women often compared the intervention of a saint to having a legal advocate. "It's like a lawyer. When you go to a court, you don't go by yourself; you take a lawyer to represent you. So those saints are representing us," Petra Guillén explained. This analogy recalled the sixteenth-century Spanish belief that a saint represented a community to God, an advocacy described as that of an *abogado* (lawyer).[43]

The comparison also reflects a difference between Mexican-origin and other American Catholics. Like Mexican Americans, Irish, Polish, and other Euro-Americans revere particular saints. But many of those devotions may be traced back to the "devotional revolution" of the mid-nineteenth century, whereas the practice among Mexican and Mexican American Catholics reaches farther back in history. Unlike the church-sponsored devotions that developed among various Euro-American Catholic groups in the later nineteenth century—the most notable exception being southern Italians—Mexican saint veneration was forged in the caldron of *mestizaje*, the racial and cultural blending that resulted from the Spanish conquest and colonization of indigenous Mexicans in the sixteenth century. The devotion to Our Lady of Guadalupe illustrates this point. The Spanish brought with them a tradition of saint veneration to Indian Mexico, where the practice of home altar worship of indigenous deities already existed. In the New World these two customs of venerating favored sacred figures fused into popular devotions of Guadalupe and other saints.[44]

In any case, women acknowledged answered prayers by fulfilling vows made to their intermediaries. Often these *promesas* took the form of a pilgrimage to a saint's shrine, such as the one Mrs. Felix Tijerina made for the Virgin of San Juan de los Lagos, Mexico. Women also prayed novenas or made an offering of money or some sort of personal sacrifice to fulfill promises.[45] Through saint veneration, women exercised their traditional role of nurturing the family and thereby contributed to the stability of the primary institution in Mexican American life.

Yet patriarchy remained a constant companion in their lives. Despite their indispensability as caretakers of the family, many women chafed at their constrained roles and felt oppressed by the collusion of two pivotal institutions in Mexican American life, family and church. Mexican American culture expected wives and mothers to devote themselves totally to the family and put the needs of their husbands and children above their own.[46] Church representatives reinforced that subordination, as Father Antonio Marañón bluntly reminded parishioners in his local newspaper column: "If it is true that husbands and wives are equals as children of God, it is also true that they are not equal with regard to each other: the husband is the master [*jefe*] and the wife owes him submission."[47]

Confronted daily by inequality, women used their religiosity and domesticity as sources of empowerment. As keepers of religion and the home, they stood at the very center of Mexican American family and community life, a position from which they exerted significant influence, directly and indirectly, and therefore commanded respect. Women often had more control than men over family matters, their influence extending not only to religion but also to the making of important decisions concerning schooling, finances, health care, and other important matters. Historically in Mexican American communities, a woman's "strength has been exercised in the home where she has become the pillar of family life. It is just this role that has brought her leadership and her abilities to the larger community." In addition, women were primarily the ones who maintained the extended family and *compadrazgo* ties that were important to family and community well-being.[48]

Women clearly exerted their will in the domestic sphere. For example, one parishioner's mother left behind a philandering husband in Mexico City. The mother "wanted to be more independent and [have] a different life for . . . her children." She refused to live where it was acceptable for a husband to "have as many women as he wanted," the daughter recounted. So in 1956 the mother moved to Houston, taking her seven children with her; two years later the father followed.[49] In a similar vein, Mary Villagómez proudly remembered her mother's initiative and leadership in church and family matters. Villagómez described her mother as a forceful personality, a whirlwind of energy and resolve who "took the leadership that way."[50] Women's position in a mother-centered culture bolstered their dignity and assertiveness, helping them to negotiate patriarchal relationships and circumvent and temper other problems they encountered in a society that privileged men.

In asserting themselves, women drew strength from their *altarcitos*. Mrs. Janie Tijerina asserted, "I'm a great believer in my saints . . . and I believe they help me." She had been named after Our Lady of San Juan, and she always carried a small picture of the Virgin in her purse. "I think she protects me," Mrs. Tijerina stated.[51] Similarly, María López said of her favorite saint, "I have lots of faith in calling on her, [the] Virgin de San Juan," adding that "she has done many favors for me."[52] Many women prayed to the Virgin Mary and developed special lifelong relationships with her various manifestations. They revered her for her healing powers as Our Lady of St. John; sought her consolation as Our Lady of Sorrows; and saw in her a perfect role model as Our Lady of Guadalupe, a nurturing parent whose combined strength and meekness gave others vital emotional sustenance.[53]

But it is important not to exaggerate the empowering nature of home altar worship and the liberating influence of *la Guadalupana*. In reality, like other aspects of Mexican American ethno-Catholicism, this one also underscores its often contradictory nature. Saint veneration, like the tradition of the *quinceañera*, had both a positive, liberating potential, as well as a negative, constraining side. For example, while Guadalupe could inspire women to contest patriarchy, she also reinforced the pressure exerted by ethno-Catholic culture on women to emulate the "María paradox" of passivity in the face of such things as the double standard of sexual behavior.

Still, as anthropologist Kay Turner observed, Mexican American women undertook "cultural control of home and barrio life to maintain a system of values based strongly on loyalty to and respect for kin." This loyalty and sense of affiliation was "in no small way shaped and secured through an alliance formed with God and the saints, an alliance personally maintained at home by women."[54] Thus women did much more than merely assure the biological and cultural continuity of Mexican Americans. Home altar worship sustained their sense of worth, empowering them to challenge gender inequality and other harsh realities; it gave them considerable control of a crucial institution—the home—helping them to shape wholesome individuals, families, and, by extension, entire communities; and it centrally positioned them to maintain important relationships and customs that held communities together, including the *compadrazgo* networks and parish activities they dominated. In this sense, their religiosity and domesticity were hardly passive or insignificant.

INSTITUTIONAL PARTICIPATION

Mexicans and Mexican Americans attended church services less frequently than other Catholics in the United States, a source of continual complaints among clergy since the nineteenth century. Social scientists since the early twentieth century also made this observation repeatedly, and Mexican Americans themselves often confirmed it.[55] In Houston, patterns of church attendance roughly paralleled that of other Texas Mexicans. Apparently, about one-half of Mexican American parishioners regularly worshipped in their churches on a weekly basis.[56] Mexican Catholics simply did not stress frequent church attendance as heavily as the church hierarchy did, nor did they fault themselves for it. "I've always been a Catholic. I'm a very good Catholic," a prominent Houston woman insisted. "Because I don't go to church does not prove that I'm not a good Catholic. I was brought up like this."[57] Again, Mexicans defined for themselves what it was to be a good Catholic and a decent human being. Their refusal to be remade in a "better" image testified to their pride in Mexicanness and to the certainty with which they understood and lived their ethnoreligion.

Whatever their numbers, Mexican Americans who were closely

affiliated with the institutional church placed great value on attending Sunday Mass. Religion was "a main part of our lives," a dedicated churchgoer emphasized, recalling Sundays as the day at church. Before moving to the city in the 1930s, the Gonzales family rose Sunday mornings at 5 A.M. and walked five miles from their farm to the church for the 10 o'clock Mass. After services the family enjoyed "tortilla sandwiches" on the church grounds. The children then attended catechism classes before returning home at about 4 o'clock in the afternoon. This was a "commitment . . . not a sacrifice," an elderly gentleman explained, a "routine" part of family life.[58]

It was also a family tradition passed on over generations. Another parishioner, Mr. Joe Gonzales, underlined the importance of church attendance to family life. For him, going to church every Sunday was "an integral part of being a family." Grandparents, parents, and children all attended Mass together. Parents inculcated children with a sense of support for the church early in life and reinforced this value by giving weekly church attendance a high priority in the family's activities. Others recounted similar experiences of extended families worshipping together and children going to *la doctrina* (catechism classes) after services.[59]

Parents socialized their children into their ethno-Catholicism through their own modeling and by their strictness about church attendance. Children were not allowed to go anywhere else if they did not first go to Mass, a parishioner recalled. But regular churchgoing was more than a strict requirement. Esther García, a former St. Stephen's parishioner, remembered Sundays as "the highlight of the week." "[W]hen we went to church, it just made us feel good," she recalled. "I think the reason that we did practice going every Sunday was because we found . . . that *social community* that we were looking for. [T]hat was our community, and that was our way of reaching out to others . . . from other barrios, not just the one where we lived but [from] all over." Sister Agnes Rita Rodríguez, a Divine Providence nun, echoed Mrs. García's experience. The elderly nun recalled that parishioners at Our Lady of Guadalupe formed friendships and built a sense of community because the mother church in Second Ward drew Mexican worshippers from throughout the city.[60] Clearly, parishioners enjoyed Sunday Mass attendance because it reinforced the closely held cultural values of family and community. This was significant to women of the early twentieth century, whom society allowed precious few opportunities for expression and leadership. As Sister Yolanda Tarango has explained, "For my grandmother and the Hispanic women of her age, church was perceived not so much as an institution but as a community. . . . Women of this generation perceived the church as the primary means to keep the family united and cultural values alive. Their work in the church was chiefly oriented towards building the community."[61]

By the later 1960s, more clergy in the Catholic Church recognized the importance of cultural relevance in pastoral matters. Hence, one of the liturgical reforms of the Second Vatican Council was the celebration of the liturgy in the language of the people. When Spanish masses were instituted in Houston parishes, Sister Rachel Moreno noticed a positive change among parishioners at Our Lady of Guadalupe Parish in their attitudes toward the institutional church. Similarly, Immaculate Heart members indicated that they enjoyed the Mass more because they were more intimately involved by the use of their language in the service.[62]

Father Patricio Flores capitalized on the spirit of Vatican II to inject more cultural relevance into his ministry among Houston's Mexican Catholics. First, as pastor of St. Joseph–St. Stephen Parish, Flores invited the Estudiantina Guadalupana, a musical group comprised of twenty-eight girls and young women from Cuernavaca, Mexico, to perform at his church and other predominately Mexican American parishes. With their guitars, accordions, violins, and "soft hand clapping," the Estudiantina Guadalupana sang the liturgy and entertained parishioners with current popular songs after services.[63] The following year Father Flores began using a mariachi, a traditional Mexican folk band, to revive interest in poorly attended services. Flores celebrated his parish's first mariachi Mass accompanied by a local group, El Mariachi Norteño, on Sunday, October 12, 1969, during the parish's Día de la Raza (Columbus Day) festivities. The parishioners loved it. "Mariachi Masses have met with overwhelming response in two Houston churches," the Catholic press reported. Languishing services were soon "packed." Mexican American parishioners preferred the mariachi Mass, Father Flores explained, "because they feel it's their 'thing.' "[64] The innovation proved a good vehicle "for expressing the mood, temperament and emotions of the Mexican people."[65] Along with kinship networks, community ties, and language, the mariachi Mass was an important cultural ingredient that influenced patterns of church attendance among Mexicans and Mexican Americans. It also revealed how ethno-Catholic identity melded religious and social life in ways that allowed them to carve a place for themselves in the Bayou City.

Baptism and confirmation also illustrated this blending. The two sacraments ranked high among the religious duties kept by Mexican Catholics. But as with other aspects of institutional life, parishioners approached the sacraments in a distinctly Mexican way. The initiation of an infant into Catholic life was of utmost importance to Mexicans and Mexican Americans. Baptisms were great occasions, marked by a solemn ritual in the church and followed by hearty celebration in the home; they were often announced in the Spanish-language press.[66] Mexican Catholics put "all the decoration possible" into the baptism of a child. "They are accustomed to having a fiesta with tamales and beer," Father Flores explained. "If they are poor, they may have to wait a half year or a year before the baby is baptized, until they can afford the fiesta, but they consider the social aspect of the occasion very important."[67]

Baptisms were important socially because they brought together family and friends, much like the other institutional practices Mexican Catholics chose to follow. But more important, they fostered community bonds through the time-honored ritual kinship of *compadrazgo* (godparentage). In particular, *madrina* (godmother) status was much respected, given the serious commitments the relationship entailed, and it carried almost the same "social and emotional weight" as *madre*

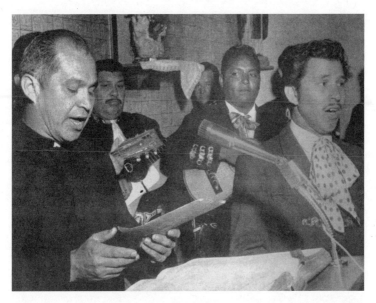

Father Patricio Flores brought more cultural relevance to Mexican American ministry in the Galveston-Houston Diocese with such innovations as the mariachi Mass, performed here at St. Joseph–St. Stephen Parish in 1969. Courtesy *Texas Catholic Herald*.

(mother). "If the natural mother dies or is otherwise unable to care for her children," anthropologist Kay Turner has explained, "the madrina frequently takes full responsibility for raising her godchildren."[68] Thus St. Patrick parishioner María López helped rear three of her godson's children. "The three children call me Godmother. They consider me their grandmother," she explained. *Compadrazgo* had a long history and an important place in the Mexican American community, as it built ties that assured lifelong emotional and material support and reciprocity between families and "a woman's sense of power in the Texas-Mexican community."[69] In reality, the use of the term *comadrazgo* is far more appropriate than *compadrazgo*, for historically it has been women—the *comadres*—who have taken the lead in perpetuating this important Mexican American institution.

The sacrament of confirmation also held great significance. Again, however, Mexican practice differed from church expectations. "The baptism rate is very high in Mexican American areas though confirmation is quite a different thing," a bishop observed in 1970. "Interest in the last years has dwindled," he lamented, "because the Confirmation age requirement is much later in a child's life and parents either forget about it or give up on Confirmation by that time."[70] The bishop's observations reflected a long-standing difference between what the church expected and how its Mexican parishioners approached the sacrament. Historically, Mexicans in Texas and the Southwest had their children confirmed as soon as possible after baptism, without first having religious instruction and First Communion, as tradition in the U.S. Church dictated. The dearth of clergy and religious institutions in the vast region compelled bishops to give the geographically dispersed Mexicans the benefit of confirmation at an earlier age. By the twentieth century, the practice was entrenched among Houston's Mexican Catholics, and the Galveston Diocese had even condoned it since 1912.[71] With time, however, churchmen pressed to bring Mexican American practices in line with those of the majority of Catholics in yet another reflection of the hierarchy's efforts to force Mexican Catholicism into the Anglo American mold. In the late 1930s, for instance, Oblate missionaries sought to change the Mexican practice so that children could receive sufficient religious instruction and be confirmed at about age twelve. "[P]astors are fully convinced," a missionary wrote, "that valuable opportunities are being wasted because of the retention of the old Spanish custom of having the children confirmed as soon as possible after baptism." However, the author anticipated difficulty in changing the practice.[72]

By the later 1960s the church held Mexican American parishioners to the same policy as other Catholics. But for the most part, Mexican Catholics in Houston and elsewhere continued their tradition; they circumvented the policy by simply crossing the border into Mexico, where they could still confirm their children without fulfilling the requirement of First Communion. Mrs. Esther García recalled the

Particular sacraments, such as this girl's First Communion, had great social, as well as religious, importance in Mexican American communities. Courtesy Houston Metropolitan Research Center, Houston Public Library.

practice during her childhood—her grandmother and mother took several of her younger siblings to Mexico to be confirmed. Mrs. García explained that the practice remained commonplace in Houston as late as the 1970s. The Oblate father's prediction a generation earlier, that it "would be difficult . . . to change this attitude," proved correct.[73] This practice again revealed some parishioners' resistance to the pressures of the institutional church as they adjusted to life in Houston in their own way, and it revealed Mexican women's leadership and initiatives in dictating the form resistance would take in some households. That independent attitude carried over into the way Mexican Catholics participated in church organizations and in how they related to the representatives of the church.

"One of the foundations of every parish is the Parish Societies," Father Esteban de Anta asserted in 1930.[74] The priest's observation was well founded, for parish organizations served important functions both for the institutional church and the *colonia*. Parish societies enhanced spiritual and social life, provided cohesion for the community, and expressed Mexican ethno-Catholic identity.

A Mexican parish typically accommodated the entire family in its organizational life.[75] Potentially, every member of a family could belong to some parish society. There were separate men's and women's organizations; young adults', as well as boys' and girls', clubs; even societies for infants. With time there were also mixed-gender societies. Different organizations came and went over the years, but some became perennial favorites that flourished for generations. Married women traditionally joined the Guadalupanas (Society of Our Lady of Guadalupe), the Socias del Altar (Altar Society), and the Socias del Sagrado Corazón (Sacred Heart Society). Later, they formed Legions of Mary, Ladies' Councils, and Mothers' Clubs, while single young women joined the Hijas de María (Daughters of Mary), young girls the Teresitas (Society of St. Therese the Little Flower), and teens the Catholic Youth Organization (CYO). Men's societies included the Sociedad del Santo Nombre (Holy Name Society), Adoración Nocturna (Nocturnal Adoration Society), and Vasallos de Cristo Rey (Subjects of Christ the King). Boys joined a Sociedad San Luis or San José (St. Louis or St. Joseph Sodality) in the early years, and later the CYO. The youngest children found their place in the Infant Jesus of Prague Society. Women's and girls' societies were more numerous than male organizations, but parish societies offered something for everyone. These voluntary organizations provided invaluable financial sustenance for parishes through their ongoing fund-raising. Moreover, parish societies offered Mexican women one of the few arenas in which they could develop their talents outside of the home (see Table A.2).[76]

Not surprisingly, parish societies often had some intimate link to

Mexican culture and history. For example, the quintessential women's organization was the Guadalupanas, a parish society that honored Mexico's patron saint, Our Lady of Guadalupe. Similarly, the Vasallos de Cristo Rey resonated with the memory of the religious wars in Mexico during the 1920s, a time when many Catholics fought to the death against the government's oppression of the Catholic Church, which, by extension, they perceived as an attack on their very identity. Mexican parishioners in Houston routinely joined the popular annual Christ the King celebrations. The citywide affair drew thousands of Catholics in its heyday of the 1950s. The event in 1950 drew over 15,000 faithful of all ethnicities, but the strong connection between Mexican history and religiosity stood out dramatically, as the press reported:

A bit of pathos was added in an incident involving three elderly Mexicans. During Solemn Benediction, as the bishop elevated the Ostensorium and blessed the assembled thousands, they knelt, made the Sign of the Cross, and the leader held up a small tattered banner on which was a picture of Christ the King. The three fixed their eyes on the Host, raised the banner and in unison exclaimed, "Viva Cristo rey!" They had come many miles from the Sierra range in North Mexico, where during the days of religious persecution, they and their little band of followers fled on Sundays to the fastnesses [sic] of the mountains, where, on bended knees, they recited the prayer, "O Christ Jesus, I acknowledge thee as the King of All."

Here were men who had come to celebrate the Kingship of Christ, men who had suffered and had deprived themselves of many things so that they could attend the great celebration. It was a display of faith rarely paralleled.[77]

In Houston's barrios people held fast to the memory of religious and historical events that entwined to define their Mexicanness. The Cristo Rey celebrations struck a chord because they were a time to honor family members and comrades killed in the Cristero Wars, as well as an expression of identity. Events like these underscored the importance of honoring the family and protecting the faith, values that were widely shared among Mexican and Mexican American Catholics. Kept alive by parish organizations and celebrations, these events unified Mexican Catholics everywhere.

At Guadalupe Parish a men's organization, the Nocturnal Adoration Society, gained great admiration and attention and flourished for several years. Pastors, bishops, and the press marveled at this men's organization, which began in the late 1920s with two groups of twenty men taking turns praying all night, twice a month. By 1934, 120 members prayed throughout the night four times a month. Men at Guadalupe Parish were also eagerly engaged in two other societies. The pastor described the men's Sacred Heart Society as a "flourishing" confraternity "with a large membership," and he heaped praise on the church band, the Banda Guadalupana. "Day after day they practice for three hours," he wrote, "and their beautiful music lends grace and animation to all the activities of the parish."[78]

The fervent participation of men in religious activities raises questions about the gendered nature of religiosity in Mexican American Catholic culture. Conventional wisdom has long held that Mexican and Mexican American Catholic men have been minimally involved in religious matters; religion has been considered something for women and children. The notoriety the men's Nocturnal Adoration Society aroused is evidence of this; the group received so much attention precisely because it was unusual to see Mexican men show such religious fervor. Reverend De Anta called the group "rare," and in describing the men's activities he used the very telling Spanish phrase— *despreciando el qué dirán* (meaning "disregarding what people might say").[79] In other words, the pastor understood that these men's allnight prayer vigils transgressed ascribed gender roles, yet the men did not care what people might say about their displays of piety. This lends credence to the conventional view about gender roles and religion in Mexican and Mexican American Catholic culture.

But rather than ask if women were more involved in religious activity than men, perhaps we should ask under what circumstances was it acceptable for men to show pious devotion? Did men monopolize some parish societies because they were considered more prestigious, or because the symbolism or activities associated with particular organizations coincided more closely with the roles and behavior society ascribed to men? Maternal symbolism and the fact that Our Lady of Guadalupe represented the ideal role model for married women certainly moved many wives and mothers to join the Guadalupana societies. As was consistent with cultural mores, too, men—not women—spent the entire night away from home praying, as members of the Adoración Nocturna. Then, too, the fact that the cry "Viva Cristo Rey!" was as much a call to arms as it was a statement of religious belief prompted men to see this organization as "theirs," linked as it was to military leadership and warfare, arenas that men historically claimed.

Preparations for and participation in the many novenas, feast days, and other ceremonies their societies sponsored further involved parishioners institutionally. The month of the Virgin Mary (May) "was celebrated with enthusiasm by the Children of Mary and the Teresitas," one proud pastor wrote in 1944. The following month, the priest added, the women of the Sacred Heart Society "put their hearts into the month of June so as not to let the Children of Mary have all the honors."[80] Likewise at Guadalupe Church in the 1920s, young girls dressed in white customarily offered bouquets to the Virgin, and individuals, families, and societies took charge of particular days during the month-long devotion. The Feast of Our Lady of Guadalupe also involved many devotees.[81] In addition, parish society members reinforced their spiritual lives by corporately partaking of the sacraments. The CYO of Immaculate Heart Parish, for instance, attended Mass and received group Communion in the 1950s. At Guadalupe Parish in the 1930s, the four children's societies took turns "to appear as a unit in church." The men's Holy Name and Nocturnal Adoration Societies at different parishes also customarily took Corporate Communion.[82]

These practices undoubtedly pleased church officials, who strove to make Mexicans "better" Catholics. Like other immigrant communities, Italians in New York and Chicago, for example, Mexican Catholics in Houston felt pressured to change their style of Catholicism to conform to the Irish American model that set the standard for "acceptable" Catholicism in America.[83] Noting what in his eyes were changes for the better among Houston's Mexican Catholics, an early-twentieth-century clergyman boasted, "The Mexicanitos . . . are being transformed into a splendid unit of people who are not only practical Catholics but Catholics who are living up to the highest Christian ideals." He offered as evidence the flourishing organizational life of the parish.[84] It would be easy, but erroneous, to interpret Mexican American participation in church societies as simple conformity to Irish American Catholicism. Rather, joining parish societies was a form of accommodation, not capitulation to total assimilation. On the one hand, participation in organizations closely associated with Mexican history and identity—the Guadalupanas and Vasallos de Cristo Rey, for instance—represented yet another tie to Mexicanness and a way to bolster ethno-Catholicism. On the other hand, by being active in parish societies, Mexicans blunted church criticism and gave the impression that they were becoming "better" Catholics. In this way, Mexican parishioners met some of the demands the church hierarchy made of them while still defining their own way of being Catholic and nurturing their sense of identity and self-worth. They made do in this way, accommodating to life in the Bayou City without disappearing into it through total assimilation.[85]

Parish societies also performed important social functions. These organizations raised money, provided community service, and had the potential for social action. Organizational fund-raising enriched individuals and whole communities by fostering ethnic identity and solidarity.[86] Societies also fostered a sense of social responsibility through community service. The sixth, seventh, and eighth graders of St. Patrick's Ave María Club, for instance, helped the Red Cross and other organizations as part of their activities. At Immaculate Heart of Mary, the teenagers of the CYO distributed food baskets to indigent families, and adults also provided emergency relief through the St. Vincent de Paul Society.[87]

In addition, parish societies were potential vehicles for social action. Since the later nineteenth century, Texas Mexicans had formed secular mutual aid societies for self-help and community assistance. Similar parish-based organizations existed since at least the early twentieth century throughout Texas as Mexicans formed chapters of the Holy Mexican Union and the Liga de Protección Mexicana (Mexican Protection League) to safeguard their civic and religious interests.[88] In the early 1910s, for instance, the Liga de Protección Mexicana in Del Rio, Texas, used court action and a boycott against local newspapers' tirades about their clergy and parishioners. At Houston's Guadalupe Parish, the men's *liga* was one of the earliest parish societies established. Significantly, some of Guadalupe's parish women formed their own *liga* the next year, in 1917.[89] Separate men's and women's parish societies were customary in the early twentieth century, and, given the often political focus of the Liga de Protección, it is not surprising that men would have their own separate organization. But the existence of a separate women's society raises intriguing questions about women forming this particular kind of organization. How different or similar were the two *ligas*? Were Mexican women in early-twentieth-century Houston pushing the limits of civic participation through this organization? The sparse available evidence leaves these particular questions unanswered, as indeed many others remain about the Mexican American religious experience.

The *cursillo de cristiandad* provided another church-based organization with implications for social change. A three-day, once-in-a-lifetime experience of spiritual renewal and dedication, the "little course in Christianity" became very popular among Spanish-speaking Catholics in the early 1960s.[90] *Cursillos* brought together priests and laypeople in a retreatlike setting that imbued participants with the Christian message of dynamic self-reform and responsibility for others. The intensity of the experience fostered a sense of empowerment that potentially could be channeled into social action.[91] Church officials, however, did not intend the *cursillo* to be a separate parish society or a means of social action. They specifically instructed participants "not to form a clique or a special organization" after completing the *cursillo*. Instead, participants were supposed to volunteer their services in parish work and "leaven the parish for God."[92] However, Mexican parishioners often disregarded these instructions. Church bulletins, diocesan reports, and the local Catholic press routinely reported the activities of those who had participated in the *cursillo* (*cursillistas*) as distinct groups.[93] The *cursillistas'* insistence on maintaining a separate identity, despite the church's instructions to the contrary, again recalled the characteristic independence of Mexican American Catholics and their tendency to circumvent church authority.

Parishioners recognized the *cursillo's* potential for social change. Many Chicanos involved in social justice movements in the 1960s and 1970s were *cursillistas*, including César Chávez and many of his lay supporters, as well as vocal Chicano clerics such as Father Patricio Flores, who introduced the *cursillo* in Houston.[94] In Houston the head of the Political Association of Spanish-speaking Organizations (PASO), Manuel Crespo, believed the *cursillo* was "one of the most important efforts in the Church" to fight for racial equality. "Since I've become a cursillista I've seen how much this activity can be of tremendous help to us and the community," Crespo stated. He believed that community political leaders who were "fallen-away" Catholics could be brought back to active membership in the church through the *cursillo*. Moreover, he saw the *cursillo* as a possible avenue for "helping eliminate discrimination against us."[95]

Padres Asociados para Derechos Religiosos, Educativos y Sociales (Priests Associated for Religious, Educational and Social Rights, or PADRES), the organization of outspoken Chicano priests who sought to involve the Catholic Church in Mexican Americans' efforts for social equality, later echoed these sentiments. PADRES believed the *cursillo* was not being used to full advantage. "[S]ocial action has not been encouraged or implemented [in the *cursillo*]," the activist priests complained.

In early 1970, they demanded a separate national secretariat for Mexican Americans and culturally sensitive priests to direct the *cursillos*. Most important, PADRES called for social action to be an integral part of the *cursillo* experience.[96]

Again, Mexican American lay and religious leaders demonstrated their self-reliance and resourcefulness. The institutional church leadership had not intended the *cursillos* to be used for social action, but at least some Mexican Americans saw them as stepping stones in that direction; they recognized the possibility of using their institutional participation to challenge their outsider status in society and the church. It is important to remember that the *cursillos* were exclusively for men when they began in 1957 and that they were structured around the notion of male bonding. The *cursillo* movement radiated intensely through Mexican American communities in an era when returning Mexican American war veterans and others were asserting themselves, mounting civil rights campaigns, and struggling to take control of their lives. This aspect of Mexican American Catholicism contrasts strongly with its more feminized nature of the pre–World War II period. An assertive expression of Mexican American men willing to publicly proclaim their spirituality and apply it to social issues, the *cursillo* fit well with the political activism stirring among the post–World War II GI generation because it offered a potential arena in which they could strive for personal and community self-determination.[97]

Language, Relationships, and Memory

Mexican parishioners usually worshipped in parishes administered by Spanish-speaking priests and sisters, especially during the first half of the twentieth century, when most of them belonged to Mexican national parishes. Church leaders appreciated the importance of having Spanish-speaking personnel, and they tried to find native speakers or Anglos who had a working knowledge of the language, as well as experience ministering to Mexicans and Mexican Americans. Often the pastors were Spaniards and had an "American" assistant.[98]

The presence of a Spanish-speaking church staff facilitated communication but did not assure closeness and confidence between clergy and parishioners. Relations between parishioners and priests were usually cordial, but they were characterized by formality, not warmth. Parishioners' recollections revealed few endearing sentiments regarding the clerics who headed the parishes. For example, an Immaculate Heart member recalled that "[y]ears back, the Church was so private and so apart from the people." In a similar vein, a Guadalupe parishioner described relations between the churchgoers and priests as "okay" and "alright."[99]

Priests were figures of unquestioned authority who demanded respect. "[P]eople respected them as the head of the church," a woman recalled, "and what we had to do was whatever they said; that was it." Some priests kept a close watch on their church members and tried to regulate their behavior. Father Esteban de Anta often surprised parishioners with his unannounced home visits, and another priest demanded that his parishioners stay away from the *aleluyas* (Mexican Protestants). But there was limited interaction with the priest. At Immaculate Heart, the priests rarely attended the fund-raisers church members put on. Even church services afforded little contact. After a service, a parishioner explained, the priest would immediately leave the church without mingling with the members afterward. Priests had a "job to do," and "whether we like it or not we just go along with it," a parishioner summarized.[100]

The social distance between priests and parishioners reflected the ambivalent Mexican tradition of respect mixed with anticlericalism. Social scientists in the early and mid-twentieth century noted the conflicted feelings Mexicans held toward the church and the clergy.[101] Because of the great wealth and political power of the church and the great vitality of Mexican Catholicism, a later scholar wrote, no other Catholic nation "experienced such extremes of anticlericalism as Mexico."[102] The long history of church-state conflict culminated in the Cristero Rebellion of 1926–29, in which thousands of Catholics carried on a bloody resistance against the Mexican government.[103] Generations of strife between Mexican civil and religious authority undoubtedly affected attitudes in Houston's *colonia*. Mary Villagómez, with her twenty years as a nun and lifelong association with the Magnolia barrio, spoke with firsthand experience. On the one hand, Mexicans had a great reverence for the habit and the cossack, she explained, but on the other hand, many people resented the fact that the church in Mexico had sided with the rich and with the oppressive government of President Porfirio Díaz. Those parishioners blamed the church for its alliance with a dictatorship that had brought on a devastating revolution in 1910 that forced many of them to flee to the United States. But Houston's parishes were also home to large numbers of immigrants who had risked their very lives to defend the church during the Cristero Rebellion in the 1920s. The issue was a paradox because Houston's Mexican parishes harbored feelings of both estrangement and loyalty toward the Catholic Church.[104]

The gulf between priests and parishioners was also partly the result of old animosities rooted in the Spanish colonial period. Some parishioners felt that priests from Spain had a condescending attitude toward Mexicans. "I had a feeling . . . that they thought they were better than us," a woman recalled, "that our culture didn't measure up."[105] Complaints by Catholic officials about the "Spanish contempt" for Mexican Americans supported the parishioner's suspicions.[106] It was not uncommon, then, as one bishop reported in 1969, to find "some well-founded complaints about lack of rapport on the part of the Pastor."[107] The parishioners' traditional deference for the priesthood probably muted this antagonism, but at times parishioners bitterly complained and demanded the removal of priests they found unacceptable.[108] Church members also tried to dissuade the hierarchy from removing priests or nuns who had been effective and respectful.[109]

Relations between Houston's Mexican Catholics and church representatives revealed some continuity in the Texas Mexican experience. The attitudes and perceptions that colored institutional parish life were a legacy of the past, and respectful but distant relations between parishioners and clergy reinforced the tradition of tenuous links with the institutional church. These lukewarm relations also revealed the people's determination to resist treatment as second-class Catholics. When parishioners demanded sensitive and helpful church personnel, in effect they were demanding respect for themselves, their communities, and their ethnoreligious identity, asserting their cultural autonomy.

A strong carrier of culture, language richly reflected Houston's Mexican ethno-Catholic culture. Religious sentiment and symbolism suffused the peoples' language and the ordinary acts of everyday life, texturing the web of Mexican American ethnoreligious memory and identity. An Oblate priest writing about Mexico in the 1930s marveled at how thoroughly the names, events, and beliefs associated with Catholicism imbued Mexican life.[110] Such names as Providence, Faith, Hope, Guadalupe, and Santiago abounded—in people's names, the names of towns and cities, in popular songs, and in the names of businesses. "Even the amusements especially among the working classes were often of a religious nature," the cleric wrote, "such as the feast of St. John, St. James, [and] the day of Holy Innocents," in addition to the "numerous religious feasts which were the occasion of much rejoicing." He added, "There is no home no matter how humble which does not have its statue or image of our Lady of Guadalupe."[111]

The author concluded that the Spanish language was "essentially Catholic." A multitude of common sayings and proverbs exuded religious feeling. To a mother, the clatter of noisy children sounded "like the Day of Judgement." In reply to a "thank you," people responded with "Let thanks be given to God." When someone took leave, saying "see you tomorrow," the response was "If God wills it" or "If God grants us life" (*Si Dios quiere* or *Si Dios nos presta vida*). The clergyman relayed many other sayings that reflected the religious imagery typical of Mexican conversation.[112]

Similarly, Houston's Mexican Catholics often expressed their reliance on an assumed sacred presence in their lives. References to *la Virgen* and *el Señor* (God) filled family letters. Time-honored phrases included *gracias a Dios* (thanks be to God); *por voluntad de Dios* (by God's will); *que el sagrado corazón de Jesús los bendiga* (may the sacred heart of Jesus bless you); and *que la Virgen los cubra con su Santísimo manto* (may the Virgin's blessed cloak protect you).[113] To invoke the protection of a sacred intercessor for a loved one was not only a conscious act of prayer in a church or at a home altar; it was just as much an unconscious way of thinking, talking, and writing—a natural part of living. Mexican American Catholics naturally entwined familial affection and the sacred this way because theirs was a world in which the temporal and the spiritual flowed continually into each other. Parishioners emphasized that confluence. "[R]eligion was our life," Mrs. Janie Tijerina asserted. Mrs. Esther García echoed, "My spirituality has a lot to do with who I am . . . especially as a Mexican, with my background and my grandmother—she's so rooted in Aztec and Mayan blood—that part of our spirituality is who we are; we can't change that. We can't divide it; we can't separate it. That's part of our being." She added that Mexican Catholics did not separate religion from politics or other aspects of life, that when they did, "that's when we stop being who we are."[114]

At times, lay and religious alike penned verses that expressed the centrality of religion in their lives and the many ways the faith sustained them. A proud Chicano's homage to his people began, "Bronze and proud are my people from the Land of Sun, Where the Virgin Guadalupe's roses blessed us new times now begin."[115] The poem not only reflected the ethnic pride and community solidarity characteristic of the Chicano movement years, but it also underlined the continuing importance of Our Lady of Guadalupe. The author invoked this sacred intercessor at the height of the Chicano civil rights movement, as many in generations before him had done in their search for social justice. Another plea for divine intervention flowed from the pen of Blas de León, a simple farmer who lived on the outskirts of Houston in the 1920s. In *"Ante el Altar de la Virgen de los Dolores,"* De León expressed his devotion to Our Lady of Sorrows, imploring her spiritual healing.[116] Rural workers often faced a harsh life in early-twentieth-century Texas, and De León's poem spoke for many immigrants and Mexican Americans who turned to favored saints for solace from drudgery and pain. "You know how I've suffered" (*Tu sabes cuánto he sufrido*), De León reminded the Virgin. Wounded by life's rocky path (*los guijarros del camino el corazón me han herido*), he needed her peace and consolation (*dadme paz dadme consuelo*).

Many clergy and sisters recognized this universal devotion to the saints among Mexican parishioners. For example, Sister Dolores Cárdenas, who spent much of her career in Houston's barrios, always ended her newspaper column with a short tribute that reflected the span of succor devotees found in Our Lady of Guadalupe: *O Virgen de Guadalupe, la más bella de las flores; Para tí nuestros afanes, alegrías y dolores* (O Virgin Guadalupe, the most beautiful of flowers, with you we share all our troubles, joys, and sorrows).[117] In 1931 Father Esteban de Anta wrote an elegant fifteen-stanza poem titled "*A la Santísima Virgen de Guadalupe*," in honor of the 400th anniversary of the Virgin's apparition. The poem, professionally printed and featuring the image of Guadalupe, was an attractive keepsake.[118]

Mexican Americans saved commemorative holy cards and other religious mementos that reflected important religious and social events in their personal lives and in the life of their communities. The cards carried images of Christ, the Virgin, or a saint, and information about celebrated events such as special missions or novenas, the entrance of a nun or priest into religious life, anniversaries of parish societies, or special feast days. Often religious mentors inscribed the cards and gave them to parishioners. Other memories might be preserved in a tattered postcard depicting the apparition of Our Lady of Guadalupe to Juan Diego, or in a faded ribbon inscribed with the date and place of an *apadrinamiento* (a godparent sponsorship). These remembrances held important meanings for Mexican and Mexican American Catholics in Houston. As "narratives of family and communal events framed in liturgical celebrations," they were tangible symbols of binding experiences shared by many individuals and communities.[119] Stored away among a family's treasures, these mementos sacralized the collective memory of a people.

Mexican ethno-Catholicism in Houston had striking parallels with

Tattered but valued: parish bulletins and other religious mementos reflected a sense of identity and community among Houston's Mexican-origin Catholics. Courtesy Houston Metropolitan Research Center, Houston Public Library.

the Catholicism of southern Italian immigrants in the late nineteenth and early twentieth centuries. Church leaders ridiculed and chastised the southern Italians' pre-Tridentine way of being Catholic in much the same way they did Mexican American faith expressions. Also like the Mexicans, southern Italians had a strong anticlerical tradition and a similar pattern of infrequent church attendance; their devotional practices centered on shrines, pilgrimages, holy cards, and other sacramentals that clergy often saw as a "peculiar kind of spiritual condition" lacking in doctrinal understanding. But what church personnel saw as spiritual deficiencies southern Italians and Mexicans understood as a source of strength. For both peoples, their "peculiar" faith helped them build community and retain the identity, pride, and values that sustained them as they struggled to create a space for themselves in a society that saw them as outsiders or even outcasts.[120]

When the Oblate Fathers of Mary Immaculate arrived in Houston in 1911, they encountered the Mexican way of being Catholic described in this chapter. It was a distinct religious tradition that often clashed with their own and one that reflected the outsider status Mexicans occupied in American society and the Catholic Church. In order to understand the relationship between Mexican Americans and the institutional church, we must next examine the perceptions and attitudes church representatives revealed about their Mexican parishioners, the topic to which we now turn.

THREE

F ather Esteban de Anta was appalled at what he saw in Houston in late 1911. One of the original band of Missionary Oblates in the city, the Spanish priest recoiled at the grinding poverty he found among Mexicans and Mexican Americans, a "poor, ignorant and despised people . . . eking out a miserable existence." Moreover, the cleric shuddered at another kind of poverty that, at least in his eyes, afflicted his parishioners—a spiritual poverty. "For many Mexicans, religion, alas! consists of having a great many *Santitos*, and in lighting a candle before them," De Anta decried. "It is impossible to make them realize the importance of the Mass and of the reception of the Sacraments."[1]

Father De Anta and officials of the Catholic Church rarely spoke about Texas Mexicans without using such phrases as "the poor Mexican" or "these poor people." But although most Texas Mexicans in the early twentieth century were in fact poor, these descriptions reflected more than their economic status. Indeed, the terminology revealed as much about the views and attitudes of church representatives as it did about the status of Mexicans in the United States. In the eyes of many church leaders, Mexicans were poor in more than the economic sense; they were spiritually impoverished as well. Thus Mexican Catholics found themselves objects of both pity and scorn, and they were usually seen as a problem for the Catholic Church.

This chapter examines changes and continuities in the way church representatives perceived Mexican parishioners in order to illustrate how those perceptions influenced and reflected the ways Mexican Catholics carved their place in Houston. Catholic officials understood the so-called Mexican problem of the early twentieth century (later called the "problem of the Spanish-speaking") as both a pastoral and a social issue. Generally, this dual perception reflected negative attitudes about Mexican Catholics, and to a large degree it contributed to their marginalization in the institutional church, especially in the early twentieth century. Over time, however, changes in the Mexican community and in societal views gradually produced attitudinal shifts among church officials. Despite a continuing tension between old stereotypes and new perceptions, by the 1960s these shifting attitudes had begun to enhance the church's ministry to Mexican and Mexican American Catholics.

THE "MEXICAN PROBLEM," 1910S–1930S

The flood of Mexican immigration in Texas and the Southwest in the early twentieth century gave rise to the so-called Mexican problem. Many Americans viewed Mexican immigrants ambivalently, as a sort of necessary evil in American society. Mexicans were wanted and needed as cheap labor, but they were also resented as economic competitors by some and as potential despoilers of the American social fabric by others. Generally, these perceptions applied equally to both native-born Mexican Americans and Mexican immigrants, for few Americans distinguished between the two groups. For the Catholic Church the "Mexican problem" was primarily a question of evangelization, a matter of combating Protestant proselytizing and making "good" (American-style) Catholics out of "nominal" ones.[2] But, in addition, church officials recognized the social side of the "Mexican problem." In the opinion of many clergy, the social aspects of the Mexicans' "problem"—their ostracism and exploitation in American society—were rooted in the racial and cultural traits of the Mexicans themselves.

Many church personnel thought of Mexicans essentially as Indians, and they often attributed to them a presumably violent "Latin temperament." However, they were also deemed polite, charming, and naturally timid.[3] Not surprisingly, some nuns felt a duty to "civilize" the Mexicans of Houston's Second Ward.[4] The perceived need to civilize Mexicans stemmed partly from the widely held view of them as nomadics.[5] Clerics noted the absence of traditional "American" values among Mexicans, especially when compared to "their more virile Northern neighbors" who were blessed, supposedly, with greater initiative. Even Bishop Christopher E. Byrne, a staunch champion of Texas Mexicans, found his flock's values deficient.[6]

In addition, it was not uncommon for representatives of the church to view Mexicans as children. The local priest was "a father indeed to the Mexicans," according to one cleric. Childlike, Mexicans were "moved more by imagination than by reason," a priest claimed, and had improvident and hedonistic tendencies.[7] An official of the Galveston Diocese, honoring a priest's work among Houston Mexicans, described his parishioners as "people who are very largely little children."[8] This tendency to infantilize the Mexican paralleled the experience of other people of color in the United States. As historian Ronald Takaki and others have shown, the ideology of the "child / savage" powerfully influenced the racialization of African Americans, Native Americans, and Asian Americans, as well as Mexican Americans.[9]

The racialization process of these groups varied, of course, depending not only on skin color but also on class, gender, geographical location, and historical era. Mexicans occupied an ambiguous place in the racial hierarchy. "As a racially mixed group," historian Neil Foley has shown, "Mexicans, like Indians and Asians, lived in a black-and-white nation that regarded them neither as black nor as white." For most white Texans, Mexicans were "a 'mongrelized' race of Indian, African, and Spanish ancestry."[10] Because of their mixed lineage, the

Mexicans' racialization experience recalls the history of other Americans whose racial classification confounded white America in the nineteenth and early twentieth centuries. Cape Verdean Americans, Afro-Portuguese Catholics from the Cape Verde Islands off West Africa, for instance, began immigrating in the 1860s mostly to southeastern New England. Considered neither white nor black in their adopted land, they came to occupy a marginal place in the Catholic Church and New England society, a situation similar to that of Mexicans in Texas.[11]

An even more striking historical parallel can be drawn between Texas Mexicans and southern Italian immigrants, especially those Italians who settled in the Deep South. Throughout the United States, Americans considered the southern Italians racially suspect and denigrated them as "kinky-haired Africans" because of their "swarthy" complexion and the fact that they were from the *mezzogiorno*, the part of Italy that is the hottest and closest to Africa. In the black and white South of the late nineteenth and early twentieth centuries, the guardians of the color line tried to keep Italian children from attending white schools and sometimes lynched adults who violated southern racial protocols by working and socializing with blacks. In the same period in Texas, Anglos treated Tejanos in much the same way and for very similar reasons. Historian Arnoldo De León has documented how whites brutalized Mexicans and held them in contempt, partly for helping slaves to escape in antebellum times but also for working, socializing, and sometimes intermarrying with blacks.[12] However, in constructing their racial views, whites emphasized the Mexicans' alleged savage Aztec Indian background.[13] This added twist distinguished the Mexicans' racialization from both the Cape Verdeans' and the Italians'. In any case, society's negative views of mixed-race people such as Mexicans existed, to some degree, in the Catholic Church in early-twentieth-century Houston. Consciously or not, these perceptions helped to perpetuate the social inequality of Mexicans in the United States.

However, racist and paternalistic clerical views nonetheless coexisted with genuine humanitarian concerns about the endemic poverty in Mexican communities. The poor were the central calling of the Oblate Fathers, a challenge reflected in the order's motto: *Evangelizare pauperibus misit me* (He hath sent me to preach the Gospel to the poor).[14] Men and women of the church agonized over the severe poverty that afflicted many Mexicans and Mexican Americans in the early twentieth century. Father Esteban de Anta observed in 1913 that Mexicans found *"[m]ucho trabajo y poco dinero"* (plenty of work but little pay) in Houston and the Southwest.[15] His superior, the Right Reverend Nicholas A. Gallagher, bishop of the Galveston Diocese, had appealed to Houston employers in 1912 for donations to ease the Mexicans' plight and carry on their evangelization. He candidly reminded "those who are benefitted most by the industrious and honest labor of this large Mexican population, namely, THE DIFFERENT RAILROADS and OTHER CORPORATIONS that employ them," of their moral duty.[16] The bishop's appeal was more than moral prodding. He recognized the importance of Mexican workers to Houston's growing economy and argued that their spiritual and temporal "uplift" was imperative for retaining them as a valuable part of the city's workforce. Contributions from area employers to the church would result in "more contented and happy" employees, the bishop reminded the corporate sector, and it would prove to Mexicans that their employers "have at heart their welfare."[17]

The Catholic hierarchy recognized the importance of the growing number of Mexicans in Houston early on and consequently began to focus more attention on their needs. But it was clear to some that the Mexicans' well-being was not a high priority among many employers. One cleric asserted that Mexicans were "more sinned against than sinning," being "heckled and brow-beaten and exploited and underpaid by avaricious and unscrupulous employers." They lived in "wretched cottages" and wore "sordid rags," another priest lamented. Sister Mary Benitia Vermeersch arrived at Our Lady of Guadalupe Parish in the summer of 1915 to find atrocious living conditions in Houston's El Segundo Barrio (Second Ward). Many railroad workers lived in company housing, usually dilapidated two- or three-room shacks. Families sometimes shared empty boxcars temporarily before finding better quarters. This dire poverty, Father L. O. Eckardt argued, made Mexican workers dependent on their employers and relegated them "to be mere machines of unskilled labor."[18]

Representatives of the church recognized that this deprivation gave rise to a panoply of other social problems. Many religious leaders criticized the indignities often heaped upon Texas Mexicans. "They came, hopeful of finding respect and love," a Houston priest observed, but found instead "only contempt and hatred. 'Greasers' they are called and looked down upon and considered as pariahs." White hostility toward Mexicans was so fierce, Bishop Byrne noted, that it sometimes exceeded that shown toward blacks.[19]

Social ostracism was widespread. "Such prejudice against the Mexicans is very strong and is shown on all sides and in hundreds of ways," a churchman reported in 1933. In an era of Jim Crow, discrimination pervaded public facilities and institutions. Mexicans were denied entry to restaurants, hotels, theaters, and other service and recreational facilities. Mary Villagómez, who grew up in Magnolia Park on Houston's east side in the 1910s and 1920s, remembered vividly that "people . . . were so prejudiced against the Mexicans." The Pine View movie theater did not even allow segregated seating, as other places sometimes did. "We could not go into Pine View," she recalled; "the Mexicans couldn't even stand at a distance to see it; no, no, you couldn't get near the place." Certain parks and residential areas were also closed to Mexicans. "We couldn't go into Mason Park . . . [or] Forest Hill; that was off limits," she recounted.[20]

Clerics readily pointed out the church's own shortcomings in this regard. "[E]ven many Catholic congregations do not want [Mexicans]," a priest wrote. Some Anglo American churches brazenly displayed signs warning, "Mexicans prohibited." Others reserved a back pew for Mexicans with a sign that read *Mexicanos.*"[21] The archbishop of San Antonio, describing a practice common throughout the Southwest, stated, "We are literally forced to erect two churches in the same localities, one for the American Catholics and the other for the Mexicans, for as one of our missionaries put it recently—'An American church for the white people and a mission church for the Helots, the Pariahs of the community, our poor Mexican Catholic people and their little ones.' "²² The archbishop's comments underscored two major aspects of the social reality of Texas Mexicans in the early twentieth century, their poverty and their status as social outcasts. The structures of the Catholic Church replicated Mexican subordination in American society.

Houston was no exception. On the city's east side, priests at Immaculate Conception, the Anglo church in Magnolia, told the neighborhood's Mexicans they had to go to the "Mexican church," Our Lady of Guadalupe, which was farther away. On the rare occasions when Mexicans were admitted into Immaculate Conception, they were allowed seating only in the back pews.²³ Newly arrived immigrants sometimes unknowingly violated this ethnic protocol. Sister Agnes Rita Rodríguez remembered her father's anguish in the late 1910s at being ordered out of Annunciation Church—the premier Anglo Catholic Church and an architectural showcase in downtown Houston. As he kneeled in prayer, Mr. Rodríguez looked up to see an usher pointing to the door and saying, "You don't belong here."²⁴

On the other hand, some men and women of the church criticized racial segregation both within churches and in society. Some were particularly critical about so-called Mexican schools. The segregation of Mexican-origin children in public schools was the "norm," and Catholic officials often decried the lack of "decent" public schools for Mexican children, pointing out how "almost hopelessly ostracized" these children were. The cruelty of Anglo children toward them, one priest remarked, frequently ended in fistfights—"a race war in minature [sic]."²⁵

Mexicans stood little chance of getting a good education. In the eyes of some church leaders, this had devastating effects, both socially and spiritually. It was this denial of schooling, in the view of one priest, that doomed the Mexican to a wretched existence of backbreaking work and economic dependency. "Poverty, destitution and misery are the fruits of his uneducated condition," asserted Father Eckardt. And most important, the priest argued, the Mexican's social condition endangered his spiritual life. As long as Mexicans remained mired in poverty, the priest reasoned, their evangelization would be useless.[26] The church's main concern, after all, was saving souls, and it was evident, at least to some, that the social aspect of the "Mexican problem" was tied to the pastoral.

The pastoral side of the so-called problem, like the social, was based on perceptions about Mexicans and their culture. Church officials shared an image of Mexican religiosity that, with few exceptions, gravely disconcerted them. According to many men and women of the church, Mexican Catholics were sadly devoid of genuine piety and badly in need of spiritual rebirth. "How pitiable was their state when we first came to Houston!" an early missionary exclaimed.[27] Many clerics thought Texas Mexicans were indifferent to religion or that they were Catholics in name only. To them, the Mexicans' infrequent church attendance was proof of an irreligious nature. One priest estimated in 1938 that only 20 percent regularly complied with their religious duties. It seemed that most Mexicans were satisfied with going to church only on special occasions, such as during the Christmas season and Holy Week, or for a christening, wedding, or funeral. "He is baptized, married and buried by the priest and '¡Esto basta!' [This is enough!]," a frustrated cleric chastised.[28]

The religious laxity many church personnel saw in Mexicans often reinforced their perceptions of them as childlike. Father De Anta considered his Mexican parishioners in Houston "our friends, yes, more, our children." Seen this way, Mexican Catholics needed the constant protection of the church because they were "such easy victims" of Protestant proselytizers. Bishop Byrne agonized over his flock, especially those so widely scattered that they were only sporadically attended by a "gypsy priest," such as Father Frank Urbanovsky. The bishop wrote that when the roving priest moved on to visit other isolated Mexicans, he left "with a dread, lest the wolves of Satan come and devour his children again." In October 1948, for example, Father

Urbanovsky noted the recently built El Divino Redentor Mexican Presbyterian Church, "[l]ess than a block away" from the soon-to-be Our Lady of St. John Parish in the Bonita Gardens barrio. "Throughout the summer," Urbanovsky reported, the *aleluya* competitors had been "using every means possible to attract the [Catholic] children and through them the parents."[29]

Conscious of the ever-present Protestants, some observers tried to absolve the Mexican for his alleged irreligiosity—only to reveal their own racial bias and misconceptions. One commentator conceded that Mexicans' supposed religious deficiencies were hardly their own fault, because "by nature" Mexicans lacked energy. Religious indifference resulted because religion required energy and, the writer claimed, Mexicans were "listless to anything requiring energy." Another clergyman attributed the alleged problem to the Mexican Indian heritage, to what he vaguely called "the native mental reactions of the race."[30] More bluntly, another priest claimed that Mexicans were "to be helped because they are not of normal intelligence and therefore poor."[31] Perceptions of Mexican cultural and racial traits meshed neatly with religious ones, and societal views reverberated with clerical attitudes.

What particularly exasperated some church officials was their belief that Mexican Catholicism was "not a Faith of reason." The Mexicans' apparent inattention to some sacraments caused many to despair, and their devotion to the sacramentals of the church—*santitos*, candles, holy water, blessings, and so forth—bordered on superstition, according to one priest.[32] In a similar vein, a high official strenuously opposed a plan to build a shrine in honor of Our Lady of Guadalupe in 1936. "I certainly am not in favor of this 'shrine-business,'" the father provincial wrote pointedly. "I think that in this country we are 'overshrined, over-grotted' [sic] and in some cases 'over-novenad' [sic]," he protested. He objected on grounds that commercial motives too often replaced religious ones in these kinds of projects. But a cultural bias showed. The cleric lamented that the "beauty and purity of *American* faith and devotion" was "victimized" by these types of religious expression, practices that were commonly favored by Mexicans and other immigrants. Much more could be accomplished among the Mexicans, the father provincial suggested, "with Masses, Holy Communions, prayers and with . . . proper limited material aid."[33] Echoing the Americanizing zeal of the era, the provincial proposed an approach that might make Mexicans "better" Catholics.

Church officials and Mexicans obviously disagreed about what comprised a "good" Catholic, as an Oblate missionary revealed: "If you ask a Mexican, 'Are you a Catholic?' he will answer: '*Sí, señor, yo soy muy católico*,' ('Yes sir, I am a good Catholic'), and as proof he will show you a medal that he wears, or point to the brightly-colored pictures which decorate the walls of his cottage."[34] Missionaries dreaded hearing Mexican parents say about their children, "O, sometimes they say a few prayers or light a candle before the picture of our favorite saint. So, you see, *Padrecito*, though they do miss Mass or Sunday-school, they are still good Catholics at home."[35] Father De Anta was understandably distressed when a religious picture he was asked to bless turned out to be that of Martin Luther! The supplicant—who insisted that the picture was not only that of a saint but of one who was *muy milagrero* (a great miracle-worker)—eventually admitted his error, "and Luther was cast into the devouring flames of the stove."[36]

Such observations were common, and they underscored the gulf between the style of Catholicism that predominated in the United States and the ethno-Catholicism of Mexican Americans that church officials considered a "problem." But in fact the problem was the inflexibility of the American Catholic Church. As a worldwide institution, the Roman Catholic Church evolved into various national forms, and in the United States what was deemed "Catholic" was the Irish American model, with its emphasis on regular Mass attendance and a more "intellectual," less overtly emotional, faith. American Catholicism was rigid, so much so that despite their deeply rooted Catholicism, Mexicans were objects of missionary activity. In Houston, where two Irish American bishops headed the diocese from 1892 to 1950, diocesan administrators saw the world through Irish eyes.[37] Their perceptions, furthermore, made little if any distinction between Mexicans and Mexican Americans. With few exceptions, church representatives saw them all as downtrodden "Mexicans"—poor, uneducated, laboring masses in dire need of spiritual and material uplift.

SHIFTING PERCEPTIONS, 1930S–1950S

A growing awareness about differences between native-born Mexican Americans and Mexican immigrants began to emerge among church officials in the 1930s. The alleged problems posed by a burgeoning Mexican population created tremendous interest among Americans, triggering a flood of literature about Mexican-origin people in the United States from the popular press and academic and clerical writers.[38] This new knowledge coincided with a general reassessment in the scientific community about the nature of race and ethnicity and its relation to social inequality. In particular, scholars and social commentators began to doubt facile explanations that historically had attributed Mexican American poverty and social marginality simply to assumed genetic or cultural deficiencies.[39] Presumably these progressive trends sensitized some church personnel to ethnic diversity, but it was their actual day-to-day involvement with Mexicans at the parish level that forced them to reexamine their attitudes toward Mexican and Mexican American Catholics.

In the 1930s representatives of the Catholic Church began making distinctions in class, citizenship status, and civic activity among Mexican-origin people. An Oblate recognized in 1933 that immigrants were not only poor workers but middle class as well, and some had even served in the U.S. Army. Similarly, Bishop Byrne reported to the American Board of Catholic Missions in 1935 that "thousands and thousands of our 'Mexicans' have never seen the other side of the Rio Grande, nor have any desire to see it."[40] Some four years later, the prelate noted the political consciousness stirring among native-born Texas Mexicans. "A movement is on foot," Byrne reported, "to get the native Texas Mexicans more interested in citizenship; to induce them to vote, and take part in every good civic movement." In the bishop's opinion, this boded well for Mexican Americans to "command a better wage, and better living conditions."[41] The growing awareness about the differences among Mexicans and Mexican Americans slowly began to change some clerical attitudes toward Mexican parishioners. At the same time, the increased awareness helped focus more attention on them from the church.

However, some of the older attitudes persisted. For example, ideas about the volatile "Latin temperament" remained intact in some quarters. According to his bishop, the priest in charge of Immaculate Heart of Mary Church near the Port of Houston had to run his parish with "a firm hand" because "being so close to the ship docks . . . he has to deal with some rather tough people." Similarly, the Oblates did not allow priests to serve alone at Mexican missions. A provincial explained that this policy was necessary "for the safety of our priests working with these rather passionate people."[42] In addition, there were occasional signs that the historical animosities between Spain and Mexico were not completely dead and continued to plague relations between Spanish priests and Mexican parishioners. Bishop Wendelin J. Nold complained in 1955 that one priest from Spain was "inclined to treat these Mexicans with a certain degree of Spanish contempt." The bishop continued to wrestle with the problem the next year. "I do not flatter myself," he confided to an Oblate official, "that I can overcome old-country prejudices on the part of certain pastors." Nonetheless, the bishop vowed to continue to seek out priests who understood Mexican Catholics.[43]

Over time, however, changing perceptions tempered older views and attitudes. In 1945, the author of a textbook for seminarians argued earnestly that they must adopt a genuinely "wholesome attitude towards the Mexican." The writer saw this as the only solution to the church's "problem" with the Spanish-speaking. For him, Mexicans were "a loveable people, gentle, polite, docile, obedient, respectful, grateful and appreciative."[44] The particular choice of words reflected both older and emergent notions held by men and women of the church about Texas Mexicans during the World War II era, attitudinally a time of flux.

One constant factor of the times, to be sure, were the social disadvantages that continued to plague Houston's Mexican community throughout the 1940s and 1950s. Poverty persisted despite the general prosperity of the times.[45] Church officials recognized the economic roots of the "Spanish-speaking problem," though their analyses and reactions varied. Bishop Nold saw the status of Mexicans as the most recent phase in the old story of immigrant adjustment and the price newcomers paid to succeed in American society. Booming industry was remaking the Gulf Coast, he explained, and Mexicans would continue to flood into Texas to meet labor-market needs. The bishop did not minimize the Mexicans' poverty and exploitation, but he stoically concluded that "like the poor, the Spanish-speaking we will always have with us," and so he urged other church leaders to cope with the problem rather than to try to solve it.[46]

Others in the Catholic Church thought the real problem was actually the Bracero Program and the new "wetbacks." In 1942 the United States negotiated an agreement with Mexico to import workers (*braceros*, literally, those who work with their arms) under contract to ease America's labor shortage during World War II. A flood of undocumented Mexican laborers also seeking work in the prosperous postwar economy soon accompanied the legal *braceros*. By the mid-1950s, however, recessionary pressures and the public outcry against Mexican immigrants prompted the Immigration and Naturalization Service (INS) to institute a draconian program, "Operation Wetback," to stem the flood of undocumented Mexican workers. More than a million Mexican nationals consequently were rounded up and deported by INS officials between 1953 and 1956, often entangling Mexican American citizens in the process.[47] Indignant churchmen, including Archbishop Robert E. Lucey of San Antonio, railed against the injustice and suffering brought on by the new deluge of Mexican immigration of the 1940s and 1950s. Immigrant labor displaced native-born Mexican Americans and made them "second-class citizens," some church leaders argued. Rev. Frank Kilday protested that Mexican Americans were "being pushed around and manhandled because they cannot produce documentary proof of their citizenship." The angry cleric denounced the INS tactics, adding that it was impossible to know how many Mexican American citizens had been illegally deported.[48]

In the meantime, another dilemma confronted urban communities, juvenile delinquency. In the 1940s and 1950s there was an alarming public perception that youth crime was rampant throughout the nation. Historians disagree about the severity of the problem; one called the rise in juvenile delinquency "staggering," while another argued that "it was not as bad as many alarmists . . . perceived it to be." The problem was real, but, as historian Karen Anderson argued, it probably was often blown out of proportion. Wartime anxiety tended to focus more attention on crime, resulting in stricter law enforcement and more arrests, which in turn skewed public perception.[49] Nonetheless, the tragic dimensions of the problem of youth crime were strongly etched in the minds of church officials, as revealed in an entry in the journal of St. Patrick Church in 1942:

> The beginning of this year found us in the middle of gang fights. From September to February we buried 5 boys of about 17 years of age who had been killed in these fights. In February we got the boys together and formed a boys club. We were not successful in converting them entirely but by hard work we kept them from killing each other. . . . One evening when the opposing team failed to show up our boys got into several cars and went over and shot a few windows out of San Felipe Courts. . . . The boys are bad in the so called "Bloody Fifth" [Ward] but they respect the church and the priests.[50]

As church representatives worked to combat delinquency, they sometimes revealed clues to their perceptions about Mexican Americans and the social ills of the barrios. Bishop Byrne, worried that all Mexican youth in Houston were being wrongly branded as "criminally inclined," shifted the blame to public school students who lacked Catholic instruction. According to the prelate, these wayward teens sullied the reputation of Catholic schoolchildren. Similarly, clerics blamed the public schools for thwarting Father Frank Brentine's efforts among the youth at Houston's "rugged" Immaculate Heart of Mary Parish.[51] Sister Mary Dolores Cárdenas, who had long ministered to the Mexicans of Houston's Fifth Ward, likewise blamed the "bad boys" of the public school for an arson plot she apparently foiled. The feisty nun, having found gasoline cans stashed on the parish school grounds, investigated and caught a suspect. She held him and threatened not to release him "until he confessed or dried up." By the time the police arrived, a group of angry mothers surrounded and taunted her. *"Parecían indias"* (They were like Indians—that is, "savages"), the nun dramatically recounted, revealing with tragic irony her own prejudice evoked by the confrontation with mixed-race women— mestizas, like herself.[52]

In the eyes of some church representatives, certain negative attributes continued to shape the Mexicans' social image. Some nuns and priests blamed the Mexicans' cultural traits for the poverty in their barrios. But while this reasoning revealed pejorative clerical attitudes, it also resulted in spirited efforts by religious men and women to try to ameliorate poverty among their parishioners. An expanded consciousness about Mexicans and Mexican Americans in the 1940s and 1950s brought them greater attention from the Catholic Church, despite the unsavory attitudes it sometimes revealed among their spiritual mentors. Likewise, perceptions about Mexican spirituality also began to change despite the fact that some church officials continued to regard Mexican religiosity as suspect.

For instance, the stereotype of religious ignorance and indifference endured. "These girls do not know much about their religion," a pastor noted about his Mexican American parishioners. Priests pleaded incessantly for expanded Catholic education, for if left to themselves, clerics warned, the Mexicans would revert to being "the neglected Catholics they have been for so long." The parochial school, nuns and priests argued, was the only way to make them "real practical [C]atholics."[53] The persistent image of religious ignorance went hand-in-hand with the enduring portrayal of Mexicans' inattention to the Catholic Church. Clerics continued to see a discouraging spiritual apathy in Houston's barrios. One census report blamed mothers, at least partly, for the "lack of Catholicity" in the parish: "Mother cannot care for the family—get Children ready & come to Mass. Lack[s] sense of duty in this regard." Another pastor sensed that religious indifference posed a greater threat than Protestantism.[54] The picture of childlike irresponsibility remained entrenched in the minds of some church personnel.

Nonetheless, some church officials during the 1940s and 1950s showed a greater appreciation of Mexican Catholicism. Some defended uniquely Mexican customs. One priest insisted that Mexicans were "essentially a good people possessed of a deep religious spirit." He went on to point out that despite severe adversity, Mexican Catholics had kept the faith.[55] Another writer asserted that Americans misunderstood the Mexicans' devotion to Our Lady of Guadalupe, the central figure and foundation of Mexican Catholicism. Though most Americans dismissed this reverence as superstitious sentimentality, Brother Joseph Buckley asked: "Why should others scoff?" Furthermore, Buckley suggested that perhaps Anglo Americans' "lack of faith has not merited a like apparition." For Buckley, Mexican Catholicism was "a living faith, tangible and vibrant" and he defended the devotion to Guadalupe as "one of the most beautiful and touching incidents in a modern world of sophistication and smug unbelief."[56]

What is most significant about these changing pastoral views is the link some officials made between the Mexicans' social status and their religious "condition." Clearly, there was more understanding shown toward Mexicans and Mexican Americans and the problems they faced. There was empathy not only for the plight of native-born Mexican Americans but also for the *braceros* and "wetbacks" who often competed with them for jobs. More important, however, some men and women of the church recognized that the supposed religious shortcomings of Mexicans were largely due to historical social and economic deprivation. Church representatives explained that Mexicans' religious indifference and conversions to Protestantism grew out of changed social conditions. Mexicans and Mexican Americans had been "forced into migratory labor," church officials argued, and this had destroyed their religious ties, practices, and education.[57] To be sure, the new thinking of the 1940s and 1950s was sometimes overstated, oversimplified, and ambivalent. One account, for example, presented the Mexican as utterly transformed from a paragon of spirituality into the epitome of materialism. Before, the writer noted, "his one desire in life was to know, love and serve God"; now, the "craze for money" was his "main objective in life." Sometimes church representatives even portrayed the Mexican as a "willing and eager wanderer," despite universal acknowledgment of the drudgery of migrant life.[58] Exaggeration notwithstanding, such observations showed an increased awareness about how entwined were the social and pastoral aspects of the "Spanish-speaking problem."

These shifting views also suggested that more individuals in the Catholic hierarchy now made clear distinctions between Mexican immigrants and Mexican American citizens. Bishop Byrne distinguished native-born from immigrant early on. By the 1940s he was convinced the Texas Mexican should consider himself "neither a Spaniard nor a Mexican" but a "Texan." The distinctions had also become obvious to Catholic leaders throughout the Southwest by the mid-1940s, when some of them formed the Bishops' Committee for the Spanish-Speaking in 1945 and began convening conferences focused on both the pastoral and the material needs of Mexican Catholics.[59]

Byrne's successor in the 1950s, Bishop Wendelin J. Nold, recognized that many of the Spanish-speaking were American-born and he understood that the ongoing nature of Mexican immigration held important pastoral and social ramifications for the Spanish-speaking apostolate. Bishop Nold challenged fellow churchmen to help assimilate Mexicans and Mexican Americans more fully into mainstream society and the Catholic Church through "generous" funding, flexibility regarding language needs, and religious leadership to combat the social and economic prejudice that hampered the incorporation of Mexicans into American life.[60] The new consciousness and changing attitudes of the World War II era would expand in the coming decades, helping to fuel a gradual improvement in the pastoral and social ministry for Houston's Mexican Catholics.

INCREASED SENSITIVITY, LINGERING DOUBTS: THE 1960S–1970S

The ascendant liberalism that shook the United States in the 1960s also reverberated strongly in global Roman Catholicism. In an effort to achieve *aggiornamento*—an "updating" of the Roman Catholic Church —Pope John XXIII convened the Second Vatican Council (1962–65), an event that initiated many liberal reforms and marked a major turning point in Catholic history.[61] How far the new liberalism evidenced among the highest echelons of the church at Vatican II actually trickled down to the parish level is hard to say. The Second Vatican Council may have promoted more liberal racial attitudes among rank-and-file church representatives in Houston, particularly considering that one of the major council reforms was the enhanced status of the laity. But what stands out in the documentary record during these years is the *absence* of a discussion about race and Mexicans; what is much more obvious is a pointed awareness of the Mexican community's growing heterogeneity and its surging politicization. The liberal ethos of the 1960s and the reforms of Vatican II encouraged progressive views among men and women of the church in Houston, but what riveted their attention and forced them to reassess their attitudes about Mexican Catholics were the demands the parishioners themselves increasingly made on the institution.[62]

The 1960s and 1970s witnessed the rise of the Chicano movement, a burst of agitation for social change that challenged many mainstream institutions and assumptions, including the Catholic Church and the perceptions its representatives had of Mexicans and Mexican Americans. Under the pressures of *el movimiento*, men and women of the church developed a more realistic picture of Texas Mexicans than the monolithic image that prevailed in the early twentieth century.

By the mid-1960s church officials in Houston were clearly more discriminating in how they viewed their parishes and the people within them. In 1966, the pastor of St. Stephen Church had a realistic if blunt assessment of his parish as "bi-lingual, inner-city, [and] slummish." He was well aware that his younger parishioners spoke a mix of English and Spanish while the older ones spoke mostly Spanish, and he knew that a continual inflow of new immigrant families constantly replenished the binational, bicultural character of the parish. These traits logically suggested that the ministry in this particular parish be a bilingual one. Bishop John L. Morkovsky also recognized the class and cultural distinctions that existed in the various parishes. He observed that St. Philip's members were mostly Spanish-speaking but that "they are not at all of the inner-city type that St. Stephen's has."[63] Morkovsky also understood the need for new and flexible pastoral strategies. English masses were needed for "the rising generation," Morkovsky advised, though Spanish services remained necessary as well.[64] But others in the diocese were less flexible. As Mexican Americans increasingly dispersed into integrated neighborhoods in the 1960s and 1970s, the new ethnic mix in once segregated parishes was difficult for some priests to accept. In 1970, for instance, the pastor at the traditionally white Immaculate Conception Church asked to be reassigned. Apparently the priest felt "a more than usual worrisome burden brought on by the continuing rapid turnover of the nature of the people of the parish, from the once predominately Anglo to Mexican American."[65]

In the 1960s and 1970s, church personnel reflected more tolerant attitudes toward Mexicans and Mexican Americans, but this did not negate all the ingrained stereotypes. According to one report, for example, most of the Mexican families moving into St. Patrick Parish in 1964 were Catholics "perhaps in name only." In another case, a pastor wondered if the catechetical work among Mexican Americans in his parish had failed because the nuns "haven't enough confidence in the capacities of our Mexican people."[66] Lack of confidence in the Mexican surfaced in other ways. There were hints about irresponsibility: "It may well be that they would neglect going to any church," a provincial worried when proposing some parish boundary changes, "for the Mexicans seem blocked from their church when things like expressways, canals and distance get between them and their church." In a similar spirit, Father Anselm Walker showed little faith in the ability of "our Mexicans" to discern and resist the wiles he saw in the ecumenicalism of the sixties. The priest conceded that "the ecumenical movement may have some praiseworthy goals to offer the Anglos," but he warned that for Mexicans it surely meant "apostasy, defection and secularization."[67] Thus the old view of the Mexican "child" retained some currency.

So, too, did the corollary of Mexican "superstition." Apparently Mexican folk healers plied their trade in Houston. A St. Stephen parishioner recalled that her grandfather was a *curandero* (healer) who considered himself a "vehicle of God." In Second Ward, *curanderas* (women healers) routinely advertised in the Spanish-language newspapers. In May 1967 pastor Emile Farge reported that *hiervistas* (herbalists), *curanderos* (faith healers), and "myriads of superstitious practices" abounded in his parish. Twice, Father Farge wrote, he had been interrupted while writing his letter by parishioners wanting him to attend to two *ensalmados* (people thought to be bewitched): "One was a sick girl, the other was a boy afraid of dogs." These were not isolated incidents. "Yesterday a mother brought a boy here who 'was seeing snakes,'" the cleric wrote. In his opinion, *curanderismo* (faith healing) among parishioners could not be called "simple faith" but was a problem needing eradication.[68]

The pastor's comments were well-intentioned. He was concerned about what he saw as a dearth of Mexican American leadership in his parish and feared the children would be "brainwashed into believing they are not as good as the Anglo." Still, the priest believed the problem lay with the parishioners themselves—with their refusal to leave their Mexican church and integrate themselves into the nearby Anglo church. The parish, the cleric claimed, suffered from "Mexican American cultural inbreeding." The solution, he believed, was for parishioners to "experience a visible, definite change from a Mexican to an American environment."[69] Mexican American culture, the priest implied, could nurture little that was spiritually wholesome or socially progressive.

Such commentary recalled the prevalent attitudes of the early twentieth century, even as it reflected some of the liberalism of the civil rights era. Among some clergy, perhaps at an unconscious level, lingering doubts remained about Mexicans ever becoming "good" Catholics. But within the Catholic Church, advocates for Mexican Americans attacked these images in the 1960s and 1970s, encouraged by the political and social changes engendered by the Chicano movement. Sister Gloria Gallardo, a cofounder of the vocal nuns' organization Las Hermanas (Sisters), spoke for many when she asserted that "Anglo priests and nuns cannot identify best with the needs of the Spanish-speaking, regardless of their good intentions." "Without meaning to," Gallardo declared, "many Anglos have a paternal attitude."[70] Some nuns and priests conceded as much. For example, a pastor attributed some of his parish's problems to "the rather patronising [sic] posture that the Church has assumed toward them [Mexican Americans] in the past."[71]

In a similar vein, Father Antonio Marañón chastised the Catholic hierarchy for alienating Mexican Catholics and trying to recast them in an Anglo image. "In all the churches," Marañón decried, "what is considered a good Mexican is a well-dressed, well-behaved but thoroughly dehumanized person." Father Marañón demanded that the Catholic Church accept the Chicanos' Mexicanness: "No!" the fiery cleric insisted, "a Mexican American cannot be the mirror image of a gringo Christian."[72] Ironically, though, even Father Marañón's defense of Chicano Catholics belied the paternalism some Spanish clerics showed toward Mexicans. "The saddest part," the priest claimed, "is that it took a Spanish priest, a *gachupín* [an old slur used by Mexicans against their Spanish colonizers], to come and teach you how to be a Mexican American."[73] By the 1970s, the attitudes and perceptions held by men and women of the Catholic Church about Texas Mexicans had undergone significant change, but they continued to coexist alongside some deeply ingrained racial attitudes from the past.

Since the 1940s, Mexican American racialization had begun giving way to ethnicization, at least in some quarters. Bishop Nold, for example, saw the Mexicans as just the latest group of immigrants slowly being assimilated into the nation's mainstream. Nold and others like him used the term "Spanish-speaking" instead of "Mexican," indicating that Tejanas and Tejanos were not a separate unassimilable race permanently fated to social inequality and outsiderhood. And yet their mestizo heritage remained an important part of the Mexican American experience in Houston even into the early 1970s. A federal judge created an uproar among Mexican Americans in 1970 when he "declared" them to be white for the purpose of desegregating Houston's public schools by integrating Mexican and African American students only, leaving white schools untouched.[74] Clearly, Mexican American racial ambiguity continued to be important even in the late twentieth century, long after the racial status of nineteenth- and twentieth-century European immigrants had been settled.

As church representatives came to understand the nature of the "Mexican problem" as something that called for action beyond the spiritual realm, they faced a twin challenge: If the Catholic Church was to save the Mexicans' souls, it had to address not only their religious needs but their material ones as well. Naturally, the church responded first to basic spiritual needs. Before anything else, churches and religious schools had to be built. How that happened and what it reveals is the theme of the next chapter.

FOUR

Father Thomas Hennessy looked out in amazement at the sea of humanity that filled his church to overflowing on December 12, 1911. Neither the reverend, pastor of Houston's most prestigious Catholic church, Annunciation, nor the city had ever seen such a large gathering of Mexican Catholics. They were there for a solemn event—indeed, a historic event—the city's first public celebration of the Mexicans' patron saint, Our Lady of Guadalupe. That special service was celebrated with "great passion and fervor," an Oblate father noted in the church journal.[1] The occasion also sent a message: Mexicans were coming to the Bayou City in large numbers and the Catholic Church needed to accommodate them.

This chapter traces the founding of Mexican parishes around the city from the 1910s to the early 1970s and shows how the Mexicans' steady population expansion and their own initiatives to build churches and parochial schools reflected their march toward greater participation in Houston's religious and social life. The Missionary Oblates who arrived in the city in 1911 found that Mexicans wanted churches of their own and would unite to bring that about. Beginning in the early twentieth century, the city's Mexican and Mexican American Catholics steadily pressed diocesan officials to increase pastoral services to them.

Over time the Catholic hierarchy responded by providing them more priests and nuns and helping to facilitate the growth of parishes to accommodate the ever-growing numbers of Mexican Catholics.

THE 1910S AND 1920S

In 1911 the bishop of the Diocese of Galveston, Nicholas A. Gallagher, entered into a contract that entrusted the spiritual care of Mexicans in Houston to the Missionary Oblates of Mary Immaculate. Bishop Gallagher chose the Oblate Fathers because their "work among the poorest of the poor along the Rio Grande [was] well known" and because apparently "so many Mexicans" in the diocese were "deprived of the consolations of Our Holy Religion on account of the scarcity of priests."[2] The understanding was that the Oblates would have "temporary charge of all Mexicans in the [D]iocese of Galveston, not otherwise provided for."[3] In Houston, this gave the Oblate Fathers a virtual monopoly on the evangelization of Mexicans in the city.

Four Oblate priests, an American, a Frenchman, an Italian, and a Spaniard, arrived in October 1911 to begin their ministry in Houston's Mexican community and to supplement the ministry to other Catholics. They established Immaculate Conception, a new parish for "American" (white) Catholics, in the suburb of Magnolia Park on the city's east side. From this "tastefully furnished" headquarters the missionaries quickly began their forays into the Mexican *colonias*, a world of stark contrast with the suburban niceties of Immaculate Conception and Magnolia Park.[4] Rev. Esteban de Anta reported that his Mexican parishioners led a "pitiful" existence, living in "sordid huts" and working for "a pittance."[5] Spiritual life, according to another priest, was equally poor. Before the Oblates arrived, the church "completely neglected" Mexican Catholics, the cleric wrote. "[D]eprived of priests who spoke their language and poorly received in the American churches," many Mexicans "lived and died without ever seeing a priest." The Oblates worked feverishly, spurred on by the ever-present Protestants, who, "[l]ike ravenous wolves," Father De Anta charged, enticed the Mexicans "with false promises . . . to abandon Mother Church."[6]

After ten months of evangelizing in the homes, stores, and meeting halls of Mexican barrios, the Oblates' labor bore fruit in the form of a two-story frame building erected to serve as a church and school for Houston's Mexican Catholics. The church was built in El Segundo Barrio at the corner of Navigation and Marsh streets. The street names perfectly suited the less-than-prime real estate where the church stood, for the area was indeed a *ciénaga*, the pastor noted, "a marsh where the runoff from the whole neighborhood collected." Undeterred, the Oblate Fathers brought in 1,500 truckloads of dirt to raise the property. Completed in August 1912, the new church was appropriately dedicated to the patron saint of Mexico, Our Lady of Guadalupe. Houston's Mexican Catholics finally had a mother church.[7]

Significantly, the dedication ceremony on September 15, 1912, coincided with the celebration of Mexican Independence Day. It took place "[w]ith a display of devotion and manifestation of zeal seldom found among even the elect and more lavishly endowed congregations," a newspaper reported. A "vast throng of Mexicans" met Bishop Gallagher when he arrived in the city, and at the parish grounds the crowd was so great that many were left outside the church, craning to see and hear what they could of the ceremony. As the prelate began the blessing of the building, parishioners formed a reverent procession behind an image of the Virgin of Guadalupe. Young girls dressed in white carried candles and accompanied the parishioners who carried *la Virgen* "in triumph" from the school to the sanctuary. "Our Lady of Guadalupe took possession of her sanctuary," the pastor wrote, "from which to protect her children, the Mexicans." A Mexican orchestra and a young women's choir added beauty and solemnity to the occasion, and the faces of the faithful beamed with pride at hearing the sermon preached in Spanish. A festive *jamaica* (bazaar) and dinner lasted long into the evening and crowned the joyous day.[8]

Toward the end of the ceremony, Bishop Gallagher administered

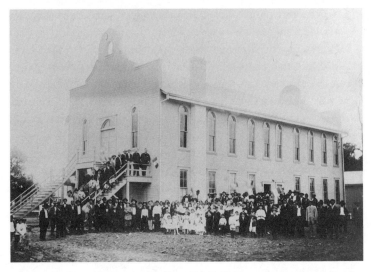

The dedication in 1912 of Our Lady of Guadalupe, the Mexican community's "mother church," was an important moment in Houston's Mexican American history. Courtesy Houston Metropolitan Research Center, Houston Public Library.

the sacrament of Confirmation to 200 men, women, and children, one of the largest such events ever held in the city. The bishop began with some revealing comments to the parishioners:

> During the thirty years I have been Bishop of this diocese, it has not seemed opportune or necessary to extend to you the privilege of having infants and children, who have not received their First Communion, receive the Sacrament of Confirmation. This privilege is always enjoyed in your own country, and now that I see your great increase in numbers in this diocese and the eagerness with which you have availed yourselves of the opportunity to advance your religious and spiritual welfare, it is with the greatest sincerity and willingness that I now grant you this right, a right to which you are entitled by reason of your loyalty to your faith amid many trials and difficulties.[9]

Bishop Gallagher's comments presaged a changing relationship between Houston Mexicans and the Catholic Church. The bishop knew that Mexicans had a different approach to the sacraments, and "granting" the parishioners the right to continue their traditional practice was more a recognition of the Mexican Catholic style than a magnanimous gesture. Before, it had not seemed "opportune or necessary" to legitimate the practice of being confirmed before having First Communion, but now their "great increase in numbers" compelled the bishop to do so. The incident showed that by insisting on defining Catholicism on their own terms Mexican parishioners could extract concessions from the church.

Mexicans' selective interest in the church's formal requirements and their initiatives to build their own places of worship became increasingly evident with time. Our Lady of Guadalupe Church became the anchor and cultural heart of the *colonia* in Houston, as a local newspaper observed in reporting that Mexican Catholics now had "a nucleus." The reporter's choice of words underlined the parishioners' self-reliance: "[T]hey seem determined to gather and to build for themselves a parish which will serve the best spiritual and temporal interests of their rapidly increasing colony."[10] The expanding community pressed for more religious services at Guadalupe Parish during the 1920s as immigration from Mexico reached unparalleled proportions. Between 1920 and 1930, Houston's Mexican population more than doubled, from about 6,000 to 15,000.[11] This obliged pastor Esteban de Anta to add two more masses each Sunday and offer Mass every day of the week, instead of only twice. Because of the availability of jobs, Father De Anta explained, "many people came to Houston and naturally following the established pattern, they flocked to the church." It became necessary to always have a priest present at the church to answer "the call of the people (*el llamamiento de la gente*)."[12] The pastor's wording was appropriate and telling because it revealed that the incessant growth and demands of the *colonia* itself prompted the increased pastoral services.

The parish school at Guadalupe also flourished. Eighty-five students enrolled during the 1912–13 school year, and this number increased to 163 by 1916–17. In the early 1920s, enrollment reached 333, and by the end of the decade some 400 students attended Guadalupe School.[13] The pastor pleaded for more teaching nuns, and with good reason because, with the exception of two school years (when there were three teachers at Guadalupe), only two teachers were assigned to the parish school during the entire decade of the 1910s. The situation improved in the 1920s, however, with an average of six teachers assigned during that decade.[14]

The growth of the Mexican community in the Second Ward prompted diocesan officials to sever Our Lady of Guadalupe from its Anglo parent church located some three miles away in Magnolia Park. In 1921, Guadalupe Church, a mission of Immaculate Conception Church since 1911, became an autonomous Mexican national parish.[15] Improvements that followed in quick succession in the early 1920s, including a convent for the resident nuns, a formidable brick church that replaced the original frame chapel, a new brick rectory, and a refurbished and expanded school, showed the vitality of the parish.[16] These initiatives reflected the parishioners' self-reliance and the importance they attached to their faith as they carved their space in the Bayou City.

Even this expansion, however, could not accommodate all those who observed the traditionally important holy days. During Semana Santa (Easter Week) in 1924, for example, the church journal noted that "the church was better with its greater space, but nonetheless it was much too small to hold the masses that turned out. Pews, aisles, sanctuary, vestries, all were filled with the faithful, and even at that many had to remain outside the church, trying to follow the services from doorways and windows."[17] Such displays of faith dramatically revealed the need for more facilities and increased Catholic officials' awareness of the Mexican presence.

As the Mexican mother church, Guadalupe brought other parishes into existence. In 1921, an Oblate superior instructed the pastor of the Anglo church in Magnolia Park to determine how many Mexicans lived within his parish. A survey discovered 230 Mexican families living "far from Father de Anta," the pastor at Our Lady of Guadalupe in Second Ward. The emergence of a barrio in Magnolia Park presented another pastoral challenge for the Catholic hierarchy in Houston. "Can you do anything?" Bishop Christopher Byrne pleaded with an Oblate superior.[18] Already since 1919 Father De Anta and other Oblates had been visiting the Magnolia Park families to administer the sacraments in their homes. Beginning in the early 1920s the Catholic leadership assigned various assistant pastors to Guadalupe specifically "to care for the growing Mexican population of Magnolia Park."[19] In 1925 one of those assistants, Father Anastacio Pérez, began holding services in a two-story family residence and business owned by Emilio Aranda at the corner of 71st Street and Navigation, in Magnolia. Aranda's property served as a temporary chapel where regular church services were held, including a daily Mass, two Sunday masses, recitation of the Rosary, baptisms, and catechism classes. In 1926 a two-story church was built in the Magnolia barrio and given the name Immaculate Heart of Mary. Two years later the Sisters of Divine Providence arrived and opened a parish school.[20]

By the mid-1920s, then, Mexican and Mexican American Catholics living on the east side of Houston had two churches and parochial schools of their own. Their counterparts in other parts of the city did not, but as they battled the difficult times of depression and war they continued to press the diocese for their own religious facilities.

The Great Depression and World War II

During the 1930s, the Catholic Church in the United States mounted a vigorous campaign to teach parishioners the essentials of Catholic doctrine. This catechetical movement was especially active in the Southwest, where the historical shortage of clergy continued. Supervised by nuns, lay volunteers established catechetical centers and taught Catholic beliefs and rituals to children, particularly those attending public schools, in any available space.[21] In Houston, several of

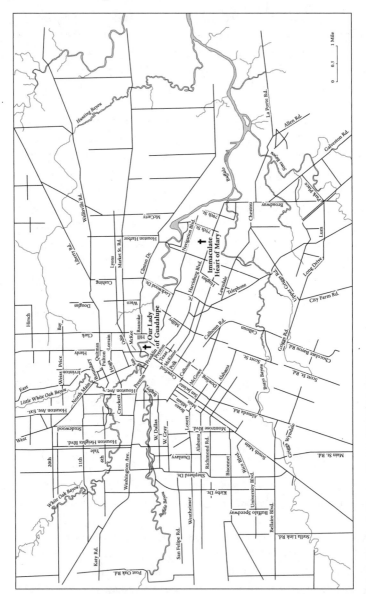

Map 3. Houston's Mexican National Parishes, 1929

these centers often became the basis for new parishes in Mexican neighborhoods.

In 1930 the school principal at Our Lady of Guadalupe, Sister Mary Benitia Vermeersch, organized a group of young Mexican American women of the parish into the Missionary Catechists of Divine Providence. Ranging in age from sixteen to twenty-two, these laywomen received religious training and, according to their bishop, had "all the zeal and consecration . . . of a nun." Initially, the group assisted the nuns in teaching catechism to public school children after school hours at Guadalupe, but their role soon expanded. The Catechists canvassed the parish territory to recruit children, and they taught catechism in several neighborhoods. In 1933 the Sisters of Divine Providence reported that eighteen "little missionaries" went out in pairs to nine catechetical centers to instruct nearly 900 children. By 1935 the Catechists had some 1,400 children under instruction in fifteen meeting places scattered throughout the city.[22] "Sister Benitia asked us if we would like to teach religion to public school Mexican children," charter Catechist Petra Guillén remembered. "So many of us volunteered to help others who were less fortunate [and] were not taught religion like we were taught in school," she explained. "I enjoyed it," another former Catechist, Rafaela Aguilar, offered. "You felt like you were giving a part of yourself to others."[23]

The Catechists brought more than the *Baltimore Catechism* to their neighbors. These lay efforts were an important part of the groundwork that preceded the spread of Catholic institutions to other Houston barrios. For instance, the second offspring of Guadalupe Parish, St. Stephen, had its beginnings as a catechetical center on Houston's west side. In 1932 the Catechists taught classes twice a week in the home of María Martínez before parishioners raised enough money to buy a property to launch St. Stephen's parish and church in their barrio.[24] In a budding area known as El Crisol, located in the Liberty Road area of northeast Houston, barrio residents repeated this pattern. There, once again the community took the initiative. José Gómez led a group that spoke with the pastor at Guadalupe Parish in 1934 and gained his

The Catechists of Divine Providence fanned out in the city to bring religious instruction and a modicum of material aid to Mexicans and Mexican Americans in the Depression era. Courtesy Mrs. Petra Guillén.

support. Soon priests were celebrating Mass and the Catechists were instructing 100 children twice a week in the Gómez home, despite some obstacles. Sister Dominic García recalled that nervous parents used to bless their children who sometimes had "to cross pastures and crawl under stalled train cars" in order to get to their religion classes. This was the beginning of Our Lady of Sorrows Parish.[25]

This pattern of religious institutional growth characterized the barrios during the 1930s and 1940s. Mexicans preserved the faith through traditional home- and community-centered worship, and their initiatives interlocked with institutional outreach efforts such as the Catechists, all of which eventually gave rise to new churches and parochial schools for Mexicans where none had existed before. While Father De Anta considered another catechetical site in the north side, the nuns and Catechists at Guadalupe sought to "broaden their field. . . to every Mexican settlement in Houston and vicinity," the press reported.[26]

As the Mexican population in Houston increased, it changed the complexion of some established neighborhoods and their parishes. St. Patrick Church on the north side is a case in point. One of the oldest parishes in Houston, St. Patrick had been the religious home of Irish Houstonians since 1880. In the 1920s Italians began moving into the area, but over the course of two decades, the number of both Irish and Italians declined as the number of Mexicans steadily increased. By the 1930s the "once fashionable" Fifth Ward was densely populated by Mexicans and Mexican Americans and most of the Irish and Italians were gone, prompting a parish history to record the "alarming" decline in St. Patrick's "English American People." The incoming pastor noted the population shift in 1941: "We found about 50 families who had belonged to the parish. There were 32 Italian grocery stores within the [parish] limits [and] about 800 [M]exican families living around about but the great majority had never seen the inside of the church."[27]

Given these circumstances, the bishop entrusted St. Patrick to his Mexican specialists, the Oblate Fathers, in 1941. St. Patrick thus became a Mexican national parish, and the Sisters of Divine Providence immediately reopened the parish school previously closed for lack of pupils.[28] St. Patrick soon exhibited a vitality that rivaled the mother church in the Second Ward. "We commenced the year 1943 with the parish on a firm footing once more," the pastor wrote. "All the societies were full of life and the school was going fine," he noted proudly. But the transition at St. Patrick may not have been entirely smooth. "The beautiful picture of Our Lady of Guadalupe was blessed and hung behind the main altar," the pastor wrote, adding that he had heard rumors "that our Italian parishioners would not have 'La Virgen Morena' behind the main altar." Apparently nothing serious developed. "The truth of the matter was that no one said a single word against the procedure," the priest wrote.[29] Were there some feathers ruffled among the Italian American parishioners? Or did the rumors originate among Mexican parishioners who feared rejection? More important than the source of the rumors or the depth of ethnic tensions is the point that the pastor noted the "incident" at all; it showed that ethnicity continued to be important as Mexicans claimed a larger place in the Bayou City. In any case, a burgeoning Mexican population, a group the Catholic hierarchy could not ignore, transformed a dying parish into a vigorous one. Despite the trying times of the Great Depression and World War II, Mexicans pressed the Catholic leadership for more institutional support, both through their continued population growth and by paving the way themselves for establishing new churches for their neighborhoods. This trend continued during the relative prosperity of the post–World War II era, and it became more evident to the church leadership when the Galveston Diocese was redesignated the Galveston-Houston Diocese and its headquarters moved to the Bayou City in 1959.[30]

Among the new enclaves of Mexicans and Mexican Americans that formed in the later 1940s and 1950s in Houston was one located just outside of the north side city limits. This neighborhood, called Bonita Gardens, had attracted the Missionary Catechists in the late 1930s. In the 1940s, the itinerant Father Frank Urbanovsky held two-week missions in the area, offering religious instruction, baptizing children, and validating marriages for area residents. Urbanovsky witnessed the fast growth of La Bonita and the "almost daily" influx of new Mexican American homeowners.[31] With the groundwork laid by the Catechists and nurtured by Padre Panchito, as parishioners called Urbanovsky, Our Lady of Sorrows Parish organized a mission chapel for the Bonita Gardens residents in 1948. The people chose to call their church Nuestra Señora de San Juan de los Lagos, honoring the Virgin's shrine in Jalisco, Mexico.[32] "As that [name] is rather long," a priest explained, "they have been using St. John of the Lakes in all business transactions." Eventually, the church's name became Our Lady of St. John, a name that pointed up the concessions some Mexican Americans made to acculturation pressures. In the end, Bonita Gardens residents gained their cultural space. They had their own church, staffed by Spanish-speaking Oblates, and named after a Mexican devotion (albeit in English). In 1957 Our Lady of St. John became a Mexican national parish, led by the only homegrown Mexican American priest in the diocese, Father Lawrence Peguero.[33]

Still more post–World War II expansion occurred on the northeast side of Houston, where a pocket of Mexican Americans formed during the 1950s on the margins of the predominately Anglo subdivision of Denver Harbor. The Anglo parish there, Resurrection, established a church mission for Mexican families in 1958. Again, the residents favored their cultural heritage in choosing a name for the church, St. Philip of Jesus, in honor of the first canonized saint of Mexico.[34] The fast growth of the city's Mexican-origin population in the 1940s and 1950s had yielded a steady expansion of churches and parochial schools in their neighborhoods, but the demographic pressures and political demands exerted by the community in the tumultuous sixties and early seventies would be unprecedented, as would the accommodations the diocese made in response.

COMING FULL CIRCLE: THE 1960S AND EARLY 1970S

The community of Jeanetta Gardens, in far southwest Houston, began as a farmworker *colonia* but was eventually swallowed up by the expanding city. Mexicans and Mexican Americans had settled in the area when farmlands were converted to modestly priced home lots in the 1940s, allowing residents to be close to agricultural jobs in the nearby towns of Rosenberg, Stafford, and Sugarland. As Houston's boundaries spread, the southwest side became affluent, surrounding Jeanetta Gardens, which remained a working-class barrio about fifteen miles from downtown and the nearest Mexican parish, St. Stephen. Maryknoll Sisters from St. Stephen held religion classes in Jeanetta Gardens homes until the mid-1950s, but the distance made the relationship untenable and an Anglo parish closer to the barrio, St. Michael, assumed the ministry to the people of Jeanetta Gardens. Eventually, community resident Francisco Aguayo donated land to the diocese for a church. The new mission church of St. Raphael was dedicated, appropriately, on the Feast of Guadalupe in December 1961. St. Raphael Parish also differed from other Mexican American parishes in its ethnic makeup. Jeanetta Gardens adjoined Piney Point, a working-class black neighborhood settled by freedmen after the Civil War. By the early 1970s, St. Raphael was 60 percent Mexican American and 40 percent black. The first black priest ordained in the diocese, Father Clifton Ransom Jr., a native Houstonian and fluent Spanish speaker, headed the parish.[35]

The creation of another mission in east Houston followed the founding of St. Raphael. In 1962 Immaculate Heart of Mary Church organized St. Alphonsus Liguori near the Port of Houston, in the Manchester addition. Mexican Catholics there had wanted pastoral services since at least the 1940s. Around 1948, Father Urbanovsky reported well-attended missions in the Manchester area. "I liked very much the spirit in general," he noted in his diary. Father Sylvester O'Toole, the priest in charge of the St. Alphonsus mission, also noted the parishioners' enthusiasm. For three years they had opened their homes to him for religion classes, prompting him to propose the mission church be elevated to parish status. "I believe that the people have worked hard for their mission Church and they have demonstrated that they will support a parish church," Father O'Toole wrote in 1966. Bishop Morkovsky responded quickly, establishing St. Alphonsus Parish within two months.[36]

The founding of St. Raphael and St. Alphonsus largely followed the established pattern of church growth in the barrios. Like their predecessors, Mexican American parishioners in the 1960s and early 1970s clearly expressed their desire to have culturally relevant religious institutions, and they laid the groundwork for them. Mexican Catholics worked to create churches that reflected their ethnic identity—by their location within the barrios, in the names they bore, through the Spanish or bilingual-bicultural services they offered, and by the communal efforts that created them. Their efforts to carve out this cultural space were yet another reflection of their ethno-Catholicism. Wherever

Mexicans and Mexican Americans set down roots, they initiated efforts that eventually prompted the church to provide pastoral services.

The evolution of St. Patrick Parish illustrated the dialectic between the changing needs and configurations of Mexican communities and accommodation by the diocese. St. Patrick had flourished in the 1940s in its Fifth Ward location on Maury Street. However, Houston's growth in the 1950s and 1960s brought changes. Progress, in the form of freeway construction and commercialization of properties, displaced Mexican families from the vicinity of the church and pushed them farther into the north side.[37] In the process, St. Patrick Church became surrounded by trains, factories, and freeway construction. "The industrialism of the section [neighborhood] has almost swallowed us up," the sisters at the parish school complained. The Oblates followed the flow of people by establishing a chapel two miles north of the parish church in 1953. By the mid-1960s, very few families remained at the parent church as the movement of parishioners toward the chapel became "a real exodus." When the last Mass was celebrated at "old" St. Patrick in 1967, only 25 families lived around the church, whereas over 400 families resided around the new chapel.[38] The late 1960s saw the construction of a new church near the chapel, as well as the reopening of the parish school and the building of a new convent and a rectory in response to the growing number of Mexican Catholics in the area. All this new construction reflected the joint efforts of parishioners and diocesan leaders "to provide adequate facilities and location where the parishioners reside."[39]

In other parts of Houston as well the expanding Mexican community compelled diocesan officials to improve existing parish facilities. The oldest parishes, Guadalupe and Immaculate Heart, undertook considerable renovation and new construction, while the more recently founded churches also upgraded their facilities.[40] Simultaneously, several Anglo congregations gradually saw their white memberships diminish as Mexican Americans became the predominate group in the parish, sometimes sparking resentment among Anglo parishioners. At Immaculate Conception Church, for instance, a white

Map 4. Houston's Majority Mexican American Parishes, 1973

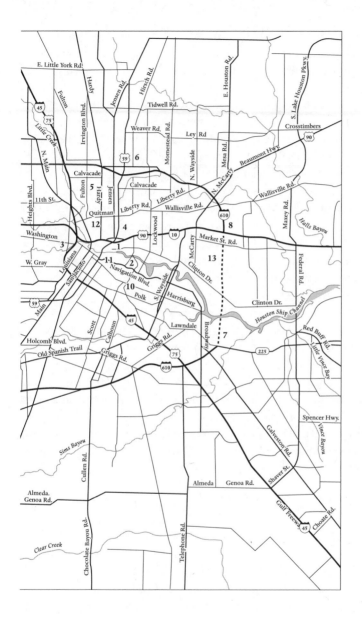

congregant complained that "the parish has gone down [because] the Spanish American people are habitating to the neighborhoods [sic]." The population in the Second Ward and Magnolia expanded so much during the 1960s that open land no longer separated the two barrios, a process that had been helped along by "white flight" to the suburbs.[41]

This demographic change in the East End, as the area was now called, resulted in predominately Mexican American neighborhoods, and it spurred Catholic officials to invite Mexicans to churches where previously they had been barred. During the late 1960s, the Catholic hierarchy instructed priests at Immaculate Conception to use Spanish in some of the masses "to attract the Latin-American element" to the historically all-white church.[42] By the early 1970s, the congregations of formerly "American" churches, such as Immaculate Conception, Blessed Sacrament, Resurrection, and Holy Name, were predominately Mexican and Mexican American. "Now they have actually taken over Immaculate Conception," parishioner Mary Villagómez pointed out.[43] With the integration of Immaculate Conception, the white parish where the Oblates' ministry to Houston's Mexicans began in 1911, the evangelization and institutional development of the Mexican community came full circle.

The experiences of those who participated in parish institutional life were not all the same, and belonging to one parish versus another said different things about the parishioners. At this point it is important to examine the distinctions among these parishes and what those differences reveal about Mexican American ethno-Catholicism in Houston.

National and Territorial Parishes

The Galveston Diocese promoted institutional Catholicism among Mexican parishioners by establishing national parishes exclusively for them, as church policy allowed.[44] The Catholic Church in the United States created these "foreign-language parishes" in response to the massive influx of "new immigrants" from southern and eastern Europe in the late nineteenth and early twentieth centuries. Nationality parishes had several functions. Through these structures, the church tried to meet the spiritual and cultural needs of immigrant Catholics while protecting them from proselytization. These segregated parishes were also meant to insulate native-born American Catholics from the newcomers so as to minimize interethnic conflict that might stir anti-Catholic nativism in the larger society.[45]

National parishes were also a handy tool for Americanization. In the early twentieth century, particularly during the anti-immigrant climate of the 1910s and 1920s, Catholic dioceses throughout the nation vied vigorously with Protestant denominations in a campaign to mold immigrants into "good" Americans. The U.S. Church fought to retain the loyalty of Catholic immigrants and to remake them into model Americans through a variety of activities that mixed social services and religious "uplift."[46] Thus a cleric's statement that Houston's new Guadalupe national parish presented "an opportunity of doing much more for the Mexicans" was laden with meaning.[47] It revealed a desire to provide a culturally more relevant ministry through the parishioners' language, but it also carried the implication that Mexican Catholics needed civic and religious improvement. Throughout the nation, armies of Catholic social workers, educators, and volunteers descended on barrios intent on making their residents "acceptable" Catholics and citizens. Working through parochial schools, neighborhood centers, and home visits, these Catholic crusaders for Americanization taught children and adults English and numerous vocational skills; gave them instruction in cooking, sewing, and sanitation; and exposed them to various aspects of American culture, including music and sports. All the while they tried to weave into these efforts an appreciation for a European American style of Catholicism. As one cleric put it, Mexicans were being given "a friendly and guiding hand to make them good citizens and better Catholics."[48] The national parish was central to these goals, although in practice Americanization was not monolithic and many individual church representatives did what they could to soften its implementation. In Second Ward's Guadalupe Parish, for example, Sister Benitia Vermeersch insisted that her students learn English to succeed in school, but she "did not try to strip the Mexicans of their cultural and religious practices and make them accept American customs."[49]

Nonetheless, virtually all Mexican Catholics, immigrants and native-born alike, belonged to national parishes during the first half of the twentieth century, having little choice in the matter. By the early 1940s the Oblate Fathers operated five national parishes in various Houston barrios (see Table A.3). As we have seen, the post–World War II years saw the dramatic growth and dispersal of the *colonia*, and, by the 1960s, Mexicans and Mexican Americans were scattered throughout the city and many were integrated into previously exclusively Anglo congregations. In the meantime, however, the American Catholic Church reverted to its preference for territorial parishes as European immigration waned and subsequent generations of immigrants assimilated. After the 1940s national parishes became increasingly rare throughout the United States. In the post–World War II years the dominant opinion among church leaders was that nationality parishes inhibited assimilation and that territorial, not national, parishes should be used to attract the Spanish-speaking for their eventual incorporation into American life.[50]

In Houston, these developments had mixed implications. For example, how did the Galveston Diocese respond to increasing Mexican immigration, given the trend away from establishing national parishes? And how did the increased residential mobility of post–World War II Mexican Americans affect Catholic institutional growth and pastoral services? The answers varied with episcopal administrations and communities, and they illuminate the changing nature of Mexican American ethnicity and religion in the city.

By the 1940s the Galveston hierarchy was well aware of the increasing heterogeneity of Houston's Mexican community. In the decades after World War II, the Mexican-origin population was increasingly bicultural, more Mexican American than Mexican, while it continued to absorb a steady flow of immigrants. Increased class stratification and social mobility accompanied Mexican Americans' acculturation, so that by the 1950s the church had to adjust its ministry to fit a community that neither warranted nor tolerated treatment as a "Little Mexico."

In 1953 Bishop Wendelin J. Nold recognized that the so-called problem of the Spanish-speaking posed a different challenge than European immigration had presented earlier in the century. Immigration restriction and the passage of time had resolved the problem of absorbing southern and eastern Europeans into American Catholic life, the bishop argued, but he suspected that this would not be the case with Mexican immigrants. Nold reasoned that Mexico's proximity and the demands for labor in the Texas Gulf Coast would make it unlikely that immigration barriers would be raised against Mexicans or that their influx would subside. "The Mexican is in Texas, and he is there to stay," he stated, and "[e]ach year will find him there in greater numbers." Nold believed that second- and third-generation Mexican Americans would be "absorbed into the American churches," only to be replaced by the continual stream of Mexican immigrants into the diocese.[51]

The bishop's assessment of "the problem" was partly right. But Nold's observations reflected the basic fallacy of trying to understand the experience of Mexicans in the United States through the lens of the European immigrant experience. Why did a distinctive "Mexicanness" still characterize the Catholicism of Houston's Mexicans even after the great majority of that population was native-born? Partly it was because, unlike the descendants of European immigrants, Mexicans in the United States continued to face racism and marginality. Mexican Americans retained the "Mexican" flavor of their Catholicism because it bolstered their ethnic identity and helped them come to grips with social subordination; it helped them confront the struggles inherent in their minority status, something with which the descendants of European immigrants no longer contended.

Bishop Nold was convinced that Houston still needed national parishes, and consequently the status of the original five Mexican parishes founded and staffed by the Oblates remained unchanged during the

1950s.[52] However, many clergy in the 1960s and early 1970s favored territorial over national parishes for the city's Mexican Catholics, and they suggested that new parishes in Mexican American neighborhoods be organized territorially rather than linguistically. Father Sylvester O'Toole, for example, successfully petitioned Bishop John Morkovsky to elevate St. Alphonsus Mission in east Houston to territorial parish status in 1966. Similarly, in 1971 Father Lawrence Peguero suggested that a proposed church for a predominately Mexican area in north Houston be one that "will not necessarily have to be considered a Church for Mexican Americans, but rather a territorial Church where all may go."[53]

Both cases illustrate the socioeconomic and cultural differences evident among Bayou City Mexicans in the second half of the twentieth century. In east Houston, about three miles from the old barrio of Magnolia, St. Alphonsus parishioners lived in a mixed neighborhood of whites and Mexican Americans. Father O'Toole reported that "Latin Americans" comprised the majority of Catholics in the area but that there were "a number of Anglo Catholic families who would add to our numbers in a most harmonious way since in this area the Latin Americans and Anglos associate with each other to the benefit of both groups." Similarly, the parishioners that Father Peguero identified in north Houston were mostly Mexican Americans who "speak English well and are well on the road to identifying with the Anglo community." These families had "made good in life," Peguero explained, and were "buying homes in the $16,000 level" outside the traditional barrios.[54] The same process affected old Guadalupe Parish, where younger parishioners were moving out of the Second Ward barrio. "This is a national parish and more and more the [L]atins move and become assimilated into their territorial parish," the pastor once complained. "As soon as they get an education and a better job, and they learn [E]nglish," the priest lamented, "they become a member of their territorial parish."[55]

These parishioners were likely younger Mexican Americans who were two or more generations removed from the immigrant experience, such as St. Philip's parishioners in one of the newer Mexican American neighborhoods in northeast Houston. Compared to the members of the old national parishes, St. Philip's parishioners were relatively younger and more affluent and able to operate with a surplus in their church budget.[56] On the one hand, they were "rather less than enthusiastic about having Spanish sermons," but, on the other hand, they named their church after Mexico's first canonized saint and turned out in great numbers every year in their Fiestas Patrias (Mexican Independence Day) celebration.[57] Bilingual or English-dominant, these Mexican American Catholics preferred a parish that reflected their middling social status, or aspirations, and their bicultural identity. This cultural middle ground expressed their accommodation to life in Houston; it was their way of fitting in, of finding a place for themselves in the city without totally giving up their Mexicanness.

In contrast, St. Stephen Parish and the old near west side barrio continued to be a magnet for Mexican immigrants. "St. Stephen's parish . . . still serves a definite need among the Spanish-speaking of Houston," Father Maurice Buckley wrote to his bishop, "for besides the many older people who speak very little English, new families from Mexico arrive here regularly."[58] The large presence of recent arrivals from Mexico gave the parish a more distinctly Mexican aura and made a bilingual pastoral approach necessary. When St. Stephen's parishioners defied their bishop and prevailed upon the diocese to let them keep their *iglesia mexicana* (Mexican church) and retain their status as a national parish, they showed that their adjustment to life in Houston involved more cultural resistance than accommodation.[59]

Differences among Mexican-origin Catholics revealed a variety of ethnoreligious consciousness. This heterogeneity resulted in slightly different ethnic identities and religious practices that distinguished Mexican Catholics not only from Anglo Catholics but also, to a degree, from each other. Their somewhat different ways of expressing their ethno-Catholicism fitted the parishioners' differences of class, acculturation, or nativity. In finding a place for themselves in the Bayou City, Mexican Catholics responded differently, some choosing to accommodate and others more openly resisting the forces of change and marginality they encountered in church and society. Significantly, however, the great majority wished to retain some of their Mexicanness, some degree of outsiderhood that helped them maintain a sense of ethnoreligious community and autonomy. In this sense, the story of Houston's Mexican Catholics recalls the experiences of other ethnoreligious peoples about whom historian R. Laurence Moore so perceptively wrote. Like American Jews and Mormons, Mexican ethno-Catholics "have been reluctant to let go completely of an outsider status" because "[t]oo much has been invested in it." Like other religious outsiders, Mexicans' "sense of outsiderhood helped turn their religion into something more than a religion. It became a separate culture, even an ethnic identity."[60]

Thus the challenge to the church in Houston in the second half of the twentieth century was not only to meet the needs of Mexican immigrants but also to provide pastoral services relevant to bilingual and bicultural Mexican Americans. In order to accomplish this, national parishes had to remain a part of the diocese's approach, though in Bishop Nold's opinion they were "not an ideal set-up." "I am convinced," he stated in 1953, "we must, if only because of language, continue to maintain separate churches."[61] Indeed, two decades later, in the early 1970s, the Galveston-Houston Diocese still maintained a handful of national parishes.[62]

Once parishes had been organized and churches and religious schools planted, Houston's Mexican communities bore the brunt of the financial cost of maintaining them. How they met that responsibility revealed much about the parishioners' ethnoreligious identity and way of life, as we shall see next.

FIVE

When Mary Villagómez and her cousins were growing up in Houston during the Great Depression, they loved going to the *jamaicas* at their church in the east side barrio of Magnolia. These festive church bazaars were something special to look forward to in those difficult years, a way to have fun with the family, see friends, and help the church at the same time. Across town in the Bonita Gardens barrio a decade later, several Mexican Americans braved snakes and mosquitos to clear some vacant lots where they would spend many evenings after work refurbishing an old army barracks into a modest chapel for themselves.[1] In separate times and places, these Mexican and Mexican American Catholics were doing the same things—creating and maintaining their own places of worship. The *jamaicas* that parishioners like the Villagómez cousins enjoyed is an example of how Mexican Catholics throughout Houston raised money to build and improve their churches and religious schools; actually doing the work of building and remodeling the structures themselves, as the Bonita Gardens residents did, provided another means to the same end.

This chapter explains how the work of funding and expanding their parishes was an important element in the lives of Mexican and Mexican American Catholics as they set down roots in the Bayou City.

Rather than presenting fund-raising efforts in Houston's Mexican parishes chronologically, this topical chapter describes the typical methods of fund-raising and interprets their impact on community-building. Working to raise money and maintain the parish reflected both the product and the process of Mexican ethno-Catholicism; that is, by participating in these activities, parishioners not only created churches and schools, but they also fashioned a strong sense of identity and community. Financing religious institutional development in the Mexican community posed a perennial challenge. The money raised to construct the first modest frame churches was only the beginning of a continual struggle to maintain and expand adequate church and school buildings for an ever-larger Mexican Catholic community. Diocesan officials tapped traditional sources of charity to meet some of the cost, but the financial viability of Houston's Mexican parishes depended primarily on the parishioners themselves. In order to meet their churches' financial needs, parishioners systematically gave money, donated materials and labor, and carried on endless fund-raising. Significantly, the occasional disagreements one would expect to surface remain silent in the historical record, and what is patently clear is the strong sense of community this labor of love produced among the many parishioners who carried it on year after year. Clearly, because the parishioners' fund-raising revealed their distinctly Mexican ethno-Catholicism and the beliefs and values that defined them as a people, this ongoing activity did far more than pay for the costs of operating the parish; it also constantly rejuvenated Mexican American culture, provided socialization, and reinforced ethnoreligious identity and cohesion in Mexican communities.

GETTING STARTED

Early in 1912 the newly arrived Missionary Oblates began planning a theatrical performance to be held on Sunday evening, February 25, in downtown Houston's Saengerbund Hall. The Oblate Fathers intended to use the proceeds of this "Dramático-Musical" to help build Houston's first Mexican Catholic church. But then tragedy struck. On February 21 a fire, one-and-a-half miles long and half a mile wide, devastated a large part of the city's Fifth Ward, jumped Buffalo Bayou, and burned down a small part of neighboring Second Ward as well. The conflagration razed some forty city blocks, leaving hundreds homeless and jobless, including many Mexicans and Mexican Americans. Flyers addressed to "MEJICANOS" soon circulated in the barrios calling for a large turn-out at the coming Saengerbund Hall performance to help their compatriots "survive the vicious blow they have just suffered." The handbills explained that the funds raised by the theatrical event would be diverted to the fire victims but that activities to raise money for a Mexican church would continue.[2]

This event in the early history of Mexican Catholicism in Houston foreshadowed a pattern of enthusiastic support among Mexicans for religious fund-raising. Entries in the Guadalupe Church journal, for example, revealed that parishioner contributions through pledges and *jamaicas* amounted to $1,354, an amount that almost matched the $1,500 seed money received from the Catholic Church Extension Society. Parishioner Dolores Ramos collected a large portion of the contributions, which financed many of the basic needs of the infant church —the painting, heating, electricity, furniture, and so forth.[3]

In subsequent years, Mexican Catholics in other barrios proved equally eager to pay for their own churches. One congregant recalled that before Mexicans in Magnolia Park had a place of worship, the Oblate Fathers encouraged them to raise money to build a church, and neighborhood residents responded enthusiastically. Mary Villagómez pointed out that her mother was "a go-getter" for the church. She and other Magnolia residents worked diligently to collect money to build the first Immaculate Heart of Mary Church in the mid-1920s.[4] This self-reliant spirit was evident in other parts of the city. In the 1930s, for instance, residents of El Crisol barrio quickly gathered $600 and located the property on which to build the first church and school of what became Our Lady of Sorrows Parish.[5]

In a similar manner, the circuit priest Father Frank Urbanovsky

MEJICANOS

1912

Considerando las circunstancias en que nos encontramos y la catastrofe de que han sidi victimas muchos de nuestros compatriotas en esta ciudad de Houston el Domingo 21 de 1912 hemos acordado dedicar los productos de la velada Dramatico-Musical, del Domingo 25 de Febrero, a las 7.30 P. M. que iba a ser dada en beneficio del proyectado TEMPLO CATOLICO para remediar en cuanto sea posible los sufrimientos de que esos infelices son objeto.

No dudamos de que todos los Mejicanos daran muestra de su amor patrio y de su caridad cristiana acudiendo numeros.

Bien poco mostrariamos que somos verdaderos hijos de Mexico, si en estas horas de tribulacion y de prueba, no nos compadecieramos de nuestros hermanos, los consolaremos ayudandoles a sobrellevar el rudo golpe que acaban de experimentar.

Sin embargo no queremos abandonar el proyecto comenzado de levantar un TEMPLO CATOLICO a la gloria de Dios y para ello daremos otra velada del mismo genero.

Con objeto de obtener mas fondos, hemos reservado algunos puestos, que podran obtenerse al precio de 50c. Admicion General 25c. niños 15c.

Salon   Saengerbund
Esquina Preston y San Jacinto
Segundo piso.

Encargados | *Padres Oblatos*
J. Gutierrez
y
C. Solsona

A flyer announcing a fund-raiser. Mexican Catholics diverted funds intended for building their first church to help people recover from a fire that razed a large section of Fifth Ward and part of Second Ward in 1912. Courtesy Southwestern Oblate Historical Archives.

noted the efforts of Bonita Gardens residents to acquire their own church in the 1940s. In mid-1947, Father Panchito reported that Mexican Americans there were "paying off the lots they bought for the future church." By the following year they had obtained four acres and two houses and were well on their way to establishing a temporary church. Urbanovsky also observed another kind of contribution typically made by parishioners—donated labor. Every bit of the work to build the first San Juan de los Lagos Church was donated by area residents. First, some twenty boys and men cleaned up the entire property, then an old army barracks was brought in sections to be reconstructed and refurbished by the men of the community. A church bell hung from a mesquite tree called volunteers to work on the project from six to eleven each evening, and, after a worker hand-fashioned an altar, the community's faithful knelt in their "new" chapel four months after setting to work.[6]

Some ten years later in another part of Houston, the people of Jeanetta Gardens launched St. Raphael Parish with equal fervor. The women of the neighborhood organized a Guadalupana Society immediately after the priest at a nearby Anglo church showed an interest in their barrio in 1958. The Guadalupanas collected money for the new church by holding dinners and rummage sales in the community. Before long, a local resident donated the land on which to build St. Raphael Church.[7] In varying degrees, outside financial sources augmented these barrio initiatives.

Catholic mission-aid societies helped finance many of the first chapels and parochial schools in Mexican communities throughout the Southwest. Organizations such as the Catholic Church Extension Society, the American Board of Catholic Missions (ABCM), and Our Sunday Visitor raised millions of dollars to fund church growth during the twentieth century. This practice followed the precedent set by the French Society for the Propagation of the Faith during the nineteenth century.[8] The founding of Our Lady of Guadalupe Church illustrates the role of institutional charity in Mexican parish development. In 1912, the Extension Society designated a gift of $1,000 toward the erection of

Guadalupe. The parish journal recorded the cost of construction at $4,515—"unpainted"—almost half of which was paid for by the Extension Society and the Oblate Fathers. Between 1915 and 1918, the Society provided an additional $1,400 to pay the interest on the remaining debt and meet other needs of the struggling infant church.[9]

Other parishes received similar aid. Churches required altars and pews, school materials, and living quarters for religious personnel, and at various times mission-aid organizations helped pay for some of these necessities.[10] From 1905 to 1950, for instance, the Extension Society gave $129,136 to the Galveston Diocese. Similarly, the American Board of Catholic Missions donated $1.5 million to the church in Texas between 1925 and 1951. Yearly sums of $15,000 to $20,000 from the ABCM were specifically designated for "Mexican work" in the Galveston Diocese from the mid-1940s to the mid-1950s.

But while the aggregate sums were substantial, they were thinly spread across many parishes and over several decades. For example, sixty-six towns and cities shared the amount given by the Extension Society to the diocese between 1905 and 1950. Houston's portion was $7,840, but, spread over some forty-five years, it averaged less than $175 per year and was parceled out to as many as six Mexican churches. In comparison, the ABCM contributions were larger, especially in the early 1950s, when donations specified for Mexican centers averaged $15,000 per year.[11] But again, Mexicans in Houston formed only a fraction of the Spanish-speaking apostolate in the large diocese.

On the one hand, Mexican parishes welcomed any help that lightened their financial loads. The contributions by mission-aid societies were, after all, an improvement over the neglect the church had shown for them in the past. On the other hand, though, the distribution of these funds showed how the pastoral needs of Mexicans took a back seat to that of Anglos. Concerning the $1.5 million distributed by the ABCM in Texas during 1925–51, historian Jay Dolan pointed out that "the Catholic population of Texas was heavily Mexican, with about two of every three Catholics being Mexican. Nevertheless, English-speaking parishes received $980,866 and the Spanish-speaking $390,000, or about one quarter of the total funds distributed by the Board. Such a distinction clearly indicated that the apostolate to the Mexicans came in a distant second to that of the Anglos."[12] Clearly, inequality still haunted Mexican Catholics in the form of the economic discrimination they faced within the church well into the twentieth century.

Institutional charity was supplemented by individuals who contributed money for the pastoral and material growth of Mexican parishes. From time to time the Catholic hierarchy made pleas for financial assistance from employers and the community at large and enlisted the support of some well-to-do individuals.[13] For example, Abe Silverman, known simply as the "Man of Providence" until after his death, contributed money anonymously to Guadalupe Parish for many years. Similarly, Mr. A. A. Hirst contributed the lion's share of funds to build the first house for the nuns at Guadalupe; Agnes Hamilton made possible the construction of a two-story convent; and the Scanlan family was a source of long-term aid to Guadalupe School.[14]

Like institutional charity, private philanthropy helped the development of religious institutions in the Mexican community. Donations of these kinds, however, hardly matched the spiraling cost of providing places of worship and religious instruction. Building costs were staggering in light of the meager financial resources of the Mexican community. In 1912, for example, Guadalupe's first frame church cost $4,515; its permanent brick structure built in 1923 cost $33,420; and a new parish school built in 1949 cost $88,000. Similarly, St. Patrick's pastor estimated the cost of a new church at $30,000 in 1944; two years later the estimate was revised upward to $40,000. By the time the new church was constructed in the mid-1960s, the land itself cost $30,000 and the building was estimated to cost $150,000.[15] Thus, given the limits of institutional and individual charity, Mexican Catholics relied on their own efforts to maintain the financial viability and continued growth of their parishes.

Mexican parishioners clearly demonstrated their willingness to contribute their money, property, and labor for the sake of having their own churches and parochial schools. The initial phases of parish development were successful in large part because of the work and financial contributions of countless parishioners, coupled with some outside support. However, this was only a beginning. The task of maintaining adequate facilities for a growing community posed an even greater challenge. Once parishes were organized and the first chapel-schools opened, church members faced the cost of upkeep and further expansion. The first frame buildings were often refurbished, but eventually they were replaced with permanent brick structures. In addition to larger churches and schools, rectories and convents had to be built and salaries and maintenance costs met. Pastors looked to their parishioners—not to the diocese or outside support—to finance most of these needs.

The construction in the early twentieth century of the Mexican mother church, Our Lady of Guadalupe, illustrates the success with which parishioners cooperated to expand their religious facilities. The parish quickly paid off its debt on the first church and collected the money to build the second church in 1923. The diocesan hierarchy made no mention of the parishioners' role in the financial success of the parish but instead lauded the "indefatigable zeal and self sacrifice" of the pastor.[16] Despite a lack of official acknowledgment, the material progress of Guadalupe Parish came largely from the parishioners' own sweat and sacrifice, as their struggles and successes continued to show over time.

Building programs at Our Lady of Guadalupe and St. Patrick in the 1940s illustrate this trend. For example, the new Guadalupe Parish School originally cost $88,000, of which a debt of $39,000 remained in 1949. Of the $49,000 already paid, all but $2,000 had been paid by church members themselves. The funds for the school were very quickly gathered and "given willingly" but at great sacrifice by the low-income parishioners. The pastor, Father Agapito Santos, realized that "money came hard" in his barrio, but he showed great confidence in the *colonia*, estimating that the debt would be paid in two years.[17] Similarly, St. Patrick's pastor confidently launched a fund drive for a new $30,000 church in the mid-1940s. The cleric sought 400 families to donate $25 or more to the project. "The donations are coming in slowly but surely and I believe that by next June we will have $15,000 in the bank," the priest noted in the parish journal. As it turned out, his optimism was justified; by 1946, some $16,000 had been raised.[18]

Raising money this way continued throughout the diocese over the years, and through the constant toil and sacrifice, several Mexican parishes achieved financial stability and self-sufficiency. But while several churches operated in the black, some of the poorer ones struggled to service large debts in the face of escalating costs and shrinking parish revenues. Our Lady of Guadalupe, for instance, had trouble paying a diocesan loan in 1971. The pastor explained that "tight money and inflation," as well as the inability to charge much for school tuition, posed serious financial problems for the parish. This was complicated by the fact that younger parishioners were moving out of the neighborhood, leaving older, less affluent members behind to support the church. "Little by little we are becoming a parish of the old whose only income is a pension or S.S. [Social Security] check which is never very much," the priest lamented. Significantly, though, the pastor reported that collections had not gone down, despite high unemployment in the parish.[19] Guadalupe's faithful still scraped together significant amounts of money for their church, as they had done traditionally. Other low-income parishes faced similar situations. At St. Raphael and Our Lady of St. John, for example, income and expenditures alternately exceeded each other in the 1960s and early 1970s.[20] As the 1970s began, the poorer parishes met their financial challenges with their customary relentless efforts and varying degrees of success.

In contrast, other parishes fared considerably better. For instance, Blessed Sacrament had a balance of nearly $4,000 at the end of 1971. Similarly, Our Lady of Sorrows Parish finished 1965 with a balance of more than $4,000, while St. Philip, another "vigorous mission," reported a balance exceeding $7,000 in 1966. Even more impressively, St. Patrick Parish had a balance of over $23,000 in 1965.[21] Hence, several Mexican parishes not only survived but flourished over the course of the twentieth century primarily through their own efforts. Spanish-speaking parishioners successfully harnessed the cooperation and meager resources of innumerable barrio residents at every stage of parish development, and, despite some setbacks, the funding strategies that Mexican Catholics used largely succeeded. How did they do it and what did their particular approaches reveal about their ethno-religion?

For many years church officials complained that "[t]he Mexican is not a collection box or envelope giver." The lament pervaded church correspondence and literature, but it revealed more about institutional racism and neglect than the reality of finances in Mexican parishes.[22] Despite this negative stereotype, the fact is that the mainstay of revenue in Houston's Mexican parishes was the regular collection of offerings on Sundays and holy days. Though the traditional (10 percent) tithe was not customary, many Mexican Catholics systematically made cash contributions to their parishes.

Parishioners recalled that parents and children regularly gave an offering at church services. Children eagerly waited to be given nickels, dimes, and quarters to "throw . . . in the basket" each week, a woman recalled. And her family was not unique in this regard; even the "truly poor" added to the collection plate: "They would say, 'Well, I only have five dollars but . . . *las monjitas* [the nuns], they need it.' And there was the five dollars in the basket, and I knew that was their last five dollars," a parishioner recounted.[23] Some families also gave money through the "envelope system" since the early twentieth century. In the late 1920s, the Guadalupe Parish bulletin listed the names of individuals who had "faithfully paid their monthly subscriptions." During January and February 1928, the paid pledges of 177 parishioners ranged from fifty cents to ten dollars, with most averaging about one or two dollars. The next year, as the economy worsened, contributions declined sharply; most donations were reduced by half, and several congregants were unable to pay the full amounts they pledged.[24] Nonetheless, regular contributions continued over the years, and by the 1960s the envelope system was part of the parochial reports, indicating the reliability and importance of this type of parishioner donation.[25] Sunday and holy day collections were by far the largest source of income reported by the Mexican parishes during the mid-1960s and early 1970s, averaging roughly one-half to three-fourths of the annual parish income.[26] But regular contributions had to be supplemented in other ways.

Pledging money for specific building projects was yet another important way of raising revenue. A member of Immaculate Heart of Mary Church explained that this was how Magnolia residents "accumulated enough to buy the land to begin with, and then to build the first church, and then again to build the big church and the school." Another member recalled "selling bricks"—soliciting pledges for construction materials—to raise money to build the new church erected in 1950. Similarly, many parish families individually or jointly sponsored the cost of stained glass windows and other items, such as religious objects and sanctuary furniture.[27] The amount of the contributions varied, from modest individual and family donations to gifts of over a thousand dollars from groups of parishioners and parish societies.[28]

All these forms of financial support were augmented by numerous smaller activities that formed an unending cycle of raising money in the parishes. Some children sold newspapers; others put on cake sales. *Rifas* (raffles) were a perennial favorite in all parishes, and some churches sponsored weekly breakfasts and lunches, bingo games, and an occasional *Gran Baile* (big dance) to fund specific parish projects.[29] Another long-standing tradition was parish "teatro," plays put on in the church hall that often featured the children of the parish. At Guadalupe Church during the late 1930s, parishioners enjoyed a nineteen-act variety show for an admission price of twenty cents for adults and ten cents for children. In addition to raising needed money, this *fiesta*

Children often performed musical numbers and plays in Our Lady of Guadalupe Church's social hall as part of their school activities, as well as for the ongoing fund-raising of the parish. Courtesy Mrs. Petra Guillén.

teatral had the added benefit, clergy and nuns pointed out, of "attract[ing] the parents and grown-up members of the family who might not otherwise attend the services." Flyers and bulletins reminded the community of upcoming events and urged the barrio residents to support the work of the church.[30]

These were valuable barrio customs. On one level, they sustained the economic life of the parish and contributed substantially to the institutional presence of the Catholic Church in Mexican communities. But equally important, fund-raising fostered ethnic solidarity. The projects involved large numbers of neighborhood residents and church members in experiences that reinforced their ethnic identity and sense of community because they were often culturally based and greatly invested with their time, money, and labor.

One particular type of fund-raising, the *jamaicas*, best revealed the implications of Mexican ethno-Catholicism. These festivals varied in size and frequency and were sometimes called *kermesses, noches mexicanas,* or simply fiestas. Some churches held several bazaars regularly throughout the year. At Guadalupe Church they were a "standard operating procedure" for generating parish revenue. Similarly, members of Immaculate Heart of Mary recalled that *jamaicas* were staged "every Sunday" during the Great Depression.[31] Often a series of small bazaars led up to a well-publicized annual affair that entailed extensive preparations, even the closing of city streets. A newspaper described one such event:

> Designers Friday were completing plans for an old Mexican village to be built in replica on the grounds of Our Lady of Guadalupe parish. . . . Gay decorations will transform the village into scenes of color and beauty for fiesta time. There will be no charge for admission to the village. Almost continuous entertainments, including typical songs and dances of old Mexico, will be staged.
>
> Refreshments will be served. Visitors may sit at tables while enjoying fast-changing spectacles of amusements.
>
> Huge loads of confetti, enough to strew Main Street from beginning to end . . . has [*sic*] been provided for revelry and merry-making at the carnival.[32]

The *jamaicas* were a way for Mexican Catholics to enjoy and propagate their culture on various levels, as the preparations involved individuals, families, and whole neighborhoods in cooperation. "Everyone would pitch in with whatever they could," one woman recalled; "everyone took part in it."[33] In the process, many of the relationships and values that undergirded Mexican American life were expressed and confirmed. For example, some of the preparations for the bazaar reinforced gender roles, as men usually did the organizing—contacting parishioners and rounding up food and other items—while women did the "dirty jobs" of food preparation and cleaning.[34]

Women often held *tamaladas*, get-togethers of family and close friends for the particularly arduous task of making tamales to sell at the *jamaicas*. "My grandmother would make tamales [for the bazaars]," a church member related. "It was a family affair; we would all help her."[35] The *tamalada* was an important occasion for both family socializing and socialization, and this tradition offers an opportunity to further examine the role of women "as agents in the production of religion."[36] The *tamalada* involved women, men, and children in long hours (even days) of intensive, gender-defined work. An assembly-line process orchestrated by a mother or grandmother, the most demanding and skilled work was carried out by women while men generally had less taxing responsibilities. Typically, storytelling, jokes, and *chisme* (gossip) punctuated the drudgery, and elders inevitably handed down their generation's wisdom to youngsters in cooking instructions laced with admonitions about proper behavior. The *tamalada* thus imparted many of the core values of Mexican American family and community life, although, like the tradition of the *quinceañera*, it, too, was a double-edged sword. On the one hand, the *tamalada* clearly illustrated the Mexican cultural norm of relegating women to food preparation. On the other hand, women's control of food—and their intimate linking of it to the religiosity they were modeling for children and community —gave them a source of domestic power and community stature. Sister Yolanda Tarango reminds us that women passed down traditions "in a uniquely female manner, teaching through stories, rituals, and example."[37] *Tamaladas* for church fund-raising illustrate this, and they reveal as well another way that women found to exert family and community influence while they propagated ethno-Catholicism. Through the *tamaladas*, then, children learned about work, internalized gender roles, and imbibed religious and other cultural values. Women thus socialized and rooted children in their ethnoreligious culture, teaching them by example that to work for the church in this way was part and parcel of being a member of a Mexican Catholic family and community. Such lessons played a crucial role in maintaining viable Mexican American communities in Houston.[38]

On another level, the preparations for the *jamaicas* linked individuals and families to the larger Mexican community through the extensive cooperation that was needed to carry out a profitable church bazaar. St. Stephen did not have "rich people," Aurora Gonzales explained, "but we had a lot of people who were willing to do the work. And we had, at the bazaars, from the little young girls who were eight or ten years old working to create something with their hands to the older ladies who could hardly walk that would come in to make tamales—the support as a group, *as a people* was fantastic."[39] Parishioners made candies, cookies, cakes, *raspas* (snow cones), and paper flowers to sell. For two or three days before the bazaar, children cut up newspapers and magazines to make confetti to sell and others solicited contributions from barrio merchants and store owners in the downtown area. Churches sponsored annual parish queen contests in which teenaged girls campaigned for cash "votes." The highly touted crowning of the parish queen culminated the laborious efforts of many neighborhood residents who contributed to a successful *jamaica*.[40]

The frequent mention of the bazaars in various parish records testified to their financial importance.[41] During the 1920s, Guadalupe Parish collected amounts of $500 to more than $3,000 a year from *jamaicas*. By 1971, the annual bazaar at Guadalupe gathered $12,000, while the event at nearby Blessed Sacrament Church brought in just under $22,000.[42] Aside from the Sunday and holy day collections, festivals were often the largest source of parish income.

But the importance of the *jamaicas* went beyond finances. Rich in human warmth, they were a true celebration of community. At these events, familiar Mexican music wafted through the evening air, creating a carefree atmosphere as people chatted and strolled around the festively decorated booths and attractions, their senses tantalized by the delicious aroma of steaming tamales, *arroz con frijoles* (rice and beans), and *mole*. Happy shouts of children pierced the night as they greeted cousins and friends, and hearty calls of ¡*Quehúbole!* (How are you?) rang out when compadres exchanged strong *abrazos* (embraces). Our Lady of Guadalupe Parish had its own band that regaled many *jamaicas* over the years. Similarly, many Second Ward and Magnolia

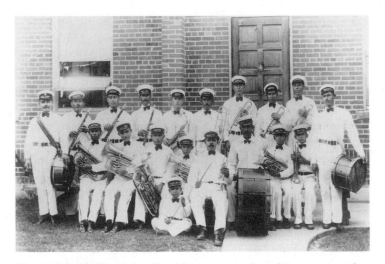

The church band of Our Lady of Guadalupe was a popular and important ingredient of the religious and social life of the Second Ward parish and barrio. Courtesy Houston Metropolitan Research Center, Houston Public Library.

Processions such as this one at Our Lady of Guadalupe Parish in the 1940s were an integral part of ethno-Catholicism. Courtesy Houston Metropolitan Research Center, Houston Public Library.

railroad workers played in the Southern Pacific Band. One parishioner proudly recounted that her *padrino* (godfather) played the tuba in the "SP" Band. "I loved to just sit there and watch him," she recalled.[43] These bazaars nurtured the important custom of godparentage by giving godparents and godchildren a chance to talk and enjoy each other's company. Mexicans preserved affectionate ties with family and friends this way, bonds of mutual support that strengthened families and sustained communities. Furthermore, the *jamaicas* introduced children to Mexican courting rituals: "The boys would stand on the outer line and the girls would walk around and the boys would throw confetti at us," a woman reminisced.[44] Thus these parish celebrations facilitated courtship and marriage, providing generational continuity among Mexican Catholics.

Clearly, the *jamaicas*, and indeed all their fund-raising efforts, served Mexican Catholics in many ways, by providing an important part of the financial base of their parishes and cementing the links between faith, identity, and community. Of course, this approach was distinctly Mexican but not unique; other Catholics had similar ways of fostering community through religion. The fusion of sacred and secular activity in Houston's barrios strongly parallels the central role Catholicism played in the lives of southern Italian immigrants in the late nineteenth and early twentieth centuries. Robert Orsi has beautifully shown how the Catholicism of New York's southern Italians totally permeated their lives and overflowed exuberantly from their homes into Harlem's streets during the feast of Our Lady of Mount Carmel. In Houston, too, Sicilian immigrants who had settled on the rural fringes northwest of the city held similar celebrations each year, complete with fireworks, processions, and bazaars.[45] In the early to mid-twentieth century, Italian American and Mexican American Catholics shared similar ways of cementing their ethnoreligious identity and sense of community.

Houston's Mexican Catholics clearly showed the depth of the connection they felt between their identity and their religious life when diocesan authorities unilaterally decided to dissolve St. Stephen, a

Mexican national parish dating back to the 1930s, and merge its members with a nearby Anglo church, St. Joseph. Seeing this as an affront to their dignity and a threat to their identity, St. Stephen's parishioners revolted.

THE ST. JOSEPH–ST. STEPHEN CONTROVERSY

In 1966 a five-year battle erupted between members of St. Stephen Church and the diocesan leadership that illustrates important links between fund-raising and Mexican ethno-Catholic identity. That fall Bishop John Morkovsky began an ill-fated attempt to merge St. Stephen, in Houston's near west side, with the historically Anglo St. Joseph Church some four blocks away. Bishop Morkovsky thought the consolidation would streamline administration and make more efficient use of resources and personnel. St. Stephen would continue to provide services and have a resident priest, but it would revert to mission status and be incorporated into the territorial parish of St. Joseph. In effect, Mexicans and Mexican Americans who historically had been barred from white churches now were the key to saving one of them from financial ruin. Apparently unmindful of the cruel irony involved, the bishop predicted that the practical effect of the merger would "probably be imperceptible." To the hierarchy, the plan seemed reasonable.[46] But St. Stephen's parishioners saw the merger very differently. Like their parents and grandparents before them, they had worked hard to raise money to build and maintain their own church. Now it seemed all their efforts might be erased, along with the bonds and memories those efforts had created over many years.

The merger took effect in early 1967. Father Patricio Flores took the helm at the new St. Joseph–St. Stephen Parish, and the diocese assigned an assistant to reside at St. Stephen's rectory. Services continued at both churches, and the new administration conducted the business of the combined parish from the Anglo church. But not even the appointment of the highly regarded Father Flores appeased St. Stephen's parishioners, and their dissatisfaction soon surfaced. On May 9,

1967, the new priest at St. Stephen confided to Bishop Morkovsky that fear and intimidation were rife in the parish. "The fear is of integration," Father Emile Farge reported, "of our people here not having *nuestra Iglesia Mexicana* (our Mexican church)." Father Farge warned the bishop that three parishioners were intimidating others into signing a petition by telling them that they would not be accepted at St. Joseph. The priest dismissed the petition drive as parish politics; the organizers feared being "dethroned" by the merger, Farge explained.[47] Father Farge also suggested a strategy to force St. Stephen's members to meld into St. Joseph: operate the mission from St. Joseph, remove the resident priest, and reduce Sunday masses from five to two or three. "I know we can't anglacize [*sic*] the Mexican but we must [A]mericanize him," the priest insisted.[48]

Three hundred signatures voicing the pleas of St. Stephen's petitioners did nothing to alter the situation, nor did they move the bishop to reappoint their former pastor as they asked. Father Farge's suggestions, in contrast, apparently carried more weight, for parishioners continued to complain about the lack of a resident priest at St. Stephen, a discord that smoldered into the next year.[49] Seeking to end the turmoil, the joint parish council agreed in October 1968 to sell both churches and begin congregational life anew under another name in a central location in the neighborhood. In early March 1969, diocesan officials announced plans to reorganize the parish at nearby Washington Avenue under the name of St. Martín de Porres, the patron saint of social justice. The proposal ignited more loud protests from both churches. Thirty "angry protestors" from St. Joseph confronted the bishop after the announcement, and, once again, over 300 members of St. Stephen signed a petition asking the bishop to let them express their feelings about the merger and the plan to relocate. At a subsequent meeting that month, "bedlam" reigned over the proposed changes.[50]

In the wake of the parishioners' opposition, Bishop Morkovsky appeared to suspend the planned sale of the churches. "There has been no decision yet on whether or not the property will be sold," the bishop stated in early March 1969. But other plans went forward. Throughout 1969 there were numerous fund-raising activities to benefit the proposed church of St. Martín de Porres. For example, Pastor Flores issued a letter soliciting donations for the proposed church on August 12. Also, in September the local Catholic newspaper reported on the *Rey Feo* (Ugly King) contest being held among the clergy to raise money for the new church. In the end, however, the plan to build a new church at a different location was laid aside.[51]

But harmony still eluded the parish. St. Stephen's parishioners remained dissatisfied with their mission status, and emotions erupted again in 1971. The congregation at St. Stephen bitterly resented not having their own pastor, wrote Mr. Raymond Lomas to the bishop. Lomas also complained that St. Stephen's members felt abandoned by the administration at St. Joseph. Poignantly he revealed the anguish that afflicted the troubled parish:

> Please forgive my boldness at writing this letter, but it must be done in order to tell you about the misfortune we find ourselves in at St. Stephen's Church. Although I imagine that you already know. As you know, since Father Buckley [the pastor prior to the merger] left, we have been without a pastor. We have had them, but not living at St. Stephen, which is what the people of the parish protest. That is why I am letting you know about this, before things deteriorate further. At this point the priests at St. Joseph apparently have a great deal of work and most of the time they're at St. Joseph and many parishioners come here asking for a priest and there is none. They [the St. Joseph priests] come here only when they celebrate a mass and then they quickly return to St. Joseph.
>
> . . . Because of this, our Reverend Bishop Morkovsky, I wish you would place your holy hand on your heart and be compassionate and send us a pastor here at St. Stephen. We have everything, thanks to God. A good house [rectory] with air conditioning and we are ready to work to support our church and the pastor who would come here. Which is all we ask of you, a pastor at St. Stephen.[52]

Lomas closed his letter rather bluntly, revealing the flip side of Mexicans' traditional reverence for the clergy, a deference now strained by a threat to their way of being Catholic: "Answer me quickly so I'll know your opinion," Lomas demanded.[53]

Bishop Morkovsky may still have been contemplating the Lomas letter when tensions flared again. St. Stephen's representatives, led by layman John Alderete, walked out of the joint parish council meeting in protest and met on their own. At their "Special Meeting" held on April 6, 1971, St. Stephen's parishioners discussed "the situation which prevails in the parishes of St. Stephens [sic] and St. Joseph."[54] Significantly, the letter to the bishop referred not to the merged parish of "St. Joseph–St. Stephen" but rather to the separate parishes. Still very much attached psychologically to their former parish, the St. Stephen's council representatives clung to their identity as an independent Mexican church. The meeting produced six resolutions that were forwarded to the bishop, along with the signatures of 309 members of St. Stephen Church. The parishioners declared that the rumored closing of St. Stephen Church had polarized the membership. They wanted to avoid any further hindrance of "the progress of our Holy Catholic Church" but were adamant about keeping their own house of worship, stating that "under no circumstances shall we accept the closing of our church." The parishioners pressed the bishop to "use his influence, as spiritual leader of the Diocese," to keep St. Stephen open. They also sought the assignment of a permanent resident pastor at St. Stephen and the continuation of the church "to the service of the Spanish-Speaking Community." In effect, St. Stephen's members called for the restoration of their previous status as an independent Mexican national parish.[55]

Scarcely two months passed before St. Stephen's members wrote to their bishop again.[56] Matters had worsened, with tensions between some parishioners and a priest reportedly escalating to an altercation. On June 25 the *Houston Chronicle* reported that Father Patout had "denied an observer's report that he had a physical scuffle" with some St. Stephen parishioners whom the priest said had been "passing out their own church bulletin at Sunday Mass, as a replacement for the official bulletin."[57] The tone and candor of the parishioners' letter to the bishop reflected the degenerating state of affairs. They poured out their indignation, accusing specific priests of "unjust and undignified" behavior. The petitioners also claimed that St. Joseph's priests slighted them. St. Stephen had not been provided the weekly parish bulletins for several weeks, the parishioners complained, and the priests offered neither explanations nor apologies.[58] Worse yet, the new schedule of reduced services at St. Stephen greatly restricted their right to receive the sacrament of confession. The letter also claimed that the clergy had misled the parishioners regarding the handling of parish funds.[59] Finally, the petitioners charged priests with unbecoming behavior. "Week after week . . . the Pastor . . . takes the opportunity [of the sermon] to hurl insults and even improprieties at the congregation," the petitioners complained, adding that the "gossiping" clergy even maligned St. Stephen's members when they visited other churches.[60]

St. Stephen's petitioners wrote that they wished to avoid any further incidents that might bring "serious calamities." Thus they issued the bishop their strongest demands to date, a "final" resolution: FIRST: that from this date on, for no reason will the presence of Father Patout be permitted in the Church of St. Stephen, where he has been the main instigator of the recent events that afflict the bosom of our parish." The petitioners also demanded action on a long-standing complaint: "SECOND: that you are given a period of two weeks, beginning with the date of this memorandum, to provide our parish of St. Stephen with its own 'PASTOR.' "[61] St. Stephen's parishioners spoke clearly and unequivocally, and it was up to the leader of the diocese to respond. They counted on Bishop Morkovsky, who had told the parish council he "would try to do what was best for the people."[62]

On July 1, 1971, about three weeks after the St. Stephen ultimatum was issued, the diocese reorganized the administration of St. Joseph–St. Stephen Parish. A new pastor and assistant were appointed, and although the merger remained, the assignment of new priests seemed to assuage the disgruntled parishioners. A relative calm descended on the joint parish. The local Catholic press noted a "revitalized" spirit in the combined parish and reported that the two congregations were cooperating, a visible enthusiasm having returned to parish organizations and activities. Many credited the tranquility to the self-effacing new pastor, Father Maurice Dho. Mr. Raymond Lomas, who earlier had appealed to the bishop, stated simply, "We are working better now because we have a better priest." More to the point, Mrs. Raymond Canales, another St. Stephen member, revealed, "We have a priest who stays here all the time, ready to serve the people." Lastly, parishioners no doubt were pleased that plans to sell the two churches and relocate were finally dropped.[63] The church hierarchy's changes apparently brought calm to the beleaguered parish. The new parish administration appeared to be to the parishioners' liking, and they had a resident priest at St. Stephen Church, something that reflected at least part of their former structure and status as an independent parish.

Still, things had not completely reverted to their former status; St. Stephen was still a mission subsumed in a territorial parish, not the autonomous *Mexican* parish it had once been. Despite the easing of tensions, both Bishop Morkovsky and Father Dho sensed a continuing dissatisfaction. On May 24, 1973, the bishop confided to the priest that, "for the good of souls," the two churches might need to be separated. Two weeks later Father Dho formally proposed "that St. Stephen be reinstated to its status, as before being united to St. Joseph and that a priest be assigned there permanently." Bishop Morkovsky concurred. "Four or five years ago," he explained, "it was thought that the people of the area of St. Joseph's and St. Stephen's could best be served from one rectory, and perhaps even as one congregation." But, the bishop conceded, "it appears now that the people will be better served by returning to the former status." Without fanfare Bishop Morkovsky restored "the dissident parish" to its original form on July 1, 1973.[64] St. Stephen once again became an independent parish for the Spanish-speaking, with its own resident pastor. St. Stephen's parishioners regained what they had temporarily lost, their cherished *iglesia mexicana*.

The merging of St. Joseph and St. Stephen embroiled parishioners and diocesan leaders in bitter controversy for six years. Throughout the painful episode, the members of St. Stephen Church refused to yield their original demands. Why did they not compromise? Why was it so important to have their own Mexican church? The answers to these questions involved notions of honor and economic justice, but, most important, they had to do with how deeply entwined were the parishioners' sense of identity and their parish life.

The controversy had to do partly with respect, or the lack of it, in the opinion of St. Stephen's members. They were surely rankled at their demotion from independent parish to mission. Moreover, the parishioners believed they were being treated as second-class Catholics —ignored, misinformed, and even maligned by the parish clergy. St. Stephen's members understood that the diocesan plan to integrate them into a white church was essentially an effort to force them to accept a different Catholic tradition—an attempt to make them "better" Catholics. Forced Americanization insulted them. Furthermore, the way in which it was carried out offended their sense of the sacred. The defiant parishioners accused one priest of behavior "unworthy of the Representative of GOD OUR LORD." The clergy's purported gossip not only tarnished "the prestige and good name" of St. Stephen's members, but, worse, it soiled "the HOUSE OF GOD."[65] In the eyes of the parishioners, these priests had violated both sacred roles and sacred space, and the affair tore deeply at their social and religious sensibilities.

The affair also had to do with economic justice. St. Stephen, like other Mexican parishes, had been built through dint of hard work and sacrifice by the parishioners. Now their efforts and money were being used to save another church and, to add insult to injury, a church whose doors had always been closed to them because they were Mexicans. The saving of St. Joseph Church, the second oldest parish in Houston, was a strong motive for consolidating the two congregations, though Bishop Morkovsky had emphasized other reasons for the merger. In the late 1960s, St. Joseph's membership had declined to the point that the weekly collections were far less than the operating expenses. At the end of the 1967–68 academic year, the parish school had to close "for economic reasons," and the church was "in dire need of repairs." Meanwhile, St. Stephen Parish "flourished," with collections sufficient to meet all its expenses.[66] Thus, in order "[t]o save St. Joseph's from the wrecker's ball," the press later reported, "diocesan officials merged St. Joseph's and St. Stephen's into one parish." St. Stephen's parishioners felt they were being used. "We have discovered," they wrote to the bishop, "that all [our] weekly collections are deposited directly in the name of St. Joseph Church, ignoring that these funds come from our Parish."[67] St. Stephen's members chafed in their roles as pawns in an economic injustice.

Aside from these questions, however, the controversy hinged on the issue of identity. Shortly after being assigned pastor of the joint parish in July 1971, Father Dho recognized the futility of trying to establish a merged parish in a new location. "It is unrealistic and too early now to try and unite St. Joseph and St. Stephen's into a third church building," he observed. Dho concluded that "[t]he two congregations—especially St. Stephen's—are not ready to give up their identities."[68] Father Dho's sense of the situation was right. When Bishop Morkovsky merged St. Stephen's and St. Joseph's parishes, he unintentionally jeopardized the sense of community and way of life among Mexican Catholics on Houston's near west side. This cultural trauma could only be righted by restoring the original status of the *iglesia mexicana*.

Mexican American Catholics developed strong bonds with their parishes not only because of the efforts they exerted to establish and maintain them but also because of the cultural nourishment they derived from the institution-building process itself. Sociologist Harvey Newman notes that parishioners have a sense of "preciousness" about their churches partly because they do not view them as commodities to be negotiated. Rather, they develop a "special relationship" with the place of worship based on the "material and psychic rewards" they associate with it.[69] Such practical things as nearness to one's home and friends and access to important services provided by social networks associated with the church contribute to a sense of community among church members and neighborhood residents. Parishioners' ties to their place of worship are "a source of identification with the status of the group and its position within the community," and "there is the sense of joining together with others who share common traits of social status and background to form an organization which stands together against others."[70]

Newman's observations capture some of the embedded meanings and relationships associated with St. Stephen Parish, and they help explain why its members fought to keep its Mexican identity. Clearly, St. Stephen's parishioners derived "material and psychic rewards" from their Mexican church. Apart from the spiritual sustenance the *iglesia mexicana* imparted, it also offered significant material and social benefits, such as access to social services and the support networks represented by nearby friends and family. All of this, to borrow anthropologist Deborah Reed-Danahay's phrase, helped them "make do."[71] The *iglesia mexicana* gave a marginalized ethnic community the wherewithal to "stand together against others"—those who wished to make them "better" Catholics or otherwise impugned their dignity.

St. Stephen Church represented a large part of the social and cultural life of Houston's near west side barrio. Church members and neighborhood residents had strong associations with St. Stephen Parish—vivid memories of their sacrifices to establish and maintain the church, and a tapestry of relationships woven together by the countless solemn and joyous events that took place there over the years, the baptisms, *quinceañeras*, *jamaicas*, and more. "Memory locates the individual in a community" and "men and women discover who they are in their memories," Robert Orsi reminds us.[72] The *iglesia mexicana* embodied the collective memory of the parishioners of the near west side community, its symbolism fused with the people's self-image. St. Stephen expressed not only the community's style of Catholicism but also its members' identity as Mexican-origin people; it was an expression of the people themselves. Thus, giving up St. Stephen was tantamount to surrendering their spiritual and cultural self-expression and losing part of what made them who they were. Keeping their independent parish, on the other hand, was a way of resisting forces that sought to remake them. Fortified by their ethno-Catholicism, St. Stephen's parishioners successfully resisted the hierarchy's coercion, however well-intentioned, to abandon their Mexicanness and adopt an "American" way of being Catholic. When St. Stephen's members regained control of their Mexican church, they preserved their ethnoreligious identity and their dignity, both of which helped them face the inequality that marked their lives as ethnic Mexicans in Houston.

As the Catholic Church expanded its pastoral ministry among Houston's Mexicans and Mexican Americans, it also began to focus more on the parishioners' social needs. Nuns and priests familiar with Mexican poverty began to go beyond their pastoral responsibilities to help parishioners gain a better material life, as the next chapter illustrates.

SIX

THE CHURCH IN THE

BARRIO: THE EVOLUTION

OF CATHOLIC SOCIAL

ACTION

ister Mary Benitia Vermeersch often trudged Houston's back alleys and streets late at night—alone. This was unheard of! Her night outings were not only dangerous, but they also flew in the face of what society expected of women, especially nuns. But Sister Benitia was well known for putting the welfare of others before her own, and neither the dangers of the streets nor the tongue-wagging of those who considered her evening forays unbecoming kept her from doing what she had to do. Sister Benitia had a mission: she was determined to do something about the crushing poverty she saw all around her in Guadalupe Parish and other poor neighborhoods in Houston. Giving fleeting thought to her personal safety and reputation, Sister Benitia went beyond her strictly religious duties and brought badly needed food, clothing, and medical attention to many indigent Mexicans and Mexican Americans in the city during the decades of the 1910s, 1920s, and 1930s.[1]

Sister Benitia's "charity work" was one way the Catholic Church in Houston responded to the material needs of Mexican parishioners from the 1910s to the mid-1960s. This chapter focuses on the changing nature of this social ministry and its impact on the Mexican ethno-Catholics living in the Bayou City. Encompassing many aspects of parishioners' lives, including the personal, vocational, financial, educational, and recreational, Catholic social ministry had implications for individuals, as well as entire communities, making it a form of social action or social reform. During the early twentieth century, Catholic Church representatives in Houston who tried to improve their parishioners' material lives worked individualistically and unsystematically, while, at the same time, Mexican Catholics had their own tradition of self-help. Over time, however, Catholic social ministry evolved from ad hoc humanitarian efforts to more systematic institutional approaches that, by the 1940s, clearly distinguished between mere charity and the need to engage the structures of society to bring about meaningful social change. Driving these changes were church leaders' awareness of an expanding and increasingly politicized Mexican American community, their continued sensitivity to Protestant proselytizing, and their evolving vision of Catholic social action as a leaven for social change.

Ad Hoc Social Action

During the first half of the twentieth century, the Catholic Church in Houston addressed the material needs of Mexicans and Mexican Americans mainly through the charitable works of individual clergy and nuns. This individual social action was wide-ranging, involving men and women of the church in making job referrals, interceding with employers on behalf of workers, helping with legal and financial matters, notifying relatives in family emergencies, and many other kinds of "personal action."[2]

Personal and family counseling formed a large part of a priest's duties. Parishioner Mary C. Villagómez recalled how people in the early twentieth century depended on the advice of local priests. Her brother, for example, sought his pastor's counsel about bringing his fiancée from Mexico to Houston. In a similar vein, when it came time to build the family house, Ms. Villagómez's father, not knowing anything about home construction or anyone who did, had the reverend look at a sketch of what he planned to build. "In other words, they looked to the priest to be not only a spiritual leader but also a material [one]," Ms. Villagómez explained. His parishioners confided in him and sought him out in times of need, Father Esteban de Anta reported in 1930. "How many 'marital differences' have thus been smoothed out!" the cleric exclaimed. "How many tears dried!"[3]

Social ministry of this kind entailed personal sacrifice, as nuns, in particular, often shared their own meager resources with needy parishioners.[4] More than any other representatives of the church, nuns seized the initiative and made personal social action an integral part of their ministry. In Houston, Mary Benitia Vermeersch and Mary Dolores Cárdenas of the Sisters of Divine Providence epitomized individual social action through their tireless work to alleviate the effects of poverty among the city's Mexicans.

Sister Benitia's ministry in Houston spanned twenty-three years as principal of Our Lady of Guadalupe School. When she arrived in the summer of 1915, the city's suffocating heat and humidity aptly symbolized the poverty that engulfed her new mission in El Segundo Barrio. Undeterred, she immediately began canvassing the parish and coordinating relief for the needy from various local sources. She firmly believed, according to one of her protégées, that people would be more receptive to the church's message if first their hunger and oppressive living conditions were alleviated. Tirelessly she trekked Houston's streets making contacts all over the city with merchants, the well-to-do, and anyone else she could enlist in her effort to meet some of the basic material needs of her students and their families. As resourceful as she was relentless, Sister Benitia salvaged discarded rugs for parishioners who often slept on cotton-picking sacks on bare floors, and she solicited food from grocers and packing houses, clothing and other provisions from affluent homes, as well as useful gifts from local charities. With seemingly endless energy she even made time to supervise the cultivation of small vegetable plots on the parish grounds for use by neighborhood families, and part of her arsenal of food included a poultry and cow yard on the church property.[5] Sister Benitia's efforts also brought medical services into the Second Ward when an influenza epidemic devastated the Mexican community in 1918–19.[6]

From 1915 to 1938, "La Madre Benita," as she was called, carried on her personal brand of social action and won the hearts of the parishioners in Houston's Second Ward and beyond. She characterized her material aid to the poor not as begging but as simply reminding others of their Christian duty. "[She] was a very compassionate person," Mrs. Petra Guillén, a longtime parishioner, recalled. "Food was given to her and she fed the poor."[7] When tensions developed between Sister Benitia and the new pastor at Guadalupe Parish, the local bishop had her transferred out of the diocese at the end of the school year in 1938 despite a petition of protest signed by more than 600 dismayed parishioners.[8]

Sister Benitia managed to work well with Father Esteban de Anta, the longtime pastor of Guadalupe Parish, despite her legendary independence. "In all of her intrepidness, she had done many things that few nuns would dare to do in those days," Missionary Catechist historian Sister Mary Paul Valdez wrote. Historian Stephen A. Privett, who described Sister Benitia as "something of an anomaly within the rigidly controlled and highly centralized structures," reported that a highly placed clergyman once marveled, "How Benitia ever got loose is an absolute miracle, given the structures and traditions of her order." Father De Anta apparently accepted her maverick style, and the two worked "unselfishly to build the parish materially as well as spiritually" for seventeen years.[9]

But that was not to be with the new pastor, Father Ladislao López. Father López apparently butted heads with Sister Benitia from the very start after arriving at the parish in late summer 1936, and he enlisted his superiors to have the nun removed. The year 1937 passed "with constant criticism and account requesting by Father López," Sister Valdez wrote. In early 1938 Bishop Christopher Byrne wrote to the superior of the Oblate Fathers in San Antonio, "I heard today that Sister Benitia of Houston still rules at Guadalupe; if you can hasten her removal I think all things would be helped." As was often the case when nuns exerted any independence, priests perceived them as a threat to their authority. Such is the tone of the correspondence between the bishop and the Oblate superior—the nun "still rules," the bishop remarked, as if the intrepid Benitia had completely taken over control of the parish; "there is some danger of her promoting herself from Vicar General to Bishop," the Oblate superior jokingly responded. In such cases, mother superiors usually obeyed a bishop's decision, but often not without resistance. In Sister Benitia's case, her mother superior stalled the pastor, his Oblate superior, and the bishop for some time. "I have had two calls from the Mother Superioress" [who] "left me with the impression that Sister would be removed, as soon as possible," Bishop Byrne wrote to the Oblate superior. "She promised to remove her when her term as Superior ended," the Oblate superior wrote to the bishop, but he added, "I could not ascertain from her when that particular time was."[10] From the time of his arrival until he was rid of Sister Benitia, Father López had to endure her way of doing things for two years. Of course, tensions like these were common between nuns and clergy. They point up not only gender-based frictions within the Catholic Church but also the uphill institutional battles individuals faced when they took on the burden of social action of an individualistic and unconventional nature. They also testify to the depth of the religious convictions that drove Sister Benitia's action on behalf of others.

In much the same style, Sister Mary Dolores Cárdenas attended to the material needs of St. Patrick parishioners in Fifth Ward, on Houston's north side. Sister Dolores was well prepared for the twenty-two years she struggled at St. Patrick; she had previously spent thirteen years doing "all kinds of jobs besides teaching" at Our Lady of Guadalupe during the years Sister Benitia was in charge.[11] "In Houston I took advantage of all the offers that came my way," she recalled. She regularly tapped government sources for surplus food to provide free lunches at St. Patrick School in the 1940s, but the government's peanut butter and similar items needed to be supplemented. So she would rise early and have a neighborhood teen take her to the wholesale produce

Nuns like Sister Dolores Cárdenas, shown here distributing clothing during the Great Depression, took the lead in ministering to the material needs of parishioners. Note the three Catechists (two behind the nun's left shoulder and one to her far right). Courtesy Houston Metropolitan Research Center, Houston Public Library.

market to try to get any leftover vegetables. A soup bone paid for with her own money completed the hot meal she gave her students. When St. Patrick's cafeteria had to be given up in favor of more classroom space, the determined nun still managed to provide free milk for her students.[12]

Providing food and other basic needs was but one form of personal social action. Often, priests and nuns also served as character references for parishioners trying to find jobs. The Southern Pacific Railroad, being a major employer of Houston Mexicans, received many letters from priests and nuns recommending "honest" and "trustworthy" workers. Sister Dolores was particularly zealous at this task. She suspected that the "SP" paid relatively better wages than other employers, so with typical inquisitiveness she looked into what was needed to apply. Soon she was hard at work tutoring young men in the barrio in math and otherwise preparing them to pass the required tests, much to the chagrin of the people in the Southern Pacific employment office, whom she exasperated and overwhelmed with referrals.[13]

Church representatives of course were very familiar with the precarious finances of many parish families, and they understood that everyone was expected to contribute to a family's income. Both Sister Benitia and Sister Dolores cajoled many potential employers, plaintively appealing to their "kind hearts" to hire students from their parishes who badly needed to work in order to help their families.[14] Clearly, many nuns thought helping parishioners find jobs was an important part of their social ministry, and they had some success at this: "Many of the young men of the parish, and even a good number of the parents of her present-day pupils," a parishioner testified about Sister Benitia, "now hold jobs obtained through her recommendations."[15]

The efforts of Sisters Benitia and Dolores were part of the long tradition of Catholic nuns and other women in U.S. history who used religious and gender ideologies "to justify, define, and expand their role in American society." Nuns like Benitia and Dolores, like all other women of their generation, had to find ways to work within the constraints imposed by a patriarchal society and church. They exploited women's ascribed role (and implicit power) as mothers—feeding, clothing, and otherwise being nurturers and caretakers of children and the poor—because these were gender-appropriate activities that paralleled women's domestic roles in the family. This "maternal feminism" allowed nuns to provide material assistance to Mexican families as they struggled to overcome marginality and make a life in Houston. It also provided avenues for nuns to develop their individual skills and to wield a certain amount of influence wherever they ministered.[16]

It would be easy but wrong to dismiss these nuns' gutsy efforts on behalf of Mexicans in the early to mid-twentieth century. Amid the widespread poverty of Houston's barrios, these women worked creatively to bring food, clothing, and other material aid to hard-pressed families. Their efforts helped to sustain many families over the years and inspired individuals to persevere in the face of inequality and discrimination. The nuns' personal interventions sometimes proved pivotal in helping individuals succeed educationally and rise above a life of poverty, later to lead the way for others. For example, Bishop Patricio Flores, a major civil rights leader during the Chicano movement, often acknowledged Sister Benitia as an important mentor in his life. Sister Benitia paved the way for Flores to become a priest, despite his disadvantage as a high school dropout. After hearing that clergymen had rebuffed Flores's idea of becoming a priest, Sister Benitia characteristically said to him: "In the Church you don't start at the bottom. You go straight to the top." With that she had the teenager drive her to Bishop Christopher Byrne's office, where she introduced him and persuaded the prelate to give the young dropout a chance at a seminary education.[17] However apolitical nuns who undertook "charity work" might seem by today's standards, they were precursors of social change who prepared the soil and planted the seeds for greater social change in the future.[18]

In addition to the efforts of Sister Benitia, Sister Dolores, and other nuns, priests also came to the aid of the working poor and the unemployed. This outreach had long-standing papal approval. In the 1891 encyclical, *Rerum Novarum*, Pope Leo XIII had ordered: "Go to the workingman, especially where he is poor; and in general, go to the poor." In 1931, Pope Pius XI decreed in *Quadragesimo Anno*: "Let our parish priests . . . dedicate the better part of their endeavors and their zeal to winning the laboring masses to Christ and to His Church." These words especially resonated among the Oblate Fathers, whose raison d'être was ministry to the poor.[19]

The outreach of bishops to the larger community complemented the initiatives of nuns and priests. Bishop Nicholas A. Gallagher appealed in early 1912 to the major employers of Mexicans in Houston to help finance the church's efforts to ease their plight. His successor, Bishop Byrne, likewise instructed pastors throughout the Galveston Diocese to solicit a special Sunday collection specifically for the work at Our Lady of Guadalupe Parish. Sometimes these appeals struck a responsive chord in the community at large. In September 1915, for example, a railroad official made an open appeal to Houstonians to help repair damage to Guadalupe Parish facilities caused by the hurricane of August 16, 1915.[20]

Bishop Byrne also voiced his support for unionization. In 1942 the prelate instructed his pastors not to be strangers to the labor unions, which, after all, were comprised of men from their neighborhoods. Byrne instructed his priests to identify and get to know any union leaders in their parishes. As the spiritual leader of the diocese, Bishop Byrne wanted to show workers that "the Church is the defender and friend of Labor," and he strongly urged pastors to convey this message.[21]

In the early twentieth century, however, church support for the working classes was mostly rhetorical. This stance was in tune with the conservative political heritage of Texas. Indeed, even in cities like San Antonio and El Paso, with their greater concentrations of Mexican workers and closer ties to American and Mexican labor unions, Mexicans and Mexican Americans struggled gamely but made few advances against powerful anti-union sentiment and tradition. Houston's Mexican workers, being fewer and less closely tied to organized labor, worked under even greater disadvantages than their counterparts elsewhere in the state. In the 1910s and 1920s, there was minimal labor activism among Mexicans in the city. It increased somewhat during the 1930s, though it apparently did not approach the scope of efforts in San Antonio and other cities.[22] Not surprisingly, the leadership in the Galveston Diocese did not move beyond verbal support for Mexican labor in the first half of the twentieth century, and thus social action in the labor arena was even more circumscribed than the personal intervention of parish priests and nuns on behalf of individual workers.

Individual efforts blended with many group activities at the parish level aimed at social needs in the barrios. Parishes implemented ongoing and ad hoc projects that, for the most part, involved the same aims and church personnel as the individual initiatives described earlier. In fact, much of the organized social work of the parishes was carried out by nuns, using the parochial school as their main vehicle. The *Houston Chronicle* noted in 1935, for example, that over 500 " 'little Americans,' members of Houston's Mexican colony [were] served with food, clothing and educational facilities at Our Lady of Guadalupe parochial school." When the Great Depression exhausted parish resources, Father De Anta appealed for the first time to the community at large. Civic and social welfare leaders joined with the parish to stage an elaborate four-day carnival and bazaar on the church grounds in December 1935 so that Guadalupe could "continue its social welfare and educational work." Similarly, funds were raised in April 1940 for the Mexican Catholic Community Center operated by Guadalupe Church on the west side of the city.[23]

Catholic schools also contributed to helping the poor; some sponsored government-subsidized lunch programs that became relatively stable features of their programs beginning in the 1940s. Though some pastors balked at the red tape involved, their superiors insisted that Mexican parishes take advantage of government assistance "to consult the good health of their children." Needy families paid minimal cafeteria charges, and church bulletins reminded parishioners that adjustments would be made for children who could not pay.[24] Concern for the welfare of parish children spurred church leaders to attack other social evils that arose from time to time. In 1932, for instance, Bishop Byrne proudly remarked that a priest's campaign against an "evil dance hall" would be long remembered. In a similar vein, Father Agapito Santos enlisted the help of the director of the Houston Settlement Association to shut down a brothel that was operating too close to Our Lady of Guadalupe Church. As one magazine article aptly stated, the Oblate Fathers in Houston were "on patrol."[25]

The clergy were particularly vigilant about juvenile delinquency in the barrios, which was a widespread concern in Houston, especially from the early 1940s to the mid-1950s. Some Mexican youths formed gangs, such as the Magnolia gang, the Scorpions, the Long-Hair gang, and others, and local authorities associated them with the rise of juvenile violence and crime that afflicted the nation during this time. By chance, the notorious "zoot-suit riots" that shook Los Angeles in the summer of 1943 coincided with a sensational murder trial involving members of the Long-Hair gang in Houston. In response to increased crime among Mexican teenagers, civic groups, such as the Federación de Sociedades Mexicanas y Latino Americanas (Federation of Mexican and Latin American Organizations), joined city officials and other groups to combat juvenile delinquency.[26]

Catholic officials entered the fray fully aware of public perceptions. "There is a cry going up and it is found in Houston," Bishop Byrne lamented, "against the Mexican youth that they are criminally inclined."[27] The diocese tried to focus more attention on parish youth as tragedies struck various barrios in the 1940s and 1950s. St. Patrick Parish buried five teenaged victims of gang fights in a span of less than six months in 1942, and Our Lady of Guadalupe Parish also suffered from gang violence. Nearby Immaculate Heart of Mary Church struggled with the same situation, as did Our Lady of Sorrows and Our Lady of St. John.[28]

But despite the gravity of the problem, the cooperation of some priests was less than their superiors expected. In 1942 an Oblate provincial heartily agreed with Bishop Byrne's idea about increasing the "boy work" in Houston's Mexican parishes. But, unfortunately, the provincial complained, "In all our parishes where the Spanish Fathers are in charge, they have refused to cooperate." The Oblate superior believed the Spanish priests in Mexican parishes generally gave "too much time to the 'Hijas de Maria' [Daughters of Mary, a parish society], and having no time for the boys, these consequently became 'Hijos del diablo' [Sons of the Devil]."[29] More than a decade later, a different bishop and provincial grappled with the same problem that, the bishop concluded, stemmed from the "old-country prejudices" that some Spanish priests had against Mexican parishioners.[30]

Efforts to eradicate delinquency had strong support at the highest levels of the Galveston Diocese. In fact, by the mid-1950s, Bishop Wendelin J. Nold considered reaching the youth the top priority in the ministry for the Spanish-speaking. Despite some priestly recalcitrance, church officials earnestly tried to find the right mix of experienced personnel and proven tactics to fight delinquency in Houston parishes.[31]

The strategies varied. Many parishes channeled youthful energy and free time into organized athletics. The nuns at the "Summer School of Catholic Action" at Guadalupe Church featured very successful football and basketball teams. Even the itinerant Padre Panchito harnessed the vigor of barrio teens. On one visit to the Bonita Gardens area, the "gypsy priest" recruited twenty boys to help with the heavy labor of clearing a lot for the future church of Our Lady of St. John. This done, he persuaded county officials to level part of the area to use as a baseball diamond.[32] Priests and nuns believed that gangs could be wiped out if only they could find more recreational facilities for neighborhood youth, and they worked hard to provide this. But sometimes their efforts were stymied. For example, Father Santos and the sisters at Guadalupe Parish wanted desperately to expand the parish playground by relocating a long-abandoned cemetery adjacent to the rectory. This "big dream" never materialized, however, for one of the few bodies that remained interned was that of Confederate war hero Dick Dowling. A local group's plans for making the cemetery a shrine for the legendary Texan overrode the need for a playground. "But what better shrine could there be to Lieutenant Dowling . . . than a playground for these Latin-American citizens?" asked a reporter who agreed with the parish's priorities. Others in the community at large disagreed.[33]

Protestant proselytizing among Mexicans also spurred Catholic social action. The competition for Mexican souls was real and long-standing. Despite the historical predominance of Catholicism, some Mexicans and Mexican Americans had been converting to Protestantism since the nineteenth century. By the twentieth century, a small but stable portion of the Mexican community, perhaps 5 to 10 percent, belonged to Protestant denominations.[34] In all of Houston's barrios, a number of small Mexican American Protestant churches existed alongside the Mexican parishes, their presence in the city dating back at least to the early 1920s. As Houston's Mexican population grew, so did the number of *aleluyas*, as the Mexican Protestants were called. In fact, by 1940 there were at least ten Baptist, Methodist, Presbyterian, Lutheran, Pentecostal, and other Mexican Protestant churches scattered among the city's barrios. The number of non-Catholic churches continued to increase in the 1950s. In the area around St. Patrick the pastor reported two Mexican Protestant churches in 1951 (Baptist and Lutheran) and a Latter-day Saints church two years later. St. Patrick's census reported five Mexican Protestant churches (two Baptist, an Assembly of God, a Church of Christ, and a Methodist), as well as a Latter-day Saints church. Catholic officials constantly agonized about the "great leakage" in the Catholic Church, that Mexicans were straying from their traditional faith.[35]

In addition to the Mexican Protestant churches, Catholic clergy worried about the Protestant "Houses of Neighborliness" and other community centers that combined social services in the barrios with proselytizing. For example, the Methodist Church sponsored the Wesley Community House, which opened in 1930 to offer recreational and other social services to the Mexicans of the near north side, while Anglo Presbyterian women operated similar centers in other barrios.[36] Of course, not all of Houston's community centers were directly affiliated with Protestant churches. The Rusk Settlement House had provided an array of social services to the residents of Second Ward since 1907. Like most settlement houses throughout the United States, Rusk Settlement purported to be a secular institution. Nonetheless, as historian María Cristina García noted, "Most settlement workers . . . came from middle-class families, their values shaped by Calvinist morality and the Social Gospel movement."[37]

No wonder, then, that Bishop Byrne grew uneasy in 1942 when he learned that the Young Men's Christian Association (YMCA) was "flirting" with "our Mexican boys." He pointed out that the YMCA had recently spent $11,000 to build a boys' club house near Our Lady of Sorrows Church, and he ordered the priests at St. Stephen and Our Lady of Sorrows to "get interested in that."[38] In a similar manner, an Oblate

Both Catholic and Protestant churches vied for the attention of Mexican American teenagers such as these pictured in Houston's Fifth Ward in the 1940s. Courtesy Houston Metropolitan Research Center, Houston Public Library.

provincial took a strong interest in the work being done by the Houston Junior Forum Community House in the late 1950s. The director seemed "a very capable woman, and at the same time most considerate even though not a Catholic." For the Catholic hierarchy, involvement in this project presented an opportunity to combat social problems, as well as shore up Catholicism in the Second Ward. Thus the hierarchy assigned Father Frank Brentine to work with the Community House director, "to direct [her] in a favorable manner."[39] Houston's predominately Protestant ethos and institutions challenged the Catholic Church to redouble its own social work in the barrios.

During the early to mid-twentieth century representatives of the Catholic Church approached social issues and material needs in Mexican communities in an indirect and individualistic manner, mainly through the personal efforts of priests and nuns acting on their own.

But an ever-growing Mexican population and shifting attitudes within the church hierarchy focused greater attention on Mexican Catholics. At the same time, Protestant proselytizing among Mexicans spurred the church to increase its social services to them in an attempt to keep them within the Catholic fold. Mexicans and Mexican Americans accepted this aid, and at the same time they continued to rely on each other, as they always had.

THE MEXICAN TRADITION OF SELF-HELP

The Mexican community had a long-established tradition of self-reliance reaching back to the Spanish and Mexican eras when a catastrophic fire struck Houston in 1912. The conflagration razed over forty city blocks and destroyed about $7 million of property in an area roughly half a mile wide and one and a half miles long. Fifth Ward suffered most of the damage, and there was some destruction in Second Ward as well, leaving many Mexicans among the hundreds of homeless and jobless victims. In a display of ethnic solidarity, the money that had been gathered by the community for its first church was diverted to the victims of the fire. As important as the projected new church was to Houston's Mexicans, the suffering of their fellow compatriots took precedence.[40]

Mexican communities throughout the Southwest had always banded together for self-preservation through mutual aid societies and other organizations. Some, like the Liga de Protección Mexicana, were fully grounded in Oblate parishes and enjoyed the blessing of the church.[41] At Houston's Guadalupe Parish, men formed a Liga de Protección Mexicana in 1917 and the following year the women there started their own chapter. Also at Guadalupe, a secular organization called the Asamblea Mejicana Pro-Raza (Pro-Mexican Congress), whose goal was "to protect Mexicans against the insults and abuses of which they are often victims," tried to recruit members by advertising in the church bulletin.[42] Little is known about these protective societies at Guadalupe Parish, but, given the Oblates' active involvement with *ligas* throughout Texas, these chapters probably pursued a mutual aid–type of social action with the blessing of the pastor. However, it is important to emphasize that this reflected traditional Mexican self-reliance and community organization, not dependency on the church. In fact, Mexican self-help organizations predated any Catholic institutional presence in the city's *colonia*.[43]

While church leaders helped to channel food and other basic needs into Mexican parishes, these same parishes, despite their own poverty, did what they could to ease the plight of others. "Although money is scarce at the church," a newspaper reported about Guadalupe Parish, "sometimes Father Agapito Santos, the pastor, must refuse cash donations because he knows the givers can't afford them." Parishioners regularly contributed to communitywide charities, such as the Community Chest and Red Cross, to the amazement of the nuns who knew the extent of poverty among them. "They somehow manage to bring a can of food for every drive," a nun pointed out.[44]

Operation Relief reflected well the parishioners' magnanimity and the church's role in helping to coordinate it. When two hurricanes devastated Tampico, Mexico, in 1955, the five Mexican national parishes of Houston responded quickly and generously. Oblate Father John Sauvageau, pastor of St. Stephen Church, coordinated the effort. Over radio and television, he appealed for donations eleven times a day while the priests of the other four Mexican parishes informed their church members. "After only a five-day campaign," Father Sauvageau recalled, "we had received $5,642.00."[45] In Mexico Father Sauvageau personally supervised the distribution of the food and medicine purchased with the contributions, while efforts continued in Houston to raise more money. The Bonita Bar donated proceeds from a barrel of beer, local musicians staged a benefit dance at the Acapulco Night Club, and the director of the Morales Funeral Home facilitated the discounted purchase of a $10,000 ambulance that was loaded with supplies and driven to Tampico by Father Sauvageau.[46]

When disasters struck, Mexicans and Mexican Americans put aside religious differences. The summer before the Tampico disaster, in July

1954, flooding along the Rio Grande devastated Mexican communities in Laredo, Eagle Pass, and Del Rio, Texas, along with their neighboring cities of Nuevo Laredo, Piedras Negras, and Ciudad Acuña in Mexico. In this case a Mexican American Baptist pastor, Reverend James L. Novarro, organized a relief drive in Houston. Reverend Novarro coordinated the collection of more than 300,000 pounds of food and clothing, as well as $5,800 in cash for medical supplies, and he personally supervised the distribution of the aid on both sides of the U.S.-Mexico border.[47]

Church leaders gave important guidance to self-help efforts, but it was the parishioners who made most of the sacrifices necessary to carry on the work. In 1957, for instance, St. Stephen's parishioners started a credit union with thirty-five members and $136.00; less than two years later the credit union had 400 members and had loaned out over $29,000. The success "was made possible by the savings of our people —25¢ . . . $1.00 . . . , and in a few rare cases, $5.00," Father Edward Murray explained, and because the parishioners themselves "were willing to utilize their talents and time to protect our people from the loan shark."[48] St. Stephen's credit union differed significantly from earlier church social action in that it combined clerical guidance with Mexican American leadership; it was not passive charity. Priests motivated by the goal of economic redemption of the working classes understood their role as nurturing self-reliance among their parishioners.[49]

The parish school also cooperated with outside groups interested in attacking educational problems in the barrios. In the late 1950s Houston's well-known entrepreneur and civic activist Félix Tijerina started a program of preschool classes for Spanish-speaking children throughout Texas. In Houston several Mexican parishes disseminated information about the program in a highly successful media blitz in April 1960.[50]

Clearly, Mexican and Mexican American Catholics in Houston maintained a tradition of self-sufficiency that often involved cooperation with the institutional church. Self-help efforts involving clergy and nuns expressed the long-standing practice of Mexicans availing themselves of church services while maintaining some distance from the institution. It also underscored the dialectical nature of their ethno-Catholicism.

Toward Institutional Social Action

By the 1940s the Catholic Church began to bureaucratize and institutionalize its social ministry, though piecemeal charity continued. The Bishops' Committee for the Spanish-Speaking (BCSS), launched in 1945, exemplified this new approach to Catholic social action. Under the firm control of the progressive archbishop of San Antonio, Robert E. Lucey, the BCSS sought the cooperation of bishops throughout the Southwest to exert a concerted "spiritual and temporal welfare work" for Mexicans and Mexican Americans.[51]

Bishop Byrne of the Galveston Diocese played at least an indirect role in the formation of the BCSS. For years he had decried the exploitation of Texas Mexicans and cast about for support. "What do you think of the idea of asking the Fathers [in Houston] to get the Mexican people more interested in the Civil life of which they are a part?" he asked an Oblate provincial. Several years before the BCSS came into being, Bishop Byrne called for action by the church. "I think, we have a field for Catholic Action," he wrote, referring to the need for an increased social ministry, "and a battle for Social Justice that we can not any longer neglect."[52] The bishop's comments reflected the more progressive attitudes that were becoming evident among some men and women of the church in the 1940s, as well as an awareness of the political implications of the growing Mexican population. Equally important, the statement was also a call to redress some of the past failures of the church.

Byrne continued emphasizing the citizenship rights of Mexican Americans as a way to end their exploitation. "I think the sooner we get these who are called Mexicans, to vote, and to use their American citizenship, they will all the sooner be regarded with greater respect and they will be accorded better wages for their work," the bishop urged. The aging prelate challenged the "energetic young Archbishop" Robert E. Lucey to take up the cause.[53] Indeed, the dynamic and influential Lucey eventually developed the BCSS as a new phase of Catholic social action. Bishop Byrne died before the committee began its tenure in Houston during 1953–55 at Immaculate Heart of Mary Parish, but he had been an important precursor of the liberal Anglo Catholics who would have significant roles in the impending civil rights era.[54]

The Bishops' Committee, it should be noted, was first and foremost Archbishop Lucey's personal vehicle for farmworker advocacy. Nonetheless, it also brought some needed services to urban Mexican Americans. In various cities the BCSS established child-care programs and clinics, promoted youth work and public housing, and worked to bring a variety of city services to neglected Mexican American neighborhoods.[55] In Houston the BCSS had slight impact, according to a former executive secretary. "I don't think that our presence in Houston had a tremendous impact on the Hispanic community there," Father William O'Connor recalled.[56] This is not surprising considering Bishop Lucey's rigid control over the committee, its primary focus on migratory workers, and the fact that Houston was not part of the "Big Swing," the perennial route made by migrant farmworkers. Still, the committee organized voter-registration drives and English classes in Mexican parishes, and it had ceremonies for those who trekked north from Houston; priests blessed the workers and their vehicles on their departure and welcomed them upon returning to their parishes.[57]

Part of the BCSS strategy was to have each diocese establish its own Catholic Committee for the Spanish-Speaking, to continue its advocacy after the regional office moved on to another diocese in its rotating schedule.[58] In spring 1964, under a newly created Catholic Community Relations Council (CCRC), the Galveston-Houston Diocese named Father Patricio Flores to head its new Committee for the Spanish-Speaking.[59] Together, the CCRC and the Committee for the Spanish-Speaking embodied Catholic social action in Houston during the 1960s.

The CCRC's director carefully stated the role of the church in social action. Father John E. McCarthy explained that the council would bring to bear the moral influence of the church on critical social problems. Significantly, however, the council would play an indirect role. Rather than offer concrete solutions to problems, it sought to clarify the ethical issues involved in disputes. "Each of these areas is one in which leadership properly belongs in the hands of the laity," Father McCarthy emphasized, partly echoing the past, as well as hinting at the direction that institutional social action would take in the future. A church representative's role in social action would be to work closely with trained and dedicated laypeople who would themselves lead efforts for social justice.[60]

The Community Relations Council, created at the height of the civil rights movement, was clearly prompted mostly by black, rather than Mexican American, concerns.[61] Nonetheless, the formation of a Committee for the Spanish-Speaking signaled an important change in the Galveston-Houston Diocese. It indicated Bishop John Morkovsky's desire for a stronger social ministry and a more systematic means of seeking social justice for Mexicans and Mexican Americans. Furthermore, the appointment of Father Flores—a former migrant farmworker keenly aware of Mexican Americans' needs and an outspoken critic of the church's treatment of Mexicans—clearly signaled a response to the increasing social and political activism among Mexican Americans in the years after World War II.[62]

Of course, it could be argued that these developments only reflected the national trend toward greater bureaucratization of charitable work and the professionalization of social action under way since the Progressive Era, evidenced in the creation of the National Conference of Catholic Charities (1910) and the National Catholic Welfare Conference (1919).[63] However, despite their prominence, these kinds of efforts did not trickle down and ignite movements for significant social change. For one thing, as late as 1960, three-fourths of American seminarians lacked training in the social teachings of the church.[64] Rather than the church changing society, the reverse occurred. As other historians have recognized, social justice movements triggered great changes in the U.S. Catholic Church.[65] This is the pattern Houston reflected in the post–World War II years. Earlier, Bishop Byrne's support for the BCSS revealed changing clerical attitudes toward Texas Mexicans in the late 1930s and early 1940s. By the 1950s, this increased awareness about the rapidly growing Mexican community and its increasing politicization moved Catholic leaders to do more to fight discrimination against Mexicans and Mexican Americans. Mexican Americans' burgeoning numbers and political agitation magnified their presence and increased the pressure on the church in Houston to provide a more effective social ministry for Mexican Catholics, as evidenced in the naming of Father Flores to head the Committee for the Spanish-Speaking.

Father Flores scheduled the first meeting of the committee to be held in Houston on October 11, 1964, announcing that education would be its major focus. The committee sought to help develop college scholarships and vocational training programs and to encourage parents to keep their children in school. Poor academic preparation denied factory and industrial jobs to many Mexicans and Mexican Americans, Father Flores stated, and was a link in the chain of poverty: "Low income forces them to take the worse [sic] in housing and poor housing conditions create many other serious problems."[66]

The Galveston-Houston Diocese moved quickly to attack the problem of education in the barrios through the Catholic Community Relations Council and other groups. In January 1965 the CCRC began a program to provide remedial instruction in math and reading at St. Stephen, Immaculate Heart, and St. Raphael nationality parishes, hoping to "eliminate academic deficiencies that lead to school drop-outs." Soon after, the diocese implemented Head Start programs at twenty-two centers, including several of the traditionally Mexican parishes in Houston. Adult education followed, with literacy classes offered by the Diocesan Council of Catholic Women at St. Stephen Parish and St. Raphael mission during the mid-1960s.[67]

The Catholic Community Relations Council, the Committee for the Spanish-Speaking, and other diocesan-level organizations, then, reflected the institutionalization of social action in the Galveston-Houston Diocese by the mid-1960s. A more coherent and systematized social ministry had developed in the post–World War II era. By the mid-1960s, with the rise of the Chicano movement, there were forces at work that eventually would propel the church in Houston into unprecedented turmoil and involvement in social issues in Mexican American communities. It is that aspect of the church's social role that we turn to next.

SEVEN

"May God protect us from guys like you," an angry young Chicano yelled at the priest. Others who had come to the meeting with the pastor also spewed bitterness as their parents watched "with glassy eyes of disbelief." The activists left Resurrection Catholic Church unable to convince the pastor to let them hold their school boycott classes at the church. "The Shepherd Refuses His Flock," a Chicano newspaper railed, adding that "the majority of the Catholic Schools, in time of need, have refused to help the people that they should be serving."[1]

This scene from a chapter in the Chicano civil rights movement (*el movimiento*) in Houston illustrates how the tumultuous years of the civil rights era rocked the Galveston-Houston Diocese. This chapter's focus is on the response of the Catholic Church to the turmoil of the Chicano movement during the mid-1960s to early 1970s, when the Mexican American quest for self-definition and inclusion in Houston climaxed. During the Chicano movement representatives of the church in Houston alternately resisted and embraced the cause for Mexican American equality. *El movimiento* unleashed a fury of demands for more social action by the church. The diocesan administration responded to many petitions in traditional ways, but the unprecedented internal and external pressures for reform forced the church hierarchy to respond in new ways as well. As individual clerics and nuns pushed efforts for Mexican American equality within the church and in society, the leadership of the Galveston-Houston Diocese cautiously supported and followed the vanguard.

THE CHURCH IS CHALLENGED

During the civil rights era many people questioned American values and institutions, and religious institutions were no exception. Indeed, churches often came under fierce attack as disaffected groups challenged their subordinate status in society.[2] Mexican Americans also questioned the role of religious institutions in their lives. Local and national leaders frequently looked to the church for help in addressing pressing social issues. For instance, when labor organizer César Chávez emerged as a national symbol of the Chicano movement in 1965, the institutional church figured prominently in his struggle for economic justice for California farmworkers. Though many individual clergy and nuns actively supported his cause, Chávez challenged the church hierarchy to throw its formidable influence and resources behind the striking agricultural workers. "We don't ask for more cathedrals," he stated, "We ask the Church to sacrifice with the people for social change, for justice."[3]

Calls for the Galveston-Houston Diocese to step up its social activism came from many quarters as hometown politicians, congressional representatives, local barrio activists, and other Chicanas and Chicanos increasingly prodded the institution. In 1965 Manuel Crespo, chair of the Houston chapter of the Political Association of Spanish-speaking Organizations (PASO), called on church leaders to do more to encourage Mexican American interest and participation in politics. Clergy "could help Latin Americans very much by mixing more with them, talk[ing] to them and encourag[ing] them in their political obligations," Crespo urged. Similarly, Texas congressman Henry B. González, in Houston to address the annual meeting of the Society of St. Vincent de Paul, a major Catholic charitable organization, suggested that clergy "redefine" and bring more relevance to their social-action programs. Likewise, local activist William Gutiérrez called for church officials to stop taking Mexican Catholics for granted and urged priests to "become deeply involved and active in the plight of the Mexican American."[4]

Over time, the voices of protest became increasingly strident. At a Houston conference in October 1969, for example, Herman Gallegos, the executive director of the Southwest Council of La Raza, a coordinating organization of Mexican American advocacy groups, denounced the institutional church's failure toward Mexicans. He charged that the institution was "too far removed" from Chicanos and Chicanas and that it was at least partly to blame for some of the social problems facing them. Gallegos challenged the representatives of Catholic charities to help remedy some of these ills by creating housing, education, and economic development programs for Mexican Americans.[5]

Others used angrier language. Lalo Delgado, a Chicano academic and activist, told a gathering of lay and clerical officials in Houston that the Catholic Church was a racist institution, that "bishops, priests and Sisters have turned it into an ugly church." Yolanda Garza Birdwell, a Mexican American Youth Organization (MAYO) leader in Houston, similarly assailed the church in a newspaper interview. "[W]hen the dogs in River Oaks [Houston's most affluent neighborhood] are eating more meat than a lot of her northside friends," the *Houston Chronicle* reported, "a woman has a right to fight back." "So it's a sin to stop having children?" Birdwell asked rhetorically. "Okay, mothers have more children and there's malnutrition and a great injustice is done. I have no doubt the Church is very responsible for this situation," Birdwell charged as she pointed the finger of blame for the poverty in Houston barrios.[6] Chicanas who attended the Conferencia de Mujeres por la Raza (National Chicana Conference), held in Houston May 28–30, 1971, echoed this anger. Many denounced the oppression of Mexican American women by men at home and in the church, and a resolution defiantly "recognize[d] the Catholic Church as an oppressive institution." The conference went on record in support of abortion and resolved "to break away" from the Catholic Church.[7]

The Chicano press voiced virulent attacks on the church during the late 1960s and early 1970s, publishing scathing editorials that condemned the failings of institutional Christianity. Chicano journalists, for example, accused church personnel of hypocrisy and insensitivity toward Mexican American parishioners. On one occasion the editor of *Compass* likened the clergy to "[p]arrots, who do not know or understand the seriousness of the doctrine being taught." In another editorial, the paper charged that clerics would rather dedicate themselves to building beautiful structures than to speaking out against discrimination and economic injustice.[8]

Another community newspaper, *Papel Chicano*, aimed most of its ire at Protestants, but it also reminded readers that "the Catholic Church [was] unmindful of the needs of the Chicano." The paper criticized the institutional church for neglecting social issues that affected both the spiritual and material welfare of its parishioners, claiming that priests did more harm than good and were "such cowards" that they were afraid to denounce bigotry, racism, and discrimination. Church officials who lacked the courage or ability "to relate Christian teachings to the community's everyday life and problems should find other vocations," the article continued, "where they will not do such damage to the parishioners' spiritual lives." The newspaper's denunciations revealed not only disillusion but also the historical anticlericalism and self-sufficiency of Mexican Catholics, who, the paper asserted, owed no allegiance to an institutional church "that pretends to teach doctrines which are alien to the spirit of the Chicano," notions such as turning the other cheek and being long-suffering.[9]

An anonymous poem in one of Houston's Chicano newspapers reflected the disillusionment many felt with the Catholic Church:

> I was hungry
> and you formed a humanities club

and discussed my hunger.
Thank you.
I was imprisoned
and you crept off quietly
to your chapel in the cellar
and prayed for my release.
I was naked
and in your mind
you debated the morality of my appearance.
I was sick
and you knelt and thanked God for your health.
I was homeless
and you preached to me
of the spiritual shelter of the love of God.
I was lonely
and you left me alone
to pray for me.
You seem so holy;
so close to God.
But I'm still very hungry,
and lonely,
and cold.
So where have your prayers gone?
What have they done?
What does it profit a man
to page through his book of prayers
when the rest of the world
is crying for his help?[10]

During the 1960s and 1970s many Chicanas and Chicanos vented a palpable anger and estrangement they felt toward the church. They lashed out at the institution's historical relationship with Mexicans— some seeing it as blatantly racist, others as paternalistic and insensitive at best—and they accused the church leadership of perpetuating their inequality. These Chicanos and Chicanas wanted more than just spiritual comfort from the institutional church; they expected it to be their ally, not their oppressor through its inaction in social matters. Prayers without social action, many Chicano Catholics felt, left them "still very hungry, and lonely, and cold." For them the institution was out of step with their struggle for social change.[11]

Some parishioners expected their churches to work for social justice in the barrios. In the fall of 1970, parishioner Eduardo López sought his bishop's support on a divisive issue. López explained to Bishop John Morkovsky that the members of Our Lady of Sorrows Parish were polarized over whether "a church [should] bury its head in the sands of complacency or . . . try to aleviate [sic] the everyday problems of the community."[12] López described what he and other members thought their church should be and do:

We feel that a church or a religion is not judged by the beautiful buildings in the parish or by the amount of money raised or the amount of money in the bank. We feel a church should be judged by the amount of faithful who participate in church activities. By the amount of faithful who are allowed to participate in its government. We feel that to preach of charity and brotherlly [sic] love is not sufficient . . . that it is imperative that we go out and actually put into practice those beautiful [C]hristian teachings; especially in the poverty level community in which we live.[13]

These parishioners urged their parish council to get involved in issues affecting their neighborhood. "We wanted to tell them how deeply we feel that our community has no recreational activities for our children, no parks, no boy scouts, no girl scouts, [that] our teenagers have no place to go," the parishioner explained. "We told them of the drug addiction problem amoung [sic] our school children; the necessity of more and better police protection." The group pleaded with their parish council for permission to use church facilities for activities "that would not only deal with the spiritual but also the material needs of our community." But those who controlled the parish council and day-to-day church activities disagreed completely with the petitioners' vision of the church, asserting that it "is a spiritual body that must not get involved in the civic affairs of the community."[14] Although this particular attempt to involve a church in social issues was staved off for the time being, the efforts of López and likeminded parishioners at Our Lady of Sorrows sent a strong message to the diocesan leadership. Chicana and Chicano laypeople increasingly stepped forward and pressed the Catholic hierarchy in Houston to join their quest for social justice.

THE CHALLENGE WITHIN: ACTIVIST PRIESTS AND NUNS

By the later 1960s the Galveston-Houston Diocese also felt pressured from within its own ranks to support Chicano social causes. The most outspoken local cleric was Father Patricio Flores, who had long ministered to Mexican Catholics in and around Houston before diocesan officials selected him in 1964 to head the local Bishop's Committee for the Spanish-Speaking.[15] Reverend Flores warned that there would be a mass exodus of Mexicans from the church unless it showed more concern and sensitivity toward them. "We, as a big body [the institutional church] are not doing enough," the priest admonished. His message was clear: Despite the fact that the great majority of Mexican Americans were Catholics, "the Church has not really been sympathetic or sensitive to us in our social, economic or educational struggle." On another occasion, the outspoken cleric decried that Mexican Americans "have been victims of . . . semi-slavery . . . , lived in conditions sometimes worse than animals in the zoo and yet the Church keeps silent."[16]

In October 1969, Father Flores was among fifty or so Chicano priests who met in San Antonio to form an organization called Padres Asociados para Derechos Religiosos, Educativos y Sociales (Priests Associated for Religious, Educational and Social Rights, or PADRES). These Chicano clerics vowed to take "the cry of our people" to the hierarchy of the church, and to involve the institution in *el movimiento*.

The formation of PADRES owed much to the pressures exerted by the Mexican American laity. Their awareness of the Chicano movement, the group's information officer told the press, was "one of the principal reasons the priests had come together."[17] Father Ralph Ruiz, the first national chairman of PADRES, explained that Mexican American Catholics resented the fact that "the Church is not Mexican American oriented." PADRES would "have to make the Church cognizant of the fact that we exist and that we wish no longer to be ignored or taken for granted," the cleric declared.[18]

A group of Chicana nuns soon joined the drive to gain the institution's attention and support. Two activist sisters, Gregoria Ortega and Gloria Gallardo, founded Las Hermanas (Sisters) in a conference held in Houston in April 1971. Gallardo and Ortega were elected president and vice-president, respectively, of the new organization dedicated to promoting social change, cultural pride, and Chicana leadership.[19] Similar to PADRES (which Gallardo also helped establish in Houston), Las Hermanas declared that they sought "revolutionary" changes within and outside of the church. Refusing to be constrained by the notion of separate sacred and secular spheres, Gallardo declared, "We agree that there should no longer be a dichotomy between religion and social aspects."[20] At the initial meeting of Las Hermanas, the conference program tantalized the participants with such questions as "Do Politics Turn You On?"; "How Do Sisters Promote Social Justice?"; and "What Is the Church's Role with La Raza?" At a national conference the sisters discussed how they might help raise the economic status of Mexicans and Mexican Americans in the United States and develop barrio leadership. In Houston they appeared at community center meetings to publicize their message and were active in barrio issues.[21]

Las Hermanas aimed to bring the Mexican community's needs "more forcibly" to the attention of the church hierarchy, declaring that they would not be ignored. If the hierarchy did not support Las Hermanas, a sister warned, it would "hear from us."[22] Clearly, these Chicana nuns had developed far beyond the "maternal feminism" that

Sister Gloria Gallardo, Chicana activist and co-founder of Las Hermanas, was one of the leaders of the Mexican American community's boycott of Houston's public schools in 1971. Courtesy Houston Metropolitan Research Center, Houston Public Library.

characterized precursors such as Sisters Benitia Vermeersch and Dolores Cárdenas in the early to mid-twentieth century. Sisters active in Las Hermanas understood themselves as political agents. In the early 1970s they understood, as activist sisters recently recognized, that being "political" did not necessarily "mean being a registered member of the Democratic or Republican party . . . [or] running for public office." Rather, it meant "to grasp one's elemental kinship with a 'people' . . . to discern, however inchoately, that one is *of* the people, which is to say that little in one's life is ever wholly private and that one's most personal spaces have import for the public weal." Las Hermanas paved the way for today's activist sisters who understand that "to be political is to incorporate into one's self-identification the fact of one's rootedness in a people and to make and act on choices that contribute to the welfare (good journeying) of that people."[23] They were important actors and companions in the Mexican Catholic pilgrimage in the Bayou City. The church clearly heard the rising chant of protest and the calls for support of the Chicano movement both from within and from outside its ranks, and began to respond.

The Institutional Rationale

Church involvement in the Chicano movement in Houston took two forms. Institutionally, the Galveston-Houston Diocese played the role of supportive ally of *el movimiento*, albeit within cautiously prescribed limits. Significantly, however, the catalysts for social change were individual priests and nuns, many acting alone or through newly formed organizations like PADRES and Las Hermanas. Political activism by religious personnel dramatically departed from the traditional patterns of church activities in Houston's Mexican communities. While some individuals within the church had long worked to improve the material lives of Mexican Americans, they had never led efforts to mobilize their parishioners on a large scale for social and political change. Nor had the diocesan leadership ever supported a movement for social change to the extent that it did in the 1960s and 1970s. The unfolding of *el movimiento* did not wait for the church's blessing. Rather, Chicanas and Chicanos were in the vanguard of social change, and the church hierarchy followed with its support.

The institutional role the church would play began to take shape in the early 1960s. During all the masses conducted on Sunday, August 25, 1963, for instance, Houston Catholics heard an explanation of the church's official position on "the race question." Pastors were instructed to read a three-page pastoral letter to their parishioners from the bishops in the United States that eloquently declared that "[d]iscrimination based on the accidental fact of race or color, and as such injurious to human rights, . . . cannot be reconciled with the truth that God has created all men with equal rights and equal dignity." The following year, the Galveston-Houston Diocese instituted "Social Justice Sunday," an annual "day of prayer focused on human rights and human dignity." In the ensuing years, Bishop John Morkovsky established committees and sponsored forums to address racial unrest and social inequality in Houston. Although these developments arose in response to the black freedom struggle, the church also recognized "the disabilities visited upon other racial and national groups."[24] The policy set forth in the early 1960s in response to the black civil rights struggle thus had a direct bearing on the diocese's response to the Chicano movement.

The declarations of the U.S. bishops and the activities of Bishop Morkovsky in Houston outlined the stance of the institutional church on social change. Although church leaders eloquently denounced social oppression, they left it to those outside the institution to actually initiate changes; the role of the church was that of moral suasion in support of progressive change. "We should do our part," the U.S. bishops stated, "to see that voting, jobs, housing, education and public facilities are freely available to every American." In the same spirit, Bishop Morkovsky declared that minority grievances in Houston were moral issues and "definitely concerned" the church. But official church policy made it very clear that "civic action" in defense of human rights was primarily the concern of the laity and, particularly, of course, the prime duty of civil authorities.[25]

In Houston, the Bishop's Interracial Committee promoted interracial justice by working with Catholic lay organizations in the city. The committee "[did] not feel that it should . . . react toward civic problems or enter into the field of community relations" because it recognized "that there were already existing organizations which were formed to react to interracial injustice in the community." The role of the Interracial Committee was, therefore, "to use every persuasive means available to bring about interracial justice." "Necessary persuasion" then demanded "action on the part of the committee and its lay working group." This approach implied a strictly facilitatory role for the institutional church, such as providing forums, finding ways to air issues, and bringing together parties in conflict. Thus the U.S. bishops suggested that Catholics work for social justice "through various lay organizations . . . as well as with civic groups of every type," and that the places to discuss social issues should be the parish and diocesan societies, political gatherings, and civic and neighborhood associations.[26] This policy of guidance and facilitation recalled the position church personnel took in the past, when they encouraged the formation of parish-based mutual aid societies like the Liga de Protección Mexicana and other self-help organizations. It was within this framework that the Catholic Church in Houston responded to *el movimiento*. In the meantime, individual sisters and priests seized opportunities to spearhead social causes themselves, beginning with the key events of 1966.

INDIVIDUAL RESPONSES OF CLERGY AND NUNS

The Chicano movement in Texas was sparked by *La Marcha*, a dramatic protest march staged by striking farmworkers from the Rio Grande Valley of South Texas to the state capitol in Austin during the summer of 1966. The march originally aimed to publicize the strikers' demands by staging a pilgrimage from Rio Grande City to nearby San Juan Shrine Church, a place of special religious significance for Mexican American Catholics. However, it quickly assumed a broader purpose with larger ramifications; it became instead the "Minimum Wage March," a 490-mile trek to the capitol steps that marked a pivotal event for Texas Mexicans. Father Antonio Gonzales, the assistant pastor of Houston's Immaculate Heart of Mary Church, co-led the march, along with labor organizer Eugene Nelson, of the National Farm Workers Association, and Rev. James L. Novarro, the Mexican American pastor of Houston's Kashmere Baptist Temple.[27]

As the farmworkers' strike unfolded in Starr County in June 1966, Gonzales and Father Lawrence Peguero of Our Lady of St. John visited the area to assess the conditions surrounding the conflict. Father Gonzales reported that there was a dire shortage of basic necessities among farm laborers and that families were "going hungry."[28] The two priests collected food and clothing among their parishioners in Houston for the strikers, and delivered still more donations as the strike garnered support from Houston labor unions.[29] A Valley Workers Assistance

Committee was soon formed in Houston, and, with Father Gonzales as its chairman, the group held rallies at different parishes and coordinated the flow of support from Houston to the strikers.[30]

On July 4, seventy-five farmworkers began the pilgrimage to San Juan Shrine, accompanied by Father Gonzales and some forty supporters from Houston. Four days later in San Juan, the strikers and other state leaders decided to march to the state capital to demand that the Texas legislature include farmworkers in a new minimum wage law of $1.25 per hour. The purpose of the protest thus shifted from the demands of a fledgling farmworkers' union to the larger issue of economic justice for Mexican Americans. Gonzales agreed to remain with the farmworkers until Labor Day (when they planned to present their demands on the steps of the capitol), and thus he emerged as one of the leaders of the "march for justice."[31]

As the marchers inched their way toward the capital under the scorching Texas sun, tremendous demonstrations of support buoyed their spirits. Hundreds of Chicanos and Chicanas joined the caravan at different points, and thousands attended the rallies in the larger cities along the way. But five days before reaching their destination, Governor John Connally and an entourage of officials suddenly confronted the marchers on the highway. Father Gonzales and co-leader Reverend James Novarro warmly greeted the governor but were soon disappointed. Although he complimented the peaceful nature of the protest, the governor lectured the marchers on the possibility of violence if they continued. Furthermore, he bluntly told them he would not meet with them in Austin or call a special session of the legislature to consider a minimum wage bill. The governor's words stunned Father Gonzales like a slap to the face. "We feel that the lamentation and the sufferings of so many poor people in Texas were directed to the governor and . . . they were not heard," the dejected priest reported. Another marching cleric noted that Connally's demeanor was "a pat on the head, a great white father-type of thing" that angered the marchers. The governor's rebuff backfired and only strengthened the protesters' resolve. The march continued.[32]

Striking Texas farmworkers and supporters march to the state capital in summer 1966. Note woman (middle) carrying a picture of Our Lady of Guadalupe. Courtesy Houston Metropolitan Research Center, Houston Public Library.

Supporters listen to leaders of the Texas farmworkers' Minimum Wage March of 1966. Father Antonio Gonzales (holding crucifix) is flanked by co-leaders Rev. James Novarro to his right and Eugene Nelson on his left. Courtesy Migrant Farm Workers Organizing Movement Collection, University of Texas at Arlington Libraries.

The demonstrators finally reached the state capitol in Austin on September 5, 1966 (Labor Day), where they were greeted by some 10,000 clamoring supporters. Drama and poignancy reigned that afternoon. A former farmworker himself, Father Gonzales visibly moved the crowd when he introduced his parents, migrant workers for forty years. His mother had borne eighteen children and his father recently had been stricken with cancer, the priest revealed, and yet they still depended on back-breaking migrant work for a living, earning wages that were a "disgrace" to Texas and the nation. Gonzales then declared a "Vigil for Justice." He would bless two farmworkers—"two of the poorest of the poor"—and station them in front of the capitol, where they would remain until the state legislature passed a minimum wage law. Amid thunderous cheers that afternoon, César Chávez and other labor, political, and religious leaders demanded social justice for Mexican Americans, loudly echoing the success of the "march in the sun."[33]

Father Gonzales and Reverend Novarro moved quickly after the march to capitalize on their success. Gonzales met with Governor Connally three days after the rally and reported that the governor had agreed to cooperate. The same week the Valley Workers Assistance Committee met at Immaculate Heart of Mary Church in Houston and announced the next stage of the struggle for fair wages. Stating that their work had "just begun," Gonzales and Novarro outlined an ambitious agenda. First of all, they planned to organize thirty-six secondary assistance committees to help impoverished workers in South Texas. In addition, the clerics announced that before 1968 they hoped to organize Mexican and other workers in sixteen states throughout the Southwest and Midwest.[34]

But despite the success and momentum of *La Marcha*, its immediate goals were lost: the farmworkers' strike failed, and in their next session the state legislature failed to pass a minimum wage law. Yet in a more important sense the minimum wage march produced profound results and proved to be a pivotal historical moment. During and after the march Mexican Americans across the state showed an increased political awareness and a heightened ethnic consciousness that gave

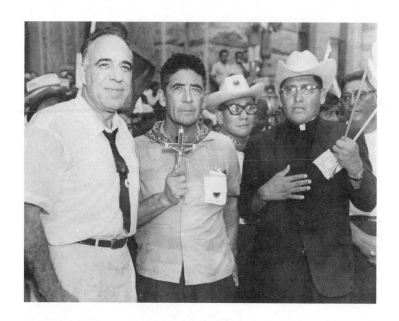

Above: Father Antonio Gonzales (right) with one of "the poorest of the poor" (farmworker holding crucifix) and Texas congressman Henry B. González at the culminating rally of *La Marcha* in 1966. Courtesy Houston Metropolitan Research Center, Houston Public Library.

Left: Chicano lay and clerical activists. Father Patricio Flores (left) meets with labor organizer César Chávez in Houston in 1969. Courtesy *Texas Catholic Herald*.

direction to their long-held resentments and energized the budding Chicano movement in Texas.[35] Strike organizer Eugene Nelson neatly summed up the new mood when he observed, "The Tejanos no longer tip their hats to the *gabachos* (Anglos)."[36] Mexican deference to the white establishment crumbled in the aftermath of the march. Early in *el movimiento*, clerical leadership fueled the fire of Chicano resistance to subordination.

In addition to Gonzales, another priest, Father Patricio Flores, earned a reputation as a leading social activist and advocate of Mexican Americans in Houston. He forcefully reminded his colleagues and the public, for example, not to let the plight of farmworkers be "swept under the rug."[37] Many of his fellow priests disapproved of Flores's support of César Chávez and the United Farm Workers' grape boycott, but the cleric stood firm. He encouraged the Houston grape boycott committee to meet at his parish, and at rallies and meetings he eloquently defended the strikers, whom he felt worked under "inhumane conditions."[38]

As director of the Committee for the Spanish-Speaking in Houston, Flores demanded greater material support from the diocese for programs for Mexican Americans. But many of Houston's Catholic churches refused to allow the use of their parish facilities to implement federal antipoverty programs, and even his own committee, Flores complained, lacked sufficient staffing and cooperation from the diocese.[39] Flores particularly decried the lack of educational opportunities for Mexican Americans and he tried to focus church attention on it. Like other social reformers, Flores realized that low educational achievement locked Mexican Americans out of good jobs and in turn created other serious problems. In addition, educational underachievement precluded the development of a significant body of homegrown priests and sisters to serve their own people.[40] Himself a high school dropout, Flores understandably placed frequent and heavy emphasis on education as a key to social progress. Father Flores also worked for change through his involvement in PADRES, though his activities in this regard were not in Houston proper. PADRES was not established in

Houston until about a year after its founding and after Flores departed to the episcopacy in San Antonio.[41] Flores escalated his advocacy after his elevation to bishop and as PADRES national chairman in the early 1970s. The Houston PADRES, bereft of a powerful leader, never evolved into an activist organization comparable to its counterparts elsewhere in Texas and the Southwest.[42]

While priests like Gonzales and Flores agitated for Chicano rights, Chicana nuns also confronted the Catholic hierarchy and society with demands for social change. Sister Gloria Graciela Gallardo, for example, went to Houston in early 1970 after being active in community organizing in her native San Antonio. Recruited by Father Flores to help in his work in Houston, Gallardo became a coordinator for the Bishop's Committee for the Spanish-Speaking in the Galveston-Houston Diocese and immediately took up various Chicano causes.[43] In autumn of 1970 Houston public school officials subverted a court-ordered desegregation plan by integrating schools that were predominately black and Mexican American, leaving Anglo schools virtually unaffected. Outraged, community leaders formed the Mexican American Education Council (MAEC), headed by prominent lay activist Leonel Castillo. MAEC quickly organized a boycott of Houston's public schools and set up a number of *huelga* (strike) schools to tutor the boycotting students.[44] Sister Gallardo played an integral role in the lengthy campaign that followed. Reinterpreting the traditional role of a nun and her ascribed role as a Mexican American woman, she participated in protest rallies and spoke publicly for MAEC, for a time serving as its acting director.[45]

The activities of Father Gonzales, Las Hermanas, and PADRES were clearly a break from any social action undertaken in the past by church personnel on behalf of Mexicans in Houston. Unlike the individual efforts of nuns and priests in the past, these religious activists mobilized Mexican Americans on a large scale for social change. Acting on their own initiative, they sought social justice by engaging in political protest and by using church facilities and religious forums to help propel the Chicano movement. Individually and in concert, these religious men and women played an important part in moving the Catholic Church toward its role as an ally of *el movimiento*. Thus pressured, the Galveston-Houston Diocese responded with institutional programs that complemented the individual actions of religious personnel.

INSTITUTIONAL ACTIONS

One of the ways the Galveston-Houston Diocese responded to the Chicano movement was by continuing its charitable works among Mexican parishioners. During the 1960s and 1970s, the diocese expanded some of its long-standing social services to barrio residents, particularly health services of various kinds. For example, one of the oldest Catholic charitable institutions in Houston was the San José Clinic. Started in 1924 as the "Mexican Clinic," San José provided free medical services to all the poor but was begun specifically to stem the alarming mortality rates among Mexican children in El Segundo Barrio during the 1920s. In 1970, the diocese significantly expanded the clinic's services, doubling the size of the facility and adding new medical and social services. Appropriately, newly appointed Bishop Patricio Flores presided over the dedication ceremonies.[46] The diocese also sponsored many ad hoc projects at predominately Mexican American parishes, including nutrition programs, tutoring and cultural enrichment activities, and summer recreation programs. Coordinated with public agencies and community groups, these efforts channeled more money to "less fortunate" parishes through Bishop Morkovsky's personal initiatives and a greater emphasis on the Christian obligation of charity.[47]

Some of these efforts were ecumenical and cross-ethnic. In the post–Vatican II years, the Galveston-Houston Diocese joined with various white, brown, and black Protestant groups to attack poverty in Houston barrios. One such initiative was the Latin American Community (LAC) Project, sponsored originally by the United Church of Christ and Houston Metropolitan Ministries but soon designated a project of Volunteers in Service to America (VISTA). The LAC Project aimed to empower the "hard core poor" of Houston's East End, a predominately Mexican American section of the city. Between 1965 and 1972, LAC tried to organize residents "to attack the root causes of deprivation, alienation and discrimination." Its operations included educational and employment services, coordination of emergency relief and recreational services, as well as nonpartisan political activities. LAC's programs involved local church personnel and facilities, including some of the Catholic parishes in the targeted ship channel area, Guadalupe, Immaculate Heart, Blessed Sacrament, and St. Alphonsus.[48] These parishes and others provided volunteer workers, trustees, and material and moral support for LAC projects.[49]

By far the most ambitious ecumenical and interethnic venture was the building of Oxford Place, a $2.7 million interfaith housing project cosponsored with the Episcopal Church. The apartment complex in Houston's north side offered government-subsidized rent and a number of social services for its residents (the majority of whom were Mexican Americans and blacks), including English lessons, basic education, and child care. The diocese also helped to sponsor the Centro de la Raza community center, which had aims and activities similar to the LAC Project.[50]

Projects like Oxford Place and some of the social services provided by the diocese were in keeping with established practices yet different in an important respect. Church-sponsored social services had a long history, but the idea of developing self-help in the barrios was more recent. Hence, a project director insisted that a literacy program for Mexican Americans was "not looked upon as a handout, but rather as one that will train them to develop leadership within their own community."[51] Similarly, the LAC Project claimed it was vastly different from "traditional welfare agencies" in that it aimed to "help people break their dependency on 'charity,' paternalism and on the welfare system."[52] The church's support for self-help projects meshed with its policy of indirectly nurturing social change rather than leading frontal assaults on social problems. As evidenced by the religious and ethnic diversity of the Oxford Place staff, led by Baptist Reverend Lupe Maciel, it also reflected a shift from competition to more cooperation with local Protestants and other ethnic communities.

The Texas farmworkers' strike of 1966 illustrated the church's policy of indirectly supporting social change. When Father Antonio Gonzales became a co-leader of the Minimum Wage March in July 1966, the Galveston-Houston Diocese explicitly gave him its blessing. "I am happy to have you take leave of absence from Immaculate Heart of Mary until Labor Day," wrote Bishop Morkovsky to Gonzales, "to represent myself and this diocese in the efforts for just wages for the working man in the Valley Marchers' project." The prelate even authorized the priest to use the parish car and credit card in these activities. Gonzales's religious order, the Oblates, also approved his participation, thanking Bishop Morkovsky for his support of "the cause of the underdog."[53]

Soon after the beginning of the strikers' march, the Galveston-Houston Diocese and four other Texas dioceses publicly supported the farmworkers' right to unionize. Bishop Morkovsky gave his "blessing to the efforts of those who are directly concerned with the problems of justice and the dignity of man."[54] Less publicly, Anglo diocesan officials carried on behind-the-scenes activities to support the Chicano movement. For example, the diocese gave some direct financial and material support to the farmworkers' cause. Bishop Morkovsky donated money to help with Eugene Nelson's living expenses while he was in Houston in early 1966 organizing a grape boycott to support striking California farmworkers, and Father John McCarthy and other Houston priests guaranteed Nelson a small monthly income during his organizing efforts among the Rio Grande farmworkers. Father McCarthy also headed the diocesan Community Relations Council, which brought together the handful of religious and labor leaders in Houston, San Antonio, and Amarillo to form the Valley Workers Assistance Committee used to channel money and supplies to the strikers in South Texas. McCarthy gave important support to the farmworkers' cause even though he purposely kept a low profile because, as he explained, "I was always very sensitive about being an Anglo cleric who did not even speak Spanish."[55]

These actions by Catholic officials in Houston revealed their stance on social issues. Bishop Morkovsky was careful to emphasize the intermediary role of the church. The first step toward settling the Rio Grande Valley strike was "the voicing of problems by the people involved," Morkovsky explained, and "an appraisal of the problems by mutual trust and communication."[56] On the one hand, such wording reflected the hierarchy's belief that both labor and management had the right to organize to protect their interests, a position that had encyclical precedent. On the other hand, this position also expressed the diocesan leadership's desire to facilitate, rather than directly lead, efforts for social change. The diocese consistently reflected this position in the ensuing years. As the farmworkers' strike wore on in the Rio Grande Valley, the Community Relations Council under Father Emile Farge continued to send aid to the strikers from Houston parishes.[57] On another front, Bishop Morkovsky joined other Houston clerics who voiced support of the California farmworkers' grape strike. Again, Houston's highest Catholic cleric reiterated that church teachings and papal encyclicals emphasized the right of workers to organize collectively.[58] The limits of this policy became quite clear, however, when Father Gonzales overstepped the boundary set by the hierarchy for political activism among its clergy.

The Limits of Church Support

Gonzales continued to be active in political circles in Houston after the Minimum Wage March. In an address to a PASO convention in August 1967, however, he incurred the wrath of the political establishment when he called for more Chicano militancy. "PASSO doesn't throw bricks and cause riots, but some Negroes have caused some riots, and I compliment them because they stirred up the cities," the priest reportedly declared. Gonzales could not condone violence but he understood the reasons why it occurred. Father Gonzales also called for Chicanos and blacks to form a powerful political coalition. He believed his work toward this goal would be supported by his superiors.[59] But he was mistaken.

Democrats and Republicans alike quickly attacked Gonzales in the press. Within a day of the press accounts, Bishop Morkovsky mildly reprimanded the activist priest and explained the church's position. The bishop stated that he did not intend to curb efforts to promote "Christian principles of justice and charity" but that it was "to the disadvantage of justice and charity for the Church or its leaders to engage in political controversy." The priest's role was to teach laypeople Christian principles, the bishop explained, and "it is up to the lay people to put these in practice in the political arena."[60] The prelate also rebuked Gonzales for attacking politicians "by name." The local press had reported that Gonzales had "swapped verbal blows" with the former Texas attorney general who had been in the entourage that tried to dissuade the farmworkers' march on the capital.[61] "Whether they needed this criticism of yours or not," the bishop lectured Gonzales, "it was not fitting nor is it going to help the promotion of Christian principles for the Church or its representatives to take up this kind of attack."[62]

Bishop Morkovsky offered a contemporary example to explain his reasoning. In Morkovsky's opinion, the Reverend Martin Luther King Jr. had "lost some of his effectiveness by publicly expressing himself against the government policies in Viet Nam." "His cause for peace may certainly be right," Morkovsky argued, "but possibly it was a mistake in leadership on his part to publicly adopt one side of a concrete application of principles in which there are sincere Christians on both sides." The bishop reiterated that Gonzales could be most effective by giving his people "spiritual guidance" and "in this way help to develop leadership among them." After this incident, Father Gonzales was ordered to clear his public appearances beforehand with his superior and the bishop's office.[63]

Gonzales's predicament illustrated that the Galveston-Houston Diocese would pursue social justice within clearly defined limits and protocol. The diocese supported the Chicano movement by allowing and even encouraging some activism among its clergy, such as Father Gonzales's involvement in the Minimum Wage March. It also took a public stand on certain principles, such as the right of workers to organize and strike, and it even gave some financial and material support to the striking farmworkers. But Father Gonzales's remarks at the PASO convention went beyond what the church leadership in Houston saw as its proper role in social issues, and, consequently, the priest's activities were reined in. After his controversial speech, Gonzales was reassigned to a rural outpost in East Texas, "to help him settle down to the regular parochial duties." In February 1968, the priest's superior wrote to Bishop Morkovsky that Gonzales now recognized "his limitations in the social action field and in the jungle world of politics."[64]

The church hierarchy wanted to remain above "the jungle world of politics," to seek out high-minded influential people upon whom to exert moral persuasion in order to effect social change. In 1966, the Catholic Community Relations Council (CCRC) moved into the chancery (the main headquarters building of the diocese) and was integrated into the diocesan structure, thereby gaining "more of a handle on power than before," according to Father Farge, the CCRC director.[65] Father Farge claimed he alone controlled social action activities in the diocese, that neither the bishop nor the diocesan chancellor had tried to "keep this office out of delicate or possible explosive affairs." Still, Farge admitted that "[t]he difficulty with this alliance is that one must act in a socially acceptable way."[66] Bishop Morkovsky sought "to get people influential in the establishment to meet together and to find that they have the same high ideals." This circle of people would then be "broadened step-by-step so that the establishment would be influenced."[67] Obviously, maverick political actions by individuals like Gonzales fitted neither the philosophy nor the strategy of institutional social action in the Galveston-Houston Diocese.

FAILING TO DELIVER?
THE HUELGA SCHOOLS AND OXFORD PLACE

During the Chicano boycott of Houston public schools, the Catholic Church failed its children, at least in the opinion of one community newspaper, *Papel Chicano*. The newspaper was bitterly disappointed by pastors who refused to allow religious facilities to be used as *huelga* schools. In 1971 the paper reported that one parish wanted $400 a month rent, plus cost of utilities, which prompted the editor to charge that the church put "exploitation" ahead of the education of children.[68] Another article assailed a pastor as "a racist gringo priest" who had "no right" ministering to Mexican Americans, and claimed that the majority of the Catholic schools had refused to support the school boycott.[69] Although several parishes and individual priests did help the boycott in different ways, backing for the *huelga* schools was uneven, and some Chicanas and Chicanos obviously resented the lukewarm support.[70]

Papel Chicano also considered the diocese's involvement in Oxford Place harmful to Chicano interests in Houston. About a year and a half after the opening of the housing project, the newspaper denounced it as "Another Well-Meaning Instant Slum." *Papel Chicano* argued that Oxford Place was an example of misguided thinking by churches "who were very rapidly destroying the very people [they] sought to help." The newspaper charged that the project was plagued by overwhelming problems: poor race relations between Chicanos and blacks in the complex and in the surrounding white neighborhood, high unemployment and student dropout rates, and lack of public transportation to outside areas with good jobs. *Papel Chicano* further argued that the church-related managing agency (and by association the Galveston-Houston Diocese) was to blame for not providing the necessary support to ensure success for Oxford Place residents.[71]

The project administration had failed to provide tutoring for students to succeed in the white schools of the area, the newspaper charged, and there had been no leadership training, no education in race relations, and no programs to organize the residents to protect themselves from the racism of the surrounding community. "To have done this kind of work would have caused the people in Oxford Place to stand up for themselves in the schools and community," the editorial asserted, "and neither of these two religious sects [Catholic and Episcopalian] want any whites to actually know these minorities are living in 'their' communities." Ultimately, the writer argued, the problem at Oxford Place was "the unwillingness of the churches to really break the poverty cycle."[72]

At least some Chicanos considered the diocese's indirect approach to social change a failure. Some of the more disaffected voices in the community charged that it was not only ineffective but also disingenuous—not only did it not work, but it was not really *supposed* to work, they implied. However, that conclusion reflected more the time's political hyperbole and personal estrangement some felt toward the church than it did an accurate understanding of the diocese's policies and actions toward Chicano social issues. Clearly, racial conflict between Chicanos and blacks had marred the early history of Oxford Place.[73] That is not to say, though, that the Catholic Church in Houston had conspired to thwart Chicano aspirations for equality. The church had indeed been supporting *el movimiento*, albeit through more conservative means than appealed, understandably, to more militant Chicanas and Chicanos.

LEGITIMATION OR CONTROL? THE *ENCUENTROS*

The activism of the late 1960s and early 1970s culminated in an institutional response by the hierarchy of the U.S. Catholic Church called an *encuentro*, a meeting to address problems. Father Edgard Beltrán, an activist priest from Latin America, suggested the idea in the fall of 1971 while visiting the Archdiocese of New York. The idea soon gained support in the U.S. hierarchy and thus the first Encuentro Hispano de Pastoral (Pastoral Congress for the Spanish-Speaking) became a reality in June 1972. For the first time, the Catholic Church in the United States provided a national forum for leaders of Spanish-speaking communities throughout the nation to air their grievances. Two hundred and fifty delegates met in Washington, D.C., to examine the place of the Spanish-speaking in the church. "It was a meeting," said Bishop Patricio Flores, "called by the [C]hurch not to praise, but to make a self-evaluation and correct what is wrong." What was "wrong," essentially, was that Mexican-origin and other Spanish-speaking peoples—25 percent of the U.S. Catholic population—had virtually no voice in the institutional church and were not adequately served by it, pastorally or socially. Adequate representation was the central theme of the national *encuentro*: "[I]f we are 25 per cent of the church, we should participate in 25 per cent of . . . the committees of the national church," Bishop Flores demanded.[74] The three-day meeting produced seventy-eight conclusions and demands calling for "greater participation of the Spanish-speaking in leadership and decision-making roles at all levels within the American church."[75]

The crescendo of Chicano demands struck a responsive chord within the U.S. Catholic Church. On the national level, for instance, the church responded by naming more Mexican American bishops.[76] Locally, Houston's Bishop Morkovsky opened the door to greater Mexican American participation and voice in the church. In the months after the national *encuentro*, similar regional and diocesan meetings took place, and the findings of these smaller forums and the motions of the national meeting were then presented to the U.S. bishops in November 1972 to serve as a basis for a comprehensive pastoral plan for Spanish-speaking Catholics.[77] Houston hosted the Southwest regional *encuentro* in October 1972. Prior to the meeting, in July, Bishop Morkovsky named Father John McGrath, the Oblate pastor of St. Patrick Parish, as interim coordinator of the ministry for the Spanish-speaking. In appointing an Anglo to this position, Bishop Morkovsky was not slighting Chicanos or their social activism. Morkovsky made clear to Father McGrath that his was a temporary position, one meant to start discussions about developing a "pastoral" plan; "the social part" of the ministry remained in the hands of such people as the well-known activist sister Gloria Gallardo and Father John McCarthy, who earlier had facilitated much of the diocese's support for the striking farmworkers. In addition, Bishop Morkovsky ordained more Mexican American laymen as permanent deacons in Houston's predominately Mexican parishes. In July 1972 the local Catholic newspaper featured three such appointees, Manuel Betancourt, Benigno Pardo, and Valeriano Leija, proudly posing in surplice and cassock. Coming in the wake of the national *encuentro*, Bishop Morkovsky's actions signaled his recognition that Chicanas and Chicanos comprised at least 25 percent of the diocese and, therefore, their needs were one of the hierarchy's "special areas of concern."[78]

As the year 1972 drew to a close, Mexican Catholics in Houston and throughout the nation entered a changed relationship with the institutional church, especially as it affected their struggle for social equality. The Galveston-Houston Diocese, like the national church leadership, had begun to respond systematically to pressures from Chicanas and Chicanos. It had put in place the *encuentro*, an institutional structure that could serve as a springboard for further changes. It now seemed possible to build a critical mass of homegrown clergy and sisters who could leverage their power in the struggle for social justice. Those who interpreted these developments optimistically saw in the *encuentros* legitimation of Chicano protest and concessions from the Catholic Church in the United States; some even called the *encuentro* process the "Magna Charta of Hispanic Catholics."[79]

But others were less optimistic. Had the church co-opted the Chicano movement, channeling protest into a controlled environment of its own creation? At the Houston regional *encuentro*, poet Lalo Delgado extemporaneously harangued attendees for seventy minutes about the long-standing neglect of Mexicans by the Catholic Church in the United States and the festering discord many Chicanas and Chicanos felt toward the institution. At the same meeting, national lay leader Pablo Sedillo hinted at co-optation, reminding listeners that similar meetings had taken place before, with nearly identical conclusions, yet nothing had changed. Sedillo voiced what many Mexican Catholics had experienced historically: "To date there has been a com-

The Diocese of Galveston-
Houston responded to Mexi-
can American pastoral needs
in part by ordaining more per-
manent lay deacons. Here (left
to right) Manuel Betancourt,
Benigno Pardo, and Valeriano
Leija pose outside St. Mary's
Seminary in 1972. Courtesy
Texas Catholic Herald.

mitment of words, lip service, but no real action."[80] Ultimately Sedillo
offered a cautiously optimistic assessment of the *encuentros* and the
juncture Mexican Catholics and the institutional church had reached.
Although he did not see the *encuentros* as a panacea, Sedillo perceived a
significantly altered relationship between Mexican Americans and the
institution in 1972. "The Mexican Americans are not asking for pity, for
handouts, for a box of groceries. We're beyond that traditional help,"
Sedillo explained. The Catholic Church in the United States was "beginning to respond" to the needs of Mexican Catholics, Sedillo stated,
adding that he hoped the rhetoric would beget meaningful action.[81]
The lay leader viewed the reactions of the church hierarchy in the
1960s and early 1970s in historical perspective and correctly recognized
them for what they were, a response to activism by Chicanas and
Chicanos.

In 1972 Mexican and Mexican American Catholics in Houston faced the future with mixed feelings. Some looked forward to brighter times; for others, the clouds of the past darkened the vista. But few would deny that their particular way of being Catholic and their relationship with the Catholic Church had been deeply entwined as they journeyed toward greater self-determination.

EPILOGUE

National and international developments in the last three decades of the twentieth century brought significant changes to Houston and the nation. In particular, three overlapping developments underscore striking changes in the social and religious landscape of the Bayou City that have affected ethno-Catholicism since the 1970s: the dramatic increase in Latin American immigration, the waning of liberal politics, and the rise of Latino evangelical Protestantism.

A new wave of Latin American immigration to the United States began in the 1970s. Driven by economic crises in Mexico, civil wars and political violence in Central and South America, and changes in U.S. immigration laws that stimulated Latin American migration, this rising tide of migrants sharply increased and diversified the nation's Hispanic population in the last three decades of the twentieth century.[1] By the year 2000, Latinos in the United States numbered some 35.3 million, accounting for 12.5 percent of the country's 281.4 million residents. The 20.6 million Mexican-origin people in the United States comprised the largest group of Hispanics, or 58.5 percent of the total Latino population. At 3.4 million, Puerto Ricans, who made up 9.6 percent of the Latino population, remained the second largest group, while Central Americans (1.7 million) and South Americans (1.4 million) eclipsed the number of Cuban Americans (1.2 million).[2]

In Houston, the 1970s saw an increase of 88 percent in the city's Hispanic residents (from 149,727 to 281,331), making them 17.6 percent of the city's population by 1980. In the early 1980s, droves of Central Americans began fleeing their war-torn homelands. Of this exodus from Guatemala, Honduras, and especially El Salvador, only Los Angeles received more immigrants than Houston. By 1990, Houston's Hispanics numbered 450,483 (or 27.6 percent) of the city's population of 1.6. million. Latino growth and diversity persisted, and by 2002 Houston was a city of about 2 million people whose roughly 772,000 Hispanic residents represented 39 percent of the city's population, while whites made up 29 percent and blacks 26 percent, reflecting a pattern evident in many urban areas throughout the country.[3]

As the number of Central and South Americans has grown in Houston, their distinct dialects, foods, and folkways have also become more evident alongside those of the Mexican community. Today, vendors of Salvadoran *pupusas* (a popular tacolike food) are as easily found as Mexican taco stands, and a variety of music pulsates in many city streets and homes—from Mexican *música norteña* to Caribbean salsa beats to Colombian *cumbias* and Latin rock—mirroring a changing Latino community. In today's shifting ethnic landscape, Houston's roughly 568,000 Mexicans and Mexican Americans remain a large numerical majority of the city's Hispanic population (73 percent). But they share the city with a significant number of other Latinos (some 205,000) who trace their roots to Central and South America or the Caribbean.[4] In light of this increased Hispanic diversity, what has happened to ethno-Catholicism in Houston and other places where "Spanish-speaking" historically has meant "Mexican"?

For one thing, it is abundantly clear that Mexican American ethno-Catholicism continues to flourish in Houston and the Southwest. In the decades since the 1970s, newspapers, popular literature, and scholarly studies consistently have reported a vibrant lived religion among Mexican American ethno-Catholics.[5] For example, Our Lady of Guadalupe still commands a fervent following. As parishioner Petra Guillén noted, the annual December 12 Guadalupe Feast Day celebrations at Our Lady of Guadalupe Church in Houston's Second Ward have grown "more and more" in recent years; in the year 2003 some 15,000 to 20,000 devotees jostled for seating space at the masses held in honor of *la Morenita*. "We keep the church open from the eleventh at night until the twelfth at midnight," Mrs. Guillén recounted. "It's open with mariachis all night through, *matachines* (Indian dancers) all night through . . . it's open regardless—whether it's raining or freezing, they are there."[6] Similarly, talk of a divine sign from *la Guadalupana* can electrify a community, sending legions of faithful to the site of a reported apparition, as has twice been the case in recent years in the Bayou City.[7] And, as they did in the past, Mexican and Mexican American Catholics in Houston and other cities in Texas and the Southwest continue to make pilgrimages, raise funds to maintain their parishes, and in other ways distinguish and celebrate their Mexican ethnoreligious identity and way of life.[8]

In addition, the 2000 census showed a significant Mexican presence outside of the Southwest, where ethno-Catholicism has begun to reveal its importance in new settings such as New York City and Washington, D.C., as well as in the Carolinas, Georgia, and other places in the Deep South. In Chicago's Mexican American community, which, like Houston's, dates back to the early twentieth century, religious traditions in barrio homes and streets echo those of Houston.[9] Similarly, in New York City—where the 2000 census reported a Mexican population of more than 186,000 (plus some 100,000 undocumented immigrants)—"[Mexican] music, dance and street festivals are often intertwined with religion, politics and the struggle for legal rights."[10] Thus significant growth and continuity have characterized the lived religion of Mexican and Mexican American ethno-Catholics since the 1970s. Especially as it structures family and community life and expresses ethnic identity, ethno-Catholicism continues to play an important role in helping immigrants and native-born alike meet the daily challenges of modern urban life.

In the process, of course, some aspects of ethno-Catholicism show signs of change and adaptation. According to Luís León, for example, Mexican American *curanderismo* (faith healing) in Los Angeles "has shifted from the familiar intimate space of home to the public space of commodity consumption." In today's urban capitalist culture, *curanderismo*, "once restricted to private homes and kinship networks," may be evolving into a tradition that is as concerned with folk healing as it is with profit-seeking, as entrepreneurs establish *botánicas* (stores) in which contracted *curanderas* (faith healers) perform their traditional healing services and "both religious and secular items are bought from a wholesale distributor, marked up, sectioned off into discrete display areas, tagged with prices, and sold for profit."[11] Clearly, as folklorist Ilana Harlow states, "You have to look at how people have to adapt their culture to survive in the new environment, but also how they adapt the new environment to support their culture."[12] Ethno-Catholicism historically has provided ways for Mexicans to adjust to U.S. society, and it continues to do so. Mexican and Mexican American Catholics still celebrate *quinceañeras*, kneel before *altarcitos*, and otherwise conserve age-old traditions that define them as a people and help them make sense of life, even as some aspects of those traditions undergo change. However altered and evolving, ethno-Catholicism still functions in much the same way it has historically, and it continues to be a foundational element of the Mexican American urban experience.

Ironically, however, despite the vitality of their ethno-Catholicism and even as their numbers have grown dramatically in the U.S. Catholic Church and society, in one sense, the influence of Mexican Americans within the structures of the church has lessened. In the post–civil rights era, Mexican American pastoral and social concerns have been diluted by the institutional church's approach that treats them as "Hispanic"—and increasingly as "multicultural"—issues rather than as Mexican American concerns per se. In the heyday of civil rights, Chicanas and Chicanos awakened the Catholic Church to their needs and gained concessions from it, including the naming of more Mexican American bishops, the creation of the Mexican American Cultural Center in San Antonio, and the elevation of the Division of the Spanish-speaking to Secretariat of Hispanic Affairs.[13]

However, the subsequent *encuentros* took place against the background of increasing U.S. Latino diversity and interethnic tensions as Mexican Americans and other Latinos competed for the church's resources.[14] By the time of the Second National Encuentro, held August 18–22, 1977, in Washington, D.C., the perception existed "that Mexican Americans, because of their numbers, were dominating the other Latino groups."[15] Consequently, church historian Moisés Sandoval has argued, the church hierarchy "appropriated the process of the *encuentro*" so that "it could no longer be considered part of the *movimiento* [the Chicano movement], coming from and controlled by the people."[16] Thus, despite eloquent rhetoric about resolving "to correct injustices both inside and outside the Church," the concrete actions that resulted from the Second Encuentro were clearly pastoral, not social.[17]

The church hierarchy's control of the *encuentro* process and the primacy of pastoral over social justice concerns became even clearer when Washington, D.C., hosted the Third National Encuentro during August 15–18, 1985.[18] By that time Latinos other than Mexican Americans had increasingly captured the attention of the church leadership. Moreover, the country's political climate had shifted dramatically by the 1980s—the backlash against minority demands that had started in the 1970s stood clearly ascendant and embodied in the neoconservative policies of the so-called Reagan Revolution. In an atmosphere in which minority demands for equality were increasingly labeled "reverse discrimination," the resolutions of the Third Encuentro focused not on social justice but at finally developing a national pastoral plan for Hispanics. But even that important achievement reflected a lack of urgency as the church presented the plan as "a beautiful new car without wheels," a mandate without funds to implement it.[19]

Encuentro 2000 took place July 6–9 in Los Angeles. With the title "Many Faces in God's House" and multiculturalism as its hallmark, this latest *encuentro* focused on "the richness of the Church's racial, ethnic and cultural diversity." Indeed, ethnic diversity reigned—mariachi music and Native American drumbeats opened the celebration as 5,000 Catholics representing 150 dioceses and 153 ethnic backgrounds streamed into the Los Angeles Convention Center. In the ensuing days the press highlighted the proceedings' sensory and ethnic richness—the sounds of conch shells announcing prayer services, the wail of Celtic bagpipes, the tempo of African American hymns, the aroma of Asian incense, and the striking colors of Korean, Polish,. Filipino, Middle Eastern, and other dance spectacles.[20] Amid this rainbow of humanity, the U.S. bishops urged the participants to confront the challenges of Catholic diversity, and pastoral matters clearly occupied center stage, although some individuals made eloquent statements about social justice.[21]

The decline of PADRES as a Chicano activist organization also reflected the more conservative tenor of the post–civil rights era and paralleled the multiculturalist and pastoral trajectory of the post-1972 *encuentros*. Since its founding in 1969, PADRES had aggressively promoted Mexican American equality in both the church and the larger society. But after some gains in the 1970s, the organization became increasingly polarized into two camps, the pastoralists who focused on reforming the structures of the church and the liberationists who wanted to concentrate on changing oppressive societal structures. Despite liberationists' insistence that "the major thrust of PADRES should not be in trying to get more Hispanos appointed bishops but in political action on behalf of the poor," they found themselves increasingly isolated in the conservative climate of the 1980s as the organization adopted a more cooperative and conciliatory stance toward the church leadership.[22] Not surprisingly, the decline of liberal politics and the conservative papacy of John Paul II coincided with the death of PADRES. In 1990 the organization ceased to exist when it merged with two other groups made up mostly of foreign-born Spanish and Latin American clerics to form Asociación Nacional de Sacerdotes Hispanos (National Association of Hispanic Priests, or ANSH), an organization that, at least in some eyes, "seems intent on avoiding" social and political issues in favor of concerns that "directly affect the priests themselves."[23] The disappearance of PADRES into ANSH undoubtedly further submerged Mexican American social concerns in the U.S. Catholic Church.

Unlike PADRES, the activist sisters' organization, Las Hermanas, weathered repressive forces and changing times and has been able to continue its mission of championing Latina equality both within the church and in society at large.[24] Although the Chicano movement fueled both organizations and shaped their liberationist postures and goals, Las Hermanas made changes in its identity and mission that proved crucial to its survival. While PADRES remained exclusively an organization of Chicano priests, Las Hermanas started as a Chicana nuns' group but soon expanded its membership to include not only other Spanish-speaking sisters but also Catholic laywomen. Moreover, Las Hermanas evolved from a group that sought primarily their own empowerment as Chicana nuns within the Catholic Church to one that struggles for a broader goal, "the promotion of the Hispanic woman." These changes allowed the organization to find support outside the male-dominated institutional church and to become a larger and more diverse group that promoted Latina issues, not only within the Catholic Church, but also in a number of social and political arenas.[25] Las Hermanas has thus continued as a voice for Mexican Americans in the face of the changes of the last thirty years.

And potentially the most far-reaching of those changes has been the prolific increase of evangelical Protestantism among U.S. Latinos. What the *New York Times* called "a huge cultural transformation that is changing the face of religion in the United States" understandably has led to much hand-wringing among Catholic clergy and laity alike. It is "a sad thing," conceded Bishop Joseph A. Fiorenza of the Galveston-Houston Diocese, "a serious problem" that is difficult to combat given the lack of homegrown Hispanic priests. The marked increase of Latino evangelical Protestants is also quite evident to parishioners who resent their more frequent and aggressive proselytizing in Houston's Mexican American neighborhoods.[26] Estimates vary, but probably at least one million Hispanics had left the Catholic Church by the beginning of the twenty-first century. Whereas historically "Mexican American" and "Spanish-speaking" invariably meant "Catholic," today perhaps only 65 percent to 75 percent of U.S. Latinos are Catholics.[27] Only time will tell if the "great leakage" will continue.

However, there are at least two factors countering this trend, the continuing vitality of Mexican American ethno-Catholicism and the fact that the relationship between the church and Mexican Americans has been irrevocably altered. Clearly, the lived religion of Mexican American Catholics is flourishing and spreading throughout the United States, and, given Mexico's proximity and historical ties to the United States, this will continue. Equally important, Mexican American and Latino Catholics have created their own church within the larger U.S. Church. This is no small matter, as it has reversed the church's historical stance of strongly promoting assimilation at the expense of ethnic consciousness and traditions.[28] Consequently, today's Catholic leadership is more acutely aware than ever of the Mexican American presence, and church representatives point to initiatives such as a new Hispanic ministry plan and the appointment in the Galveston-Houston Diocese of Bishop James Anthony Tamayo, a native Tejano, as evidence of their increased responsiveness to Mexican American pastoral needs.[29]

But what of social justice? How have the political shifts to the right and the growth of evangelical Protestantism—a faith expression not known for its engagement in social issues—affected the quest for Latino social equality? At first glance, the developments of the last thirty years do not augur well for progress on the social and political front, particularly the fight to tame the beasts of poverty and racism that still tear at Latino communities. The prospects appear dim in a time when "American Catholics in general do not put much support behind efforts specifically designed to help members of minority groups" and, arguably, the institutional Catholic Church promotes a type of "multiculturalism without a transformative political agenda [that] can be just another form of accommodation to the larger social order."[30] Who will provide the leadership for an effective social ministry in the twenty-first century?

The struggle for Latino social equality will continue much as it has in the past, that is, largely through lay initiatives that enlist the support of the churches. Not all the organizations rooted in the activism of the 1960s and 1970s have disappeared, nor has their capacity to inspire new recruits totally faded. The fire of liberation theology still fuels the efforts of many Latino Catholic activists working in behalf of the most vulnerable of barrio residents; the San Antonio–based Communities Organized for Public Service (COPS) and the West Coast–based Pacific Institute for Community Organizing (PICO) are but two examples.[31] In Houston, Mexican American Catholics continue to seek social justice through The Metropolitan Organization (TMO). Since the late 1970s, several predominately Mexican parishes have successfully used "the not-so-gentle prodding" of this interdenominational grassroots organization to gain better city services, establish antidrug campaigns, and otherwise improve their low-income neighborhoods; more recently they have turned their attention to helping poor immigrants.[32] At St. Philip of Jesus Parish on Houston's East End, TMO leader Lillian Quiñones recently launched a crime-fighting effort in the surrounding El Dorado barrio, and at Our Lady of Guadalupe Parish, a twenty-five-year tradition of feisty community activism continues.[33]

In addition to these continuing efforts, there will be—indeed, there already are—new configurations in religious-based social activism among Mexican Americans and Latinos. One of the fruits of the rise of Latino evangelical Protestantism is, surprisingly, evidence of a budding social consciousness.[34] According to recent studies, Latino Pentecostals in particular have been developing a ministry to attack social ills that plague urban Mexican Americans and Puerto Ricans since at least the 1970s. The rise of the Religious Right, sociologists Ana María Díaz-Stevens and Anthony Stevens-Arroyo argue, "moved Latino Pentecostal and Evangelical congregations toward direct political engagement" as they sought to stem drug abuse and other problems that threatened their communities. Evidence of a Pentecostal social ministry is seen in the work of individuals and organizations from Los Angeles to Philadelphia and New York.[35] Pentecostal women have been especially active in these efforts, even to the point of transgressing the strict gender restrictions often imposed on them by their faith traditions.[36] Finally, in recent years Latino Pentecostalism has begun to elaborate the theological underpinnings for social action, as well as the organizational vehicles, such as the Alianza de Ministerios Evangélicos Nacionales

(National Alliance of Evangelical Ministries, or AMEN), to implement it—recalling the elaboration of liberation theology and the founding of PADRES and Las Hermanas in an earlier era.[37]

Still, Latinos sorely lack decision-making power in today's institutional Catholic Church, and they lack the political clout to significantly improve their status in society. This is ironic, given the profound changes they have brought to the American religious scene and the fact that they are the nation's largest minority. Anthropologist Peggy Levitt sums it up well: "Latinos enjoy greater power and autonomy with respect to their own church-based activities, but this has not translated into greater power within the institution as a whole or into a more prominent role in the political arena."[38]

The developments of the last thirty years, then, have had mixed effects on ethno-Catholicism in Houston and throughout the United States. On the one hand, Mexican Americans have left the church in large numbers and their influence as a separate ethnic group within the institution seems to have waned. Coupled with the unfolding sexual abuse scandals, these developments may not bode well for continued church funding for Mexican American ministries. On the other hand, the lived religion of the people remains vibrant, and although political conservatism threatens to undo hard-fought victories of the civil rights era, Mexican American aspirations and efforts for greater self-determination have hardly been stamped out. To understand the effects the developments of the last three decades have had on Mexican American ethno-Catholicism requires more in-depth study; these closing pages merely sketch a preliminary understanding. Conceivably, the last thirty years were a prelude to a great social transformation that will be played out in the twenty-first century. When the history of the "browning of America" is written, that story will have been significantly shaped by the concurrent rise of conservative politics and Latino Evangelicalism, as well as an enduring Mexican American ethno-Catholicism.

APPENDIX

TABLE A.1. Houston's White, Black, and
Mexican-Origin Populations, 1910–1970

Year	Total City Population	White (% of Total)	Black (% of Total)	Mexican-Origin (% of Total)
1910	78,800	52,832 (67.0%)	23,929 (30.4%)	2,000 (2.5%)
1920	138,276	98,268 (71.0%)	33,960 (24.6%)	6,000 (4.3%)
1930	292,352	214,687 (73.4%)	63,337 (21.7%)	15,000 (5.1%)
1940	384,514	277,959 (72.3%)	86,302 (22.4%)	20,000 (5.2%)
1950	596,163	430,503 (72.2%)	124,766 (20.9%)	40,000 (6.7%)
1960	938,219	645,547 (68.8%)	215,037 (22.9%)	75,000 (7.9%)
1970	1,232,802	754,889 (61.2%)	316,551 (25.7%)	150,000 (12.2%)

SOURCES: U.S. Bureau of the Census, *Census of the United States* (reports for 1910–70): for 1910: vol. 3, p. 852; 1920: vol. 3, p. 108; 1930: vol. 3, pt. 2, pp. 1015, 1023, and vol. 6, supplement, p. 97; 1940: vol. 2, pt. 6, pp. 1044, 1045, 1047; 1950: vol. 2, pt. 43, pp. 102, 350; 1960: Final Report PHC(1)-63, p. 15; and 1970: vol. 1, pt. 45, sec. 1, pp. 97, 118, 158. Estimates for the Mexican-origin population for each decennial year are from De León, *Ethnicity in the Sunbelt*, 7, 23, 55, 98, 147, and include other Hispanics. However, Houston's Spanish-speaking population historically has been overwhelmingly of Mexican origin (88 percent as late as 1980); see Shelton et al., *Houston*, 96. Total percentages may slightly exceed 100 percent because of rounding of numbers.

TABLE A.2. Mexican American Parish Societies,
1910s–1970s[a]

Society	Membership	Focus[b]	Active[c]
Adoración Nocturna	men	devotion to Jesus	OLG: 1928–30s, 1960s OLS: 1950s–60s OLJ: 1960s
Apostolado	adults	devotion to Jesus	OLG: 1919 OLS: 1950s
Banda Guadalupana	men	music for parish events	OLG: 1930s
Blessed Sacrament	adults	devotion to Jesus	OLG: 1919
Catholic Young Adults	young adults	socializing; religious study	OLG: 1960s Resurrection: 1970s
Catholic Youth Organization	teenagers	socializing; community service	St. Patrick: 1940s, 1960s OLS: 1950s IHM: 1960s OLG: 1960s St. Joseph: 1960s Resurrection: 1970s
Cursillo	men, later integrated	parish and civic activism	St. Stephen: 1960s–70s OLS: 1960s OLJ: 1960s St. Patrick: 1960s St. Alphonsus: 1960s
Guadalupanas	married women	devotion to Our Lady of Guadalupe	St. Patrick: 1940s, 1960s OLG: 1960s St. Stephen: 1960s–70s
Hijas de María	single women	devotion to Virgin Mary	OLG: 1917–30s St. Patrick: 1940s, 1960s OLS: 1950s–60s OLJ: 1960s
Hombres Católicos	men	parish service	St. Patrick: 1960s

Society	Membership	Focus[b]	Active[c]
Infant Jesus of Prague	young children	devotion to Jesus	OLG: 1930s St. Patrick: 1950s
Ladies' Council	women	governance	St. Alphonsus: 1960s
Legion of Mary	women	catechism instruction	OLS: 1950s St. Patrick: 1950s
Liga de Protección Mexicana	men women	social issues social issues	OLG: 1916 OLG: 1917
Men's Choir	men	religious music	OLG: 1960s
Men's Society	men	parish service	St. Patrick: 1960s
Mother's Club	mothers	parish service	St. Patrick: 1950s–60s
Movimiento Familiar Cristiano	married couples	religious study for family support	St. Patrick: 1960s
Sagrado Corazón	women	devotion to Jesus	OLG: 1920s–30s OLS: 1960s St. Patrick: 1940s, 1960s St. Stephen: 1960s
Santo Nombre	men	devotion to Jesus	OLS: 1950s–60s St. Stephen: 1960s–70s OLG: 1960s OLJ: 1960s St. Patrick: 1960s–70s
Socias / Sociedad del Altar	women	altar maintenance	OLG: 1960s St. Patrick: 1960s St. Stephen: 1960s–70s
Sociedad San José	boys	saint devotion	OLG: 1930s
Sociedad San Luis	boys	saint devotion	OLG: 1917

Society	Membership	Focus[b]	Active[c]
Sodality of Our Lady	adults	devotion to Virgin Mary	OLG: 1960s
St. Vincent de Paul	adults	charity	IHM: 1950s–70s St. Alphonsus: 1960s
Teresitas–St. Therese the Little Flower	younger girls	saint devotion	OLG: 1930s St. Patrick: 1940s OLS: 1950s–60s
Vasallos de Cristo Rey	men	Cristo Rey celebrations	St. Patrick: 1940s OLG: 1960s
Vela Perpétua	adults	devotion to Jesus	OLG: 1912 OLS: 1950s–60s St. John: 1960s
Youth Club	teenagers	socializing; service	St. Alphonsus: 1960s

Sources: Parish records, Archives of the Oblates of Mary Immaculate, San Antonio; Archives of the Congregation of Divine Providence, San Antonio; Archives of the Diocese of Galveston-Houston, Houston; and author's oral history interviews.

[a]Incomplete records preclude a full recovery of parish societies; this list is representative but not exhaustive. Some of the more popular societies (e.g., Guadalupanas, Hijas de María, Santo Nombre, Sagrado Corazón, etc.) likely had a continuous existence in most parishes.

[b]In addition to other activities, all societies raised money for the parish.

[c]Parish abbreviations: OLG = Our Lady of Guadalupe; OLS = Our Lady of Sorrows; OLJ = Our Lady of St. John; IHM = Immaculate Heart of Mary. Exact dates indicate founding.

TABLE A.3. Mexican American Parishes in Houston, 1910s–1970s

Parish	City Area / Barrio Name	Oblate Missionary Activity Since	Parish Type and Founding Date	Changes
Our Lady of Guadalupe	Second Ward El Segundo	1911	Mexican mission, 1912	Mexican national parish, 1921
Immaculate Heart of Mary	East End La Magnolia	ca. 1919	Mexican national parish, 1926	
St. Stephen	Near West Side	ca. 1930	Mexican national parish, 1932	dissolved, 1967 restored, 1973
Our Lady of Sorrows	Northeast El Crisol	ca. 1934	Mexican national parish, 1936	
St. Patrick	Fifth Ward El Quinto		Mexican national parish, 1941	reverted to territorial, 1968
Our Lady of St. John	Northeast La Bonita	1948	Mexican national parish, 1957	changed to territorial, 1964
St. Alphonsus Liguori	East End La Magnolia	ca. 1948	territorial parish, 1966	
St. Philip of Jesus	East End El Dorado	1958	territorial parish, 1967	
St. Raphael	Southwest	1950s	territorial mission, 1970	1972: 60% / 40% Mexican / Black
Immaculate Conception	East End La Magnolia		white territorial parish, 1911	mostly Mexican, ca. 1970

TABLE A.3. Continued

Parish	City Area / Barrio Name	Oblate Missionary Activity Since	Parish Type and Founding Date	Changes
Blessed Sacrament	East End		white territorial parish, 1908	mostly Mexican, ca. 1970
Holy Name	Near North Side El North Side		white territorial parish, 1919	mostly Mexican, ca. 1970
Resurrection	East End		white territorial parish, 1920	mostly Mexican, ca. 1970

SOURCES: Giles, *Changing Times*; documents, Archives of the Diocese of Galveston-Houston, Houston; and Archives of the Oblates of Mary Immaculate, San Antonio.

NOTES

ABBREVIATIONS

ABCM: American Board of Catholic Missions

ACDP: Archives of the Congregation of Divine Providence, San Antonio, Texas

ADGH: Archives of the Diocese of Galveston-Houston, Houston, Texas

ALUC: Archives of Loyola University of Chicago, Chicago, Illinois

AOMI: Archives of the Oblates of Mary Immaculate, San Antonio, Texas

CAT: Catholic Archives of Texas, Austin, Texas

FC: *Family Circular* (Sisters of Divine Providence newsletter)

HC: *Houston Chronicle*

HMRC: Houston Metropolitan Research Center, Houston, Texas

MI: *Mary Immaculate* (Oblates of Mary Immaculate magazine)

OLG *Boletín*: Our Lady of Guadalupe Parish *Boletín Parroquial*, Juan P. Rodríguez Family Collection, Houston Metropolitan Research Center, Houston, Texas

OLG *Codex*: *Codex Historicus* of Our Lady of Guadalupe Parish (Houston), Archives of the Oblates of Mary Immaculate, San Antonio, Texas

SP *Codex*: *Codex Historicus* of St. Patrick Parish (Houston), Archives of the Oblates of Mary Immaculate, San Antonio, Texas

TCH: *Texas Catholic Herald* (Galveston-Houston diocesan newspaper)

INTRODUCTION

1   David McLemore, "A Spirited Catholicism," *Gazette Telegraph*, May 18, 1996, E1, E3 (reprinted from the *Dallas Morning News*).

2   Frank Trejo, "Faithful Swarm to Mexican Shrine to Ask for Help," *Gazette Telegraph*, May 18, 1996, E1, E3 (reprinted from the *Dallas Morning News*).

3   Rev. Allan Figueroa Deck quoted in McLemore, "Spirited Catholicism," E3.

4   A note about terminology: I use the terms "Mexican" and "Mexican American" interchangeably since both native-born and immigrants make up Mexican

American communities. I also use "Texas Mexican" and "Tejano" and "Tejana" synonymously in reference to Mexican-origin residents of Texas. The euphemism "Spanish-speaking" (for "Mexican") is used in its 1940s–50s context, and "Chicana" and "Chicano" refer to politically militant Americans of Mexican descent during the 1960s and 1970s. Where the generic terms "Hispanic" and "Latino" appear, referring to any Spanish-speaking person of Latin American heritage in the United States, the discussion will place them in their proper post-1970s context. "Anglo," "Anglo American," and "Euro-American" have distinct historical meanings, but for stylistic convenience I use them interchangeably in reference to white Americans. Lastly, I use "Chicano" and "Mexican American" synonymously in discussing historiography.

5   Roberto S. Goizueta, "The Symbolic World of Mexican American Religion," in Matovina and Riebe-Estrella, eds., *Horizons of the Sacred*, 119–38, quote on 121.

6   Cogent discussions about "popular" religion include Davis, "From 'Popular Religion' to Religious Cultures," 321–41; Orsi, *Madonna of 115th Street*, xiii–xxiii; and Hall, ed., *Lived Religion in America*, vii–xiii. See also the excellent essay by theologian Orlando O. Espín, "Popular Catholicism," 308–59; the social science and theological essays in Stevens-Arroyo and Díaz-Stevens, eds., *Enduring Flame*; and Goizueta, *Caminemos con Jesús*, ch. 2.

7   On this point, see Wright, "If It's Official," and Bornstein, *Bianchi of 1399*, 3–7. See also Wright, "Popular and Official Religiosity," 1–175.

8   James C. Scott, *Weapons of the Weak*; Levine, *Black Culture*; Genovese, *Roll, Jordon, Roll*; Raboteau, *Slave Religion*; R. Laurence Moore, *Religious Outsiders*; Reed-Danahay, "Talking about Resistance"; Gibson, *Accommodation Without Assimilation*.

9   Reed-Danahay, "Talking about Resistance"; Gibson, *Accommodation without Assimilation*.

10 Timothy M. Matovina, "Hispanic Faith and Theology," *Theology Today* 54 (January 1998): 510.

11 For example, see Elizondo, *Galilean Journey*.

12 Matovina, *Tejano Religion and Ethnicity*.

13 Of the thirteen parishes in the Galveston-Houston Diocese that were predominately Mexican American by the early 1970s, six had been canonically established as Mexican national parishes between 1921 and 1957; the rest had become de facto Mexican parishes as the city's Mexican-origin populations expanded greatly in the decades after World War II. See Table A.3.

14 Grebler et al., *Mexican American People*, 456–57 (my emphasis).

15   For the revival of American religious history, see May, "Recovery of American Religious History"; Dolan, "New Religious History"; and Tentler, "On the Margins." On the growth of Chicano history, see Saragoza, "Significance of Recent Chicano-Related Historical Writing." On the dearth of studies about Latino religions, see Marty, "Editors' Bookshelf," 104, and Tentler, "On the Margins," 119–20.

16   Dolan and Hinojosa, eds., *Mexican Americans and the Catholic Church*; Matovina, *Tejano Religion and Ethnicity*.

17   Matovina and Poyo, eds., *¡Presente!*; Carroll, *Penitente Brotherhood*; Matovina and Riebe-Estrella, eds., *Horizons of the Sacred*.

18   A pioneering effort that begins to identify the basic contours of the history of Mexican American, Puerto Rican, and Cuban American Catholics is the *Notre Dame History of Hispanic Catholics in the U.S.*, 3 vols.: Dolan and Hinojosa, eds., *Mexican Americans and the Catholic Church*; Dolan and Vidal, eds., *Puerto Rican and Cuban Catholics in the U.S.*; and Dolan and Deck, eds., *Hispanic Catholic Culture in the U.S.* See also the collection of sociological and theological research contained in Stevens-Arroyo, ed., *Program for the Analysis of Religion among Latinos Series*. On the Southwest see Hinojosa, "Mexican American Faith Communities"; Sheridan, *Los Tucsonenses*; and Deutsch, *No Separate Refuge*. On the Midwest see Badillo, "Catholic Church and the Making of Mexican-American Parish Communities"; García and Cal, "*El Círculo de Obreros Católicos 'San José'*"; Crocker, "Gary Mexicans"; and Rogers, "Role of Our Lady of Guadalupe Parish."

19   Vidal, "Citizens Yet Strangers"; Lisandro Pérez, "Cuban Catholics."

20   Vidal, "Citizens Yet Strangers"; Díaz-Stevens, *Oxcart Catholicism*, 47–48.

21   Vidal, "Citizens Yet Strangers"; Díaz-Stevens, *Oxcart Catholicism*.

22   Dolan, *American Catholic Experience*, 204–8, 302–3; see also Shaw, *Catholic Parish as a Way-Station*, and Gleason, "Immigrant Assimilation."

23   Dolan, *American Catholic Experience*, 176–78, 372–76; Vidal, "Citizens Yet Strangers"; Díaz-Stevens, *Oxcart Catholicism*.

24   Lisandro Pérez, "Cuban Catholics." For more on the Cuban perspective, see Tweed, *Our Lady of the Exile*; McNally, *Catholicism in South Florida*; and McNally, *Catholic Parish Life on Florida's West Coast*.

25   Dolan and Deck, eds., *Hispanic Catholic Culture in the U.S.*, 454.

26   See Raboteau, "Black Church" and *Slave Religion*; Baer and Singer, *African-American Religion*; Lincoln and Mamiya, *Black Church*; and Sandoval, *On the Move*, 135–36.

27   In addition to the historiographical essays cited in note 6, see Stout, "Eth-

nicity"; Marty, "Ethnicity"; Butler, "Future of American Religious History"; and Hackett, "Sociology of Religion."

CHAPTER ONE

1 Juárez, "*La Iglesia Católica*," 229–32, 239. For the English version, see Juárez, "*Los Padres Rancheristas*." The bishop defused the crisis with a false promise, proffered through the mayor, to bring back the sisters sometime.

2 De León, *Mexican Americans in Texas*, 7–8, 19–20.

3 Weber, *Mexican Frontier*, 160, 44–45, 70–73.

4 Ibid., 162–77; De León, *Mexican Americans in Texas*, 27–28.

5 Doyon, *Cavalry of Christ*; James T. Moore, *Through Fire and Flood*; Diekemper, "French Clergy," 34.

6 Juárez, "*La Iglesia Católica*"; Dolan, *American Catholic Experience*, 177. See also Tafolla, "Church in Texas."

7 De León, *Tejano Community*, ch. 6; see also Doyon, *Cavalry of Christ*, 133–35, and Tafolla, "Expansion of the Church," 231–32.

8 Espín, "Popular Catholicism." See also Deck, *Second Wave*, 55–56. Quote in Dolan, *American Catholic Experience*, 16–17.

9 Hinojosa, "Mexican American Faith Communities," 19–23; Juárez, "*La Iglesia Católica*." See also De León, *They Called Them Greasers*, 1–7.

10 De León, *Tejano Community*, 153.

11 Espín, "Popular Catholicism," 338; Josef J. Barton, "Land, Labor, and Community," 198–200. On socioreligious traditions and community-building in the Spanish and Mexican eras, see De la Teja, *San Antonio de Béxar*, 146–52, and Matovina, *Tejano Religion and Ethnicity*.

12 Diekemper, "French Clergy," 29–38; Juárez, "*La Iglesia Católica*," 241–43.

13 Dolan, *American Catholic Experience*, 373, referring to Los Angeles, but the same held for Texas; see Juárez, "*La Iglesia Católica*," 241–42.

14 Tafolla, "Expansion of the Church," 225–28; Juárez, "*La Iglesia Católica*," 242–43; Sandoval, *On the Move*, 42–43; Dolan, *American Catholic Experience*, 372, 374.

15 McComb, *Houston*, 10–18; Shelton et al., *Houston*, 5.

16 Kreneck, *Del Pueblo*, 20–21; De León, *Ethnicity in the Sunbelt*, 4–5.

17 Stewart and De León, *Not Room Enough*, 29–31.

18 De León, *Ethnicity in the Sunbelt*, 6. By the late 1880s Mexicans represented only about 4 percent of the Texas population. See Jordan, "Century and a Half of Ethnic Change," 393–94.

19 Cardoso, *Mexican Emigration*, 1–17; Montejano, *Anglos and Mexicans*, 106–7; Coatsworth, *Growth Against Development*.

20 Montejano, *Anglos and Mexicans*, 91; Clark, "Mexican Labor," 476, 485; De León, *Ethnicity in the Sunbelt*, 6.

21 The census enumerated 476 "foreign-born whites" from Mexico living in Houston in 1910 (U.S. Bureau of the Census, *Thirteenth Census*, 852); De León, *Ethnicity in the Sunbelt*, 6–7.

22 McComb, *Houston*, 19–51, 92–123; Feagin, *Free Enterprise City*, 48–54; De León, *Ethnicity in the Sunbelt*, 7. A wealthy Mexican refugee passing through Houston in 1914 noted that Negroes "are being displaced by Mexican workers." See Torres, *Memorias de mi viaje*, 68.

23 *Houston Chronicle*, January 22, 1906, 8; August 10, 1908, 5; November 11, 1904, 22. For the recruitment of Mexican labor, see Cardoso, *Mexican Emigration*, 14, 27–29, 85–86, and Clark, "Mexican Labor," 475–76.

24 Shelton et al., *Houston*, 9–14; De León, *Ethnicity in the Sunbelt*, 7–8, 23; Cardoso, *Mexican Emigration*, 38–54, 71–95; Montejano, *Anglos and Mexicans*, 113–14; quote in Kreneck, *Del Pueblo*, 28.

25 Villagómez October 25, 1990, interview; Mary Catherine Villagómez, "*Memorias de mi infancia*," handwritten ms., Villagómez Family Collection, HMRC; Juan and Isidra Rodríguez interview. Lumber king John Henry Kirby transported Mexicans to his East Texas lumber mills not far from Houston. See Sitton and Conrad, *Nameless Towns*, 107. Ruth A. Allen documents a small Mexican presence in the East Texas lumber industry in the first decade of the twentieth century in *East Texas Lumber Workers*, 53, 55; see also Sitton and Conrad, *Nameless Towns*, 47, 60–61, 71, 76–77, 107–8, 122, 126, 189.

26 Guillén 1990 interview; Juan and Isidra Rodríguez interview; De León, *Ethnicity in the Sunbelt*, 9; Zamora, *World of the Mexican Worker*, 26.

27 Cary D. Wintz, "Blacks," in Von der Mehden, ed., *Ethnic Groups of Houston*, 20, table 1; U.S. Bureau of the Census, *Thirteenth Census*, 852; U.S. Bureau of the Census, *Fifteenth Census, 1930. Population*, 1023; Theodore G. Gish, "Germans," in Von der Mehden, ed., *Ethnic Groups of Houston*, 159–78. On other ethnic groups in Houston, see Von de Mehden, ed., *Ethnic Groups of Houston*; Maas, *Jews of Houston*; Collins, *Ethnic Identification*; and Beeth and Wintz, eds., *Black Dixie*.

28 De León, *Ethnicity in the Sunbelt*, 8–12, 14–16.

29 Montejano, *Anglos and Mexicans*, 179–96; Romo, "Responses to Mexican Immigration." For contemporary American and Mexican perspectives see, respec-

tively, Bogardus, *Mexican in the United States*, and Gamio, *Mexican Immigrant*, ch. 5.

30 Rosales, "Mexican Immigrant Experience," 60–61; De León, *Ethnicity in the Sunbelt*, 13–14, 18; Rosales, "Shifting Self Perceptions."

31 Zavala / Jiménez interview. The scorn for Mexicans who denied their heritage is seen in the poem *"Los abolillados,"* in *Gaceta Mexicana*, April 15, 1928, 12; see also Treviño, *"Prensa y Patria."*

32 Guillén 1990 interview; Grebler et al., *Mexican American People*, 83–84; Tilly, "Transplanted Networks."

33 Guillén 1990 interview; Villagómez October 25, 1990, interview. For *compadrazgo*, see Norma Williams, *Mexican American Family*, 23–27. Karen Mary Dávalos describes godparents as "members of the family . . . by sentiment" in her article *"La Quinceañera,"* 117–18. I have borrowed the phrase "ethic of mutuality" from Zamora, *World of the Mexican Worker*, which treats its implications for Texas Mexican labor and political struggles in the early twentieth century. For the continuing importance of *compadrazgo* see Beatriz Terrazas, "Godparents . . . and More," *Dallas Morning News*, July 11, 2001, C1–2.

34 De León, *Ethnicity in the Sunbelt*, 7, 9–10.

35 Villagómez October 25, 1990, interview; Sister Agnes Rita Rodríguez interview; Zavala / Jiménez interview; Guillén 1990 interview. The barring of Mexicans from "American" churches was commonplace; see Eph A. Kaye, "A Speedy Glimpse at Texas Oblate Work," *MI*, July 1925, 35; and Rev. G. Mongeau, "Mexicans in Our Midst," *MI*, December 1933, 345.

36 Villagómez October 25, 1990, interview; Guillén 1990 interview. Religious institutional development and worship patterns are discussed in subsequent chapters.

37 De León, *Ethnicity in the Sunbelt*, 8, 12; Beeth and Wintz, *Black Dixie*, 23, table 1; Maas, *Jews of Houston*, 34–41; Work Projects Administration, *Houston*, 189; Catholic Youth Organization Centennial Book Committee, *Centennial*, 75, 143, 150.

38 Armstrong, *Room to Grow*, 7; Bello interview; Pizaña, "Hispanic Baptists in Houston," 95.

39 "Houston's 'Little Mexico' Is a City Within a City," *Houston Chronicle*, November 9, 1930, 9.

40 Shelton et al., *Houston*, 9; McComb, *Houston*, 167–68; Rhinehart and Kreneck, " 'In the Shadow of Uncertainty,' " 23–24.

41 De León, *Ethnicity in the Sunbelt*, 45–51; McComb, *Houston*, 168.

42 Rhinehart and Kreneck, " 'In the Shadow of Uncertainty.' " For broader studies

of the repatriations, see Hoffman, *Unwanted Mexican Americans*, and Balderrama and Rodríguez, *Decade of Betrayal*.

43 Gonzales interview; De León, *Ethnicity in the Sunbelt*, 54–55.

44 On the elusive nature of the shift from "Mexican" to "Mexican American" ethnic consciousness, see Richard A. García, "Mexican American Mind"; George J. Sánchez, *Becoming Mexican American*; Rosales, "Shifting Self Perceptions"; and De León, *Ethnicity in the Sunbelt*, chs. 4–6.

45 De León, *Ethnicity in the Sunbelt*, ch. 5.

46 Weeks, "League of United Latin American Citizens"; Kreneck, "Letter from Chapultepec."

47 Shelton et al., *Houston*, 16–18; De León, *Ethnicity in the Sunbelt*, 90–91.

48 De León, *Ethnicity in the Sunbelt*, 91–92; San Miguel, *Let All of Them Take Heed*, 139–63; Zamora, "Failed Promise."

49 De León, *Ethnicity in the Sunbelt*, 98; Grebler et al., *Mexican American People*, 112–13.

50 De León, *Ethnicity in the Sunbelt*, 98–99. Father Frank Urbanovsky, a missionary who worked chiefly among rural Mexicans in the Galveston Diocese, witnessed the rural-to-urban shift. After retiring from his missions, Urbanovsky pastored Houston-area parishes where he met many people he had known previously in outlying rural communities. See Urbanovsky interview.

51 De León, *Ethnicity in the Sunbelt*, 99–104.

52 Ibid., 104–5; letter to Bishop Wendelin J. Nold, July 26, 1956, Our Lady of St. John File, ADGH; Father Nicholas [Tanaskovic] to Bishop Nold, March 12, 1952, Provincial Records, AOMI.

53 For overviews of the civil rights era, see Matusow, *Unraveling of America*, and Morgan, *Sixties Experience*.

54 Acuña, *Occupied America*.

55 Muñoz, *Youth, Identity, Power*; Ignacio M. García, *Chicanismo*.

56 Gómez-Quiñones, *Chicano Politics*, 101–53; Acuña, *Occupied America*, ch. 9; Muñoz, *Youth, Identity, Power*.

57 De León, *Ethnicity in the Sunbelt*, 147.

58 Goodman et al., *Mexican American Population*, 6–16; De León, *Ethnicity in the Sunbelt*, ch. 8; quote on 147.

59 De León, *Ethnicity in the Sunbelt*, 149–56; Goodman et al., *Mexican American Population*, 17–111, passim.

60 Shelton et al., *Houston*, 17–28; Feagin, *Free Enterprise City*, 73–96; Kaplan, "Houston."

61　De León, *Ethnicity in the Sunbelt*, 156–59; Feagin, *Free Enterprise City*, 76; Kaplan, "Houston," 203; Grebler et al., *Mexican American People*, 13–34.

62　Davidson, *Biracial Politics*, 36–40; Bullard, *Invisible Houston*, 115–17; Cecile E. Harrison and Alice K. Laine, "Operation Breadbasket in Houston, 1966–78," in Beeth and Wintz, eds., *Black Dixie*, 223–35.

63　De León, *Ethnicity in the Sunbelt*, chs. 9 and 10, esp. 172–74, 185–89, and 195–98; Ignacio M. García, *United We Win*, 178–80; San Miguel, *Brown, Not White*; "Dedicated to Community Action"; "To the Houston City Council and to [t]he Houston Independent School District Board," typed ms., Huelga Schools Coll., HMRC; Brackenridge and García-Treto, *Iglesia Presbiteriana*, 204.

Chapter Two

1　Villagómez November 9, 1990, interview.

2　Marcos Rodríguez to María Carmelita Rodríguez, June 16, 1941, Rodríguez Family Collection, HMRC.

3　See Orsi, *Madonna of 115th Street*, xix–xxiv, and Hall, ed., *Lived Religion in America*.

4　According to pious tradition, the Virgin Mary appeared to an Indian named Juan Diego outside Mexico City in 1531. On December 9 and again on December 10, the Virgin sent Juan Diego to the bishop with a request that a shrine be built in her honor. The prelate wanted proof of the apparitions, however, and so the Virgin told Juan Diego to return the next day, when she would provide a sign for the bishop. But Juan Diego's uncle became deathly ill and he did not meet the Virgin the next day as she asked. On the following day, December 12, Juan Diego went to bring a priest for his dying uncle. The Virgin again appeared to him, telling him she had made his uncle well and sending him yet again to the bishop, this time sending roses wrapped in Juan Diego's mantle as proof for the bishop. When Juan Diego revealed the roses, a portrait of the Virgin miraculously appeared imprinted on the mantle. Convinced, the bishop built Guadalupe's shrine on Tepeyac hill, the site of the apparitions. Because she appeared to one of their own, the Mexican masses made Guadalupe the center of their religious devotions and her Basilica in Mexico City became the most important pilgrimage site of her legions. Moreover, Guadalupe became "a central symbol of the Mexican nation and its destiny." See Harrington, "Mother of Death, Mother of Rebirth," 27. A classic interpretation of Guadalupe's importance is Wolf, "Virgin of Guadalupe." For an introduction into the vast literature, see the citations in the revisionist article by William B. Taylor, "Virgin of Guadalupe."

5 Francis A. Kilday, "Guadalupe is Mexico's REAL Heart!" *MI*, December 1952, 296–98, 320; Rev. G. Mongeau, "A Catholic People," *MI*, January 1934, 10–12; Joseph Buckley, "Mexicans Have a Queen," *MI*, January 1940, 12–13; see also Elizondo, *La Morenita* and *Guadalupe*.

6 Buckley, "Mexicans Have a Queen," 13.

7 Elizondo, *La Morenita*, 87–92; Meier, "María Insurgente"; Chandler, "Mexican-American Protest Movement," 237; *Papel Chicano*, December 12, 1970, 1; see also Rivera, "Power and Symbol."

8 OLG *Codex*, 2.

9 Guillén 1990 interview; Zavala / Jiménez interview; Gonzales interview; Villagómez November 9, 1990, interview.

10 SP *Codex*, 35.

11 Ibid.; Zavala / Jiménez interview; Gonzales interview; see also "Fiesta Guadalupana," *TCH*, December 10, 1976, and *TCH*, November 21, 1980, 6.

12 Guillén 1990 interview; Gonzales interview; Zavala / Jiménez interview; see also *Papel Chicano*, January 13, 1972, 12; and *El Sol*, November 17, 1972, 3.

13 "Two Masses Scheduled for Guadalupe," *TCH*, December 5, 1969, 1.

14 "Fiesta Guadalupana"; "Bishop Morkovsky Recalls," *TCH*, November 21, 1980, 6; Guillén telephone interview.

15 *Papel Chicano*, October 28, 1971, 11.

16 Ibid., January 13, 1972, 12.

17 Ibid.

18 Villagómez November 9, 1990, interview.

19 Ibid.; Zavala / Jiménez interview; Gonzales interview; Guillén 1990 interview. See also *TCH*, December 10, 1964; December 26, 1969, 1, 5; December 24, 1971, 2; and West, *Mexican-American Folklore*, 159–60, 177–78.

20 Villagómez November 9, 1990, interview; Zavala / Jiménez interview.

21 West, *Mexican-American Folklore*, 173–76; see also Waugh, *Silver Cradle*.

22 Guillén 1990 interview.

23 Orsi, *Madonna of 115th Street*, 178–80.

24 John Wheat, "*Los Pastores*: Continuity and Change in a Texas-Mexican Nativity Drama," *Journal of Texas Catholic History and Culture* 5 (1994): 51–52, explaining anthropologist Richard R. Flores's interpretation of the *pastorela* tradition. For the full and cogent analysis, see Flores, *Los Pastores*.

25 HC, March 22, 1970, 7–10 ("Texas Magazine"). Customarily the number of attendants is fourteen (one for each year of the girl's life), and the celebrant who is now fifteen years old (*quince años*) embodies the fifteenth birthday, or *quinceañera*.

26   See Dávalos, *"La Quinceañera,"* esp. 107–13; *HC*, March 22, 1970, 7–10; *El Puerto,*
     October 1959, 9; and *El Sol*, March 22, 1968, 2.

27   *TCH*, October 2, 1970, 11; *HC*, March 22, 1970, 7–8; Villagómez November 9,
     1990, interview.

28   *HC*, March 22, 1970, 10.

29   Ibid.

30   Ibid.

31   C. Gilbert Romero, *Hispanic Devotional Piety*, 72–73; Arturo Pérez, *Popular Ca-
     tholicism*, 22–23.

32   On the contradictory nature of the tradition's meanings, see Dávalos, *"La
     Quinceañera."* Men and women alike recounted the ways male privilege domi-
     nated church life in Houston's parishes. See Zavala / Jiménez interview and
     Gonzales interview. For a perspective on Aztec and Spanish colonial influences
     vis-à-vis women and religion, see Mirandé and Enríquez, *La Chicana*, 37–38.

33   Flores and Novo-Pena, *Interiores*, 21.

34   Guillén 1990 interview; Gonzales interview; García 1990 interview; Zavala /
     Jiménez interview.

35   Flores and Novo-Pena, *Interiores*, 30; Zavala / Jiménez interview. Anthropologist
     Kay Turner ("Mexican-American Women's Home Altars," 25–27, 68–71 nn. 20–
     22) suggests that home altars have their origins in the syncretism of Mexican
     indigenous and pre-Christian European religious practices.

36   Zavala / Jiménez interview; García 1990 interview; Guillén 1990 interview.

37   Gonzales interview.

38   Turner, "Mexican-American Women's Home Altars," ch. 1; Flores and Novo-
     Pena, *Interiores*, 21.

39   Quoted in Flores and Novo-Pena, *Interiores*, 24, 30.

40   García 1990 interview; Guillén 1990 interview.

41   Quoted in Flores and Novo-Pena, *Interiores*, 29.

42   Guerra and Goodman, *Content Assessment of "El Sol,"* 18; Flores and Novo-Pena,
     Interiores, 29; Zavala / Jiménez interview; García 1990 interview; Guillén 1990
     interview.

43   Guillén 1990 interview; Flores and Novo-Pena, *Interiores*, 27; Christian, *Local
     Religion*, 55–59.

44   See Rodríguez, *Our Lady of Guadalupe*, 45–46; Espín, "Popular Catholicism,"
     325–32; and Turner, "Mexican-American Women's Home Altars," 25–26. On
     the devotional revolution see Larkin, "Devotional Revolution," and Taves,
     Household of Faith.

45 Turner, "Mexican-American Women's Home Altars," 38–50, 395; Rodríguez, "Impact of Our Lady of Guadalupe," ch. 4; Flores and Novo-Pena, *Interiores*, 28–29. For the continuing importance of saint veneration in Texas and Mexico, see David McLemore, "A Spirited Catholicism," and Frank Trejo, "Faithful Swarm to Mexican Shrines to Ask for Help," both in *Colorado Springs Gazette Telegraph*, May 18, 1996, E1, E3; see also Simons and Morales, "Churches, Chapels, and Shrines," 116–18.

46 Cotera, "La Conferencia De Mujeres Por La Raza: Houston, Texas, 1971," in Alma M. García, ed., *Chicana Feminist Thought*, 155–57. See also Francisca Flores, "Conference of Mexican Women in Houston—*Un Remolino*," in ibid., 157–61.

47 "Jerarquía en el matrimonio," *TCH*, November 29, 1968, 12.

48 Turner, "Mexican-American Women's Home Altars," 38–50; Rodríguez, "Impact of Our Lady of Guadalupe," 86–91; Consuelo Nieto, "Chicanas and the Womens Rights Movement," *Civil Rights Digest* (Spring 1974), quoted in Maxine Baca Zinn, "Chicanas: Power and Control in the Domestic Sphere," *De Colores* 2, no. 3 (1976): 25. This portrait of empowered domesticity is based on recent social science research (not historical studies), but Mexican American women's influential position in the culture has long been a given in Chicano oral tradition. Mirandé and Enríquez (*La Chicana*, 116) state, "Anyone who has grown up in a Chicano family would scoff at the notion that the woman is weak, quiet, or submissive. If there is a persistent image of the woman in Chicano culture, it is that she is a strong and enduring figure." For a historical study, see Griswold del Castillo, *La Familia*. Studies since the 1970s amply contradict the stereotypical image of the Mexican American family as pathologically authoritarian and patriarchal; a good review essay is Zinn, "Chicano Family Research."

49 García 1990 interview.

50 Villagómez November 9, 1990, interview.

51 Flores and Novo-Pena, *Interiores*, 27.

52 Ibid., 25–26.

53 García 1990 interview; Gonzales interview; Guillén 1990 interview; Flores and Novo-Pena, *Interiores*; Rodríguez, "Impact of Our Lady of Guadalupe," 118–23; Turner, "Mexican-American Women's Home Altars."

54 Turner, "Mexican-American Women's Home Altars," 17–18.

55 Numerous studies and oral tradition suggest that Mexicans traditionally have attended church services less frequently than other Catholics (10–20 percent under the national average). See Stoddard, *Mexican Americans*, 90–91. See also Gamio, *Mexican Immigrant*, and Grebler et al., *Mexican American People*, 473–77.

For Mexican Americans confirming low affiliation, see Gonzales interview; Sister Mary Rachel Moreno to author, July 11, 1990; and "Need Adult Education," *TCH*, October 2, 1970.

56 In 1965–66, one study found that 58 percent of Mexican parishioners in San Antonio attended Sunday services weekly. See Grebler et al., *Mexican American People*, 472, table 19-1. In Houston between 1959 and 1966, about 54 percent of the estimated population of four parishes attended Sunday Mass weekly. See Reports on the Status Animarum, 1959–66, in Our Lady of Guadalupe, Our Lady of Sorrows, St. Patrick, and St. Alphonsus Files, ADGH. There is no definitive figure regarding church attendance; studies have shown considerable variation, and many are simply estimates.

57 Mrs. Janie Tijerina, quoted in Flores and Novo-Pena, *Interiores*, 29.

58 Gonzales interview.

59 Ibid.; Zavala / Jiménez interview; García 1990 interview.

60 García 1990 interview; Sister Agnes Rita Rodríguez interview.

61 Tarango, "Hispanic Woman."

62 *New Catholic Encyclopedia*, 1967 ed., s.v. "Vatican Council II," by R. F. Trisco; ibid., s.v. "Liturgical Participation," by P. Murray; Sister Mary Rachel Moreno to author, July 11, 1990; Zavala / Jiménez interview.

63 "Mexican Señoritas to Sing the Liturgy," clipping, *TCH*, October 25, 1968, in *TCH* Photograph Files, St. Patrick File, Chancery, ADGH.

64 Press release, March 23, 1970, PADRES Collection, CAT.

65 "Mariachi Masses," *TCH*, December 12, 1969, 6. For the importance of the innovation, see also *TCH*, October 3, 1969, 1; Rev. P. F. Flores to Bishop John Morkovsky, October 5, 1969, St. Stephen File, ADGH; and *Día de la Raza* flier, October 12, 1969, St. Stephen File, ADGH.

66 *La Gaceta Mexicana*, June 1, 1928, 11; see announcements in other issues in Mexican American Small Collections, Box 2, HMRC.

67 "Need Adult Education."

68 Turner, "Mexican-American Women's Home Altars," 44.

69 Norma Williams, *Mexican American Family*, 23–27; De la Teja, *San Antonio de Béxar*, 150–51. First quote in Flores and Novo-Pena, *Interiores*, 27; second quote in Turner, "Mexican-American Women's Home Altars," 44.

70 "Need Adult Education."

71 Villagómez telephone interview; see also Rev. Charles Serodes, "The Works and Wants of a Mexican Parish," *MI*, October 1922, 117; and "Dedication at Houston," *Southern Messenger*, September 19, 1912.

72 Rev. G. Mongeau, "The Mexicans," *MI*, March 1938, 79–80.

73 Ibid., 80; García 1990 interview.

74 Rev. Esteban de Anta, "Houston, Texas," *MI*, January 1930, 14.

75 The following summary of parish societies is a composite based on a review of documents spanning the twentieth century and oral history interviews. For specifics, see the SP *Codex* and OLG *Codex*, the annual Status Animarum reports, and *Mary Immaculate* magazine (1930s), all in AOMI; see also *Family Circular* (1930s–50s); *Texas Catholic Herald* (Houston, 1964–70); and Guillén 1990, García 1990, Villagómez, Zavala / Jiménez, and Gonzales interviews.

76 Tarango, "Hispanic Woman," 58.

77 "Greatest Religious Demonstration Ever Held," *Southern Messenger*, November 2, 1950, clipping in vertical file, CAT; see also the many references to Mexican American participation in Christ the King celebrations in *FC*, ACDP.

78 See De Anta, "Houston, Texas," 14; "Notes from Houston," *MI*, May 1931, 146; *HC*, September 9, 1934, clipping in Rodríguez Family Collection, HMRC; ABCM *Reports*, 1930, 1931, ALUC; OLG *Boletín*, July 1929, 8; Guillén 1990 interview; Zavala / Jiménez interview.

79 OLG *Boletín*, July 1929, 8.

80 SP *Codex*, 33, 35.

81 OLG *Boletín*, July 1929, 7.

82 *MI*, March 1959, 16–20; *FC*, December 1937, 61; *TCH*, November 27, 1970, 3; "Notes from Houston," 146–47.

83 See Orsi, *Madonna of 115th Street*, and Shaw, *Catholic Parish as a Way-Station*.

84 "Notes from Houston," 146–47.

85 See Reed-Danahay, "Talking about Resistance," and Gibson, *Accommodation Without Assimilation*.

86 The importance of fund-raising is treated in Chapter 5.

87 *FC*, March 1952, 116–17; Don LeBlanc, "Waterfront Priest," *MI*, March 1959, 16–20; Villagómez November 9, 1990, interview.

88 De León, *Tejano Community*, 194–96; Gamio, *Mexican Immigration*, 121–22. The tradition of self-help is more fully discussed in Chapter 6.

89 Zamora, *World of the Mexican Worker*, 80; OLG *Codex*, 8.

90 The *cursillo de cristiandad* originated in Spain in the late 1940s and was brought to the United States in 1957 by two Spanish air cadets temporarily stationed in Texas. Father Patricio Flores, a pioneer in the cursillo movement, held the first cursillo in the Galveston-Houston Diocese at the predominately Mexican Guardian Angel Parish in Pasadena, a Houston suburb. See "Just Six Years

Ago," *TCH*, October 29, 1964, 2; "Hundreds Attend," *TCH*, November 12, 1964, 2; and *New Catholic Encyclopedia*, 1967 ed., s.v. "Cursillo," by J. F. Byron.

91 Grebler et al., *Mexican American People*, 467; Hough, "Religion and Pluralism," 188–89.

92 Typescript, ca. 1963, Provincial Records, AOMI; Grebler et al., *Mexican American People*, 467.

93 St. Stephen Parish Bulletin, June 6, 1971; Status Animarum, 1966, St. Alphonsus File; and Status Animarum, 1964, Our Lady of Sorrows File, all in ADGH; *TCH*, November 5, 1964, 12; November 12, 1964, 12; December 10, 1964, 10; January 7, 1965, 8.

94 Grebler et al., *Mexican American People*, 467; Sandoval, *On the Move*, 84.

95 *TCH*, February 11, 1965, 10.

96 Tucson Convention Resolution, PADRES Collection, CAT.

97 Significantly, women began participating in cursillos in 1963, showing yet again that Mexican American women's agency and initiatives predated the feminism of the Chicano movement (*TCH*, October 29, 1964, 2).

98 The correspondence between religious orders and bishops of Galveston-Houston is filled with discussions about the importance of having Spanish-speaking personnel, especially priests, in Houston's Mexican parishes. Besides the Oblates, other priests in the diocese were beginning to enroll in classes to learn Spanish by the early 1970s. For references to Spanish-speaking priests, see Rev. A. Antoine to Bishop Christopher Byrne, January 21, 1919; Rev. E. Lecourtour to Byrne, August 9, 1922; Rev. Theodore Laboure to Byrne, September 27, 1931; Rev. Walter Arnold to Byrne, June 10, 1943; Rev. Nicholas Tanaskovic to Bishop Wendelin Nold, October 20, 1951; and Rev. John Hakey to Bishop John Morkovsky, January 31, 1967, all in Provincial Records, AOMI; and *TCH*, May 28, 1971, 2. For references to sisters, see Father Nicholas [Tanaskovic] to Bishop Nold, February 2, 1951, Provincial Records, AOMI; Father Augustine Pérez to Nold, February 25, 1953, Our Lady of Sorrows File, ADGH; Rev. M. Buckley to Bishop Morkovsky, June 24, 1966, St. Stephen File, ADGH; and Father A. Goossens to Buckley, July 4, 1966, St. Stephen File, ADGH. See also Villagómez interviews; Guillén 1990 interview; and García 1990 interview.

99 Zavala / Jiménez interview; Guillén 1990 interview.

100 Zavala / Jiménez interview; Guillén 1990 interview. Parishioners added, however, that priests tended to interact more with the people in the post–Vatican II years.

101 Gamio, *Mexican Immigrant*; Woods, *Mexican Ethnic Leadership*.

102 José M. Sánchez, *Anticlericalism*, 183.

103 See Meyer, *Cristero Rebellion*; James W. Wilkie, "The Meaning of the Cristero Religious War against the Mexican Revolution," *Journal of Church and State* (Spring 1966): 214–33; for a contemporary assessment, see Galarza, *Roman Catholic Church*.

104 Villagómez November 9, 1990, interview. The deference Mexicans showed toward priests and nuns is evident in a diary of Sister Delphine Marie [Mary Villagómez], 1944, photocopy in author's possession. See also F. Arturo Rosales, "Mexicans in Houston: The Struggle to Survive, 1908–1975," *Houston Review* 3, no. 2 (Summer 1981): 234; and Rosales, "Mexican Immigrant Experience," 62.

105 Zavala / Jiménez interview.

106 See Bishop W. J. Nold to Rev. Father Nicholas [Tanaskovic], October 19, 1955; Tanaskovic to Nold, October 22, 1955; and Nold to Tanaskovic, May 21, 1956, all in Provincial Records, AOMI; see also Gamio, *Mexican Immigrant*, 163. Grebler et al., *Mexican American People*, 451, reported "a fairly widespread impression" of Spanish priests as "authoritarian."

107 Bishop John L. Morkovsky to Rev. Clifford Blackburn, December 1, 1969, Provincial Records, AOMI.

108 See the explicit complaints against some clerics' undignified and insulting behavior in Resolution, June 10, 1971, St. Stephen File, ADGH.

109 For example, over 650 parishioners signed a petition protesting the transfer of the highly regarded Sister Benitia Vermeersch; see Toribio Cano, President of Diocesan Council, to Mother Superior M. Philothea, May 16, 1938, Our Lady of Guadalupe File, ACDP. Similarly, children from St. Patrick petitioned their bishop to keep a popular priest, Father Anthony Moreno; see Mr. Ralph R. Vásquez, basketball coach, to Bishop Wendelin Nold, March 23, 1963, and St. Patrick children's choir to Nold, March 23, 1963, both in Provincial Records, AOMI.

110 Mongeau, "Catholic People."

111 Ibid., 12.

112 Ibid., 11–12.

113 Ángela Pérez de Rodríguez to Carmelita and Margarita Rodríguez, August 14, 1939; Marcos Rodríguez to Carmelita Rodríguez, August 29, 1939; Ángela Pérez de Rodríguez to Carmelita Rodríguez, July 8, 1940; and Marcos Rodríguez to María Carmelita Rodríguez, June 16, 1941, all in Rodríguez Family Collection, HMRC.

114 Flores and Novo-Pena, *Interiores*, 29; García 1990 interview. See also Gonzales interview for similar comments about religion and identity.

115 Roberto Santoya, "Bronze and Proud—My People," *Papel Chicano*, February 20, 1971, 8.

116 Blas de León Poetry File, Mexican American Small Collections, Box 3, HMRC. I am thankful to Thomas H. Kreneck for this information.

117 *El Sol*, November 17, 1972, 3.

118 Folding commemorative, Rodríguez Family Collection, HMRC.

119 See the numerous holy cards and other religious mementos in the Rodríguez Family Collection and the Gómez Family Collection, HMRC; religious postcard and "Apadrinamiento" ribbon, Villagómez Family Collection, Box 1, folder 7, HMRC; quoted phrase from Tarango, "Hispanic Woman," 57.

120 See Orsi, *Madonna of 115th Street*, xvi–xvii; 55 and passim.

Chapter Three

1 Rev. Esteban de Anta, "Missionary Work in the Diocese of Galveston," *Extension Magazine*, August 1913, 5, 22.

2 Montejano, *Anglos and Mexicans*, 179–96. For a Catholic perspective on the "problem" see Charles J. Taylor, "The Mexicans of Texas," *MI*, December 1915, 7–8; Taylor, "Our Mexican Problem in Texas," *MI*, June 1923, 30–32; and Rev. G. Mongeau, "The Mexicans—A Rural Problem of the Catholic Church in the Southwest," *MI*, March 1938, 78–81, 94–95.

3 "Among our Brethren Exiled from Mexico," *Extension Magazine*, January 1915, 9; Rev. Esteban de Anta, "A Missionary Tour among the Mexicans," *MI*, December 1924, 101. See also Most Reverend Arthur J. Drossaerts, "The Children of Guadalupe," *Extension Magazine*, October 1937, 4; and Mongeau, "Mexicans," 78.

4 *FC*, November 1912, 23.

5 Rev. L. O. Eckardt, "The Oblate Fathers in Texas," *MI*, June 1917, 137; Mongeau, "Mexicans," 78.

6 Taylor, "Our Mexican Problem," 32; ABCM *Reports*, 1929, 63, ALUC.

7 Rev. Esteban de Anta, "Houston, Texas," *MI*, January 1930, 14; Mongeau, "Mexicans," 78; Rev. Charles Serodes, "The Works and Wants of a Mexican Parish," *MI*, October 1922, 117.

8 "Honored by Churchmen," *HC*, April 30, 1935, 9.

9 Takaki, *Iron Cages*, 101, 106, 187, 113–17, 125–26, 223, 269, 275.

10 Foley, *White Scourge*, quote on 5. See also Foley, "Becoming Hispanic," 53–70.

11 Halter, *Between Race and Ethnicity*.

12 Orsi, "Religious Boundaries"; De León, *They Called Them Greasers*.

13 De León, *They Called Them Greasers*, 65–66, 69. See also De León, *Racial Frontiers*, 31–32.

14 Very Reverend H. A. Constantineau to Bishop Nicholas A. Gallagher, August 26, 1911, Provincial Records, AOMI; De Anta, "Missionary Work," 22.

15 De Anta, "Missionary Work," 22. The poverty in Mexican American communities is documented in Clark, "Mexican Labor in the United States," and Selden C. Menefee, *Mexican Migratory Workers of South Texas* (1941), reprinted in Cortés, ed., *Mexican Labor in the United States*; for Houston, see De León, *Ethnicity in the Sunbelt*, 11–12, 16–17, 26–27, 46–56.

16 Bishop Gallagher, form letter, January 9, 1912, File 8H59, AOMI (emphasis in original). Many of Houston's Mexicans, perhaps as many as 25 percent, worked for the numerous railroad lines. See De León, *Ethnicity in the Sunbelt*, 8–9.

17 Gallagher letter, January 9, 1912, File 8H59, AOMI.

18 Taylor, "Our Mexican Problem," 32; Rev. L. O. Eckardt, "Conditions in Our Missions," *MI*, December 1922, 176; Valdez, *History of the Missionary Catechists*, 5–6. See also De León, *Ethnicity in the Sunbelt*, 12. For Mexican immigrant labor in this period see Reisler, *By the Sweat of Their Brow*.

19 De Anta, "Missionary Work," 6; Bishop C. E. Byrne to Very Reverend A. C. Dusseau, June 11, 1938, Provincial Records, AOMI. See also Tafolla, "Expansion of the Church," 235.

20 Rev. G. Mongeau, "Mexicans in Our Midst," *MI*, December 1933, 327, 345; Zavala / Jiménez interview. See also Montejano, *Anglos and Mexicans*, 157–254, and De León, *Ethnicity in the Sunbelt*, 26–27.

21 Mongeau, "Mexicans in Our Midst," 345.

22 Drossaerts, "Children of Guadalupe," 4.

23 Villagómez October 25 and November 9, 1990, interviews; Zavala / Jiménez interview.

24 Sister Agnes Rita Rodríguez interview. See also Cárdenas interview and Guillén 1990 interview.

25 Drossaerts, "Children of Guadalupe," 4; "The Growing Need for Mission Schools," *Extension Magazine*, February 1916, 5; Mongeau, "Mexicans in Our Midst," 327. For the Mexican American struggle against segregated schools see San Miguel, *Let All of Them Take Heed*; for Houston's Mexican schools see De León, *Ethnicity in the Sunbelt*, 12–13, 27–28, 57–58.

26 Taylor, "Our Mexican Problem," 32; Eckardt, "Conditions in Our Missions," 176.

27 Gallagher letter, January 9, 1912, File 8H59, AOMI; De Anta, "Missionary Work," 5, 22.

28 Serodes, "Works and Wants," 117; Mongeau, "Mexicans," 78; Eph A. Kaye, "Texas Talking," *MI*, April 1924, 4–5.

29 De Anta, "Missionary Work," 5; Byrne to Dusseau, June 11, 1938, AOMI. Between 1937 and 1954, Father Frank Urbanovsky ministered to the Mexicans in isolated rural areas of central and southeast Texas in his trailer-chapel, *Espíritu Santo* Mission. He periodically visited Houston to attend to scattered pockets of Mexicans who had no churches of their own. Endearingly called Padre Panchito by parishioners—the nickname for Francisco, or Frank, is Pancho—Father Urbanovsky eventually settled in Houston and pastored Resurrection Parish, in the predominately Mexican American neighborhood of Denver Harbor, where he died in 1991. See Urbanovsky diary, CAT, and obituary, *TCH*, February 22, 1991, 10.

30 Kaye, "Texas Talking," 5; Mongeau, "Mexicans," 78.

31 Monsignor A. Verhagen to Archbishop Arthur J. Drossaerts, October 18, 1937, Religious Congregations of Women Collection, Hermanas Guadalupanas File, 1930–40, Archives of the Archdiocese of San Antonio, San Antonio, Texas.

32 Eckardt, "Conditions in Our Missions," 176; Serodes, "Works and Wants," 118; Mongeau, "Mexicans," 78.

33 Letter to Bishop Byrne, February 14, 1936, Provincial Records, AOMI (emphasis added). Father José A. Prieto wanted to erect a shrine for Texas Mexicans in Austin, Texas, modeled after the great Basilica of Our Lady of Guadalupe in Mexico City. See Rev. José A. Prieto to Rt. Rev. E. E. Byrne, February 12, 1936, Provincial Records, AOMI.

34 Eckardt, "Conditions in Our Missions," 176.

35 Serodes, "Works and Wants," 118.

36 De Anta, "Missionary Work," 22.

37 On the dominance of Irish Catholicism and the adjustment of various ethnic groups to that model, see Dolan, *American Catholic Experience*, 143–44, 294–303, and passim. On Irish prelates in the Galveston-Houston Diocese see Giles, *Changing Times*, 28–29, 56–59.

38 Mongeau, "Mexicans in Our Midst," 345. For a sampling of clerical and academic literature see Linna E. Bresette, *Mexicans in the United States*; Manuel, "Mexican Population of Texas," 29–51; Paul S. Taylor, *American-Mexican Frontier*; and Gamio, *Mexican Immigration*.

39 Anthropologist Franz Boas and sociologist Robert Park were instrumental in

shaping the discourse on race. See Gossett, *Race*, and Matthews, *Quest for an American Sociology*.

40 Mongeau, "Mexicans in Our Midst," 327; ABCM *Reports*, 1934–35, 75, ALUC.

41 ABCM *Reports*, 1939–40, 58, ALUC.

42 Bishop C. E. Byrne to Very Reverend Walter Arnold, November 29, 1940, Provincial Records, AOMI; Arnold to Byrne, March 22, 1942, Provincial Records, AOMI.

43 Bishop Wendelin J. Nold to Very Reverend Father Nicholas (J. Tanaskovic), October 19, 1955, Provincial Records, AOMI; Nold to Tanaskovic, May 21, 1956, Provincial Records, AOMI.

44 Simon, *Pastoral Spanish*, xviii, xxiii.

45 De León, *Ethnicity in the Sunbelt*, 99–104.

46 "Spanish Speaking Problems," *TC*, July 25, 1953, clipping, Nold File, Episcopal Collection, CAT.

47 Galarza, *Merchants of Labor*; Juan Ramón García, *Operation Wetback*.

48 Rev. Frank A. Kilday, "Second Class Citizens," *MI*, July–August 1953, 2–3; Kilday, "The New Challenge," *MI*, January–February 1956, 16; Sandoval, "Effects of World War II," 350–51. On the varied responses to the Bracero Program and Operation Wetback, see Mario T. García, *Mexican Americans* and *Memories of Chicano History*; and Gutiérrez, *Walls and Mirrors*.

49 See Perrett, *Days of Sadness*, 347–49; Karen Anderson, *Wartime Women*, 95–105; De León, *Ethnicity in the Sunbelt*, 105–10; and Mazón, *Zoot-Suit Riots*, 60–61.

50 SP *Codex*, 24. Longtime parishioners Juan and Isidra Rodríguez recalled that Mexican Americans used to refer to the Fifth Ward as the *Quinto Infierno* (the hellish Fifth or, literally, the fifth hell). See Juan and Isidra Rodríguez interview.

51 Bishop Byrne to Very Reverend Walter Arnold, June 11, 1943, Provincial Records, AOMI; Don LeBlanc, "Waterfront Priest," *MI*, March 1959, 16–20. For references to delinquency in other Mexican neighborhoods see Bishop W. J. Nold to Very Reverend Lawrence J. Seidel, July 9, 1957, and Seidel to Nold, August 13, 1957, Provincial Records, AOMI.

52 Cárdenas interview. On the issue of color sensitivity among Mexican-origin people see Gamio, *Mexican Immigration*, ch. 4; Paul S. Taylor, *American-Mexican Frontier*, passim; McWilliams, *North from Mexico*, ch. 2; and Forbes, "Race and Color."

53 SP *Codex*, April 19, 1945, 33; Rev. F. A. Santos to Rev. Mother Angelique, July 12, 1948, Our Lady of Guadalupe File, ACDP; Rev. Augustine Pérez to Bishop Wendelin J. Nold, November 21, 1955, Our Lady of Sorrows File, ADGH. See also Mother Angelique to Fr. A. Santos, September 11, 1951; letter from Sr. M. of

the Nativity, December 4, 1943; and Rev. F. A. Santos to Rev. Mother Angelique, May 4, 1948, all in Our Lady of Guadalupe File, ACDP.

54 Census, 1951, St. Patrick File, ADGH; Census, 1953, St. Stephen File, ADGH.

55 Simon, *Pastoral Spanish*, xv, xxi. Positive views of Mexican Catholicism existed before the World War II era, of course, but they did not appear as frequently. See Rev. G. Mongeau, "A Catholic People," *MI*, January 1934, 10–12; for more paternalistic views see Drossaerts, "Children of Guadalupe," 34, and *FC*, November 1935, 34–35.

56 Brother Joseph Buckley, "Mexicans Have a Queen," *MI*, January 1940, 12–13.

57 Kilday, "Second Class Citizens"; Kilday, "New Challenge"; Sandoval, "Effects of World War II," 350–51; Simon, *Pastoral Spanish*, xvi–xvii, xxii.

58 Kilday, "New Challenge," 16.

59 Bishop Byrne to Most Reverend Walter Arnold, June 16, 1943, Provincial Records, AOMI; National Catholic Welfare Conference, *Spanish Speaking*, 10; Dolan, *American Catholic Experience*, 377.

60 "Spanish Speaking Problems."

61 Dolan, *American Catholic Experience*, ch. 15.

62 Historian Jay P. Dolan has argued that civil rights agitation in the later twentieth century more profoundly affected changes in the Catholic Church than did the Second Vatican Council. See "Religion and Social Change."

63 Rev. M. Buckley to Bishop John L. Morkovsky, June 24, 1966, St. Stephen File, ADGH; Morkovsky to Very Reverend John A. Hakey, February 24, 1967, Provincial Records, AOMI. See also Morkovsky to Hakey, February 9, 1967, Provincial Records, AOMI.

64 Morkovsky to Hakey, September 19, 1966, Provincial Records, AOMI; Pastoral Letter from Bishop Morkovsky, January 8, 1965, Provincial Records, AOMI.

65 Letter to Bishop Morkovsky, August 28, 1970, Provincial Records, AOMI.

66 Letter to Monsignor Harris, April 27, 1964, St. Patrick File, ADGH; Father A. Goossens to Father Buckley, July 4, 1966, St. Stephen File, ADGH.

67 Hakey to Morkovsky, March 8, 1967, Provincial Records, AOMI; "Ecumenical Movement Offers Little to the Texas Mexicans," *TCH*, October 31, 1969, 5. See also Father Anselm Walker, "Texas Mexicans: Target for Marxist Revolution," *TCH*, October 24, 1969, 5, for similar perspective.

68 García 1990 interview; *El Sol*, October 31, 1969, 2; Father Emile J. Farge to Bishop Morkovsky, May 9, 1967, St. Stephen File, ADGH. See also Romano, "Charismatic Medicine," and Trotter and Chavira, *Curanderismo*.

69 Farge to Morkovsky, May 9, 1967, St. Stephen File, ADGH.

70 *Houston Post*, April 21, 1971, clipping in Joe Torres / Huelga Schools Collection, HMRC.

71 "Synopsis of Problems," January 30, 1971, St. Raphael File, ADGH.

72 *Papel Chicano*, June 1, 1972, 12.

73 Ibid.

74 San Miguel, *Brown, Not White*.

CHAPTER FOUR

1 OLG *Codex*, 2.

2 Copy of contract, October 5, 1911, Provincial Records, AOMI; Oblate Provincial H. A. Constantineau to Bishop N. A. Gallagher, August 26, 1911, Provincial Records, AOMI.

3 Memorandum from Bishop Gallagher, December 18, 1911, Provincial Records, AOMI; see also October 26, 1911, clipping in Oblata File, AOMI; and "Parish History of Our Lady of Guadalupe, Houston, Texas," Parish Collection, CAT.

4 Rev. Esteban de Anta, "Missionary Work in the Diocese of Galveston," *Extension Magazine*, August 1913, 5–6, 22; OLG *Codex*, 1.

5 Rev. Esteban de Anta, "Houston, Texas," *MI*, January 1930, 13.

6 "This Is Our Story," typewritten document (copy in French), Box 4, Mexican American Small Collections, HMRC; De Anta, "Missionary Work," 6.

7 De Anta, "Houston, Texas," 13; "House of Houston," *MI*, October 1929, 306; OLG *Boletín*, April 1928, 2; OLG *Codex*, 5.

8 "Dedication at Houston," *Southern Messenger*, September 19, 1912; OLG *Codex*, 4–5.

9 "Dedication at Houston."

10 Ibid.

11 Cardoso, *Mexican Emigration*, ch. 2; De León, *Ethnicity in the Sunbelt*, 23, 55.

12 OLG *Codex*, 10–12.

13 Sister M. Lucinda Schuler and Sister M. Rachel Moreno, comps., "History of Our Lady of Guadalupe School," ACDP; Chancery office questionnaire, ca. 1929, Parish Collection, CAT.

14 Rev. E. de Anta to Mother Superior Florence, May 1, 1923, and Faculty list, both in Our Lady of Guadalupe File, ACDP.

15 Giles, *Changing Times*, 123; "House of Houston," 306. Our Lady of Guadalupe became the first of several "national" parishes exclusively for Spanish-speaking parishioners in Houston.

16 OLG *Codex*, 18, 28; "House of Houston," 306–7; see also Valdez, *History of the Missionary Catechists*, 12.

17 OLG *Codex*, 29.

18 Letter to Father Tonson, November 30, 1921, Provincial Records, AOMI; Bishop C. E. Byrne to Father Lecourtour, August 12, 1922, Provincial Records, AOMI.

19 Chancery office questionnaire, Immaculate Heart of Mary (Houston) File, Parish Collection, CAT; Villagómez October 25, 1990, interview; letters to Bishop Byrne, January 9, 1924, August 9, 1922, August 22, 1922; and letter to J. M. Kirwin, August 22, 1925, all in Provincial Records, AOMI.

20 Giles, *Changing Times*, 138–39; "House of Houston," 307; ABCM *Reports*, 1930, 57, ALUC.

21 Dolan, *American Catholic Experience*, 377.

22 "The Catechists in Houston," *MI*, May 1933, 151–52; "Silver Jubilee," *MI*, June 1935, 181; "Modern Lay Apostles," *MI*, September 1935, 233–34; ABCM *Reports*, 1931–35, ALUC; *FC*, March 1933, 128. The Catechists received papal approval and became an adjunct of the Sisters of Divine Providence in 1946; see Valdez, *History of the Missionary Catechists*.

23 "Missionary Catechist: Sister Benitia," *TCH*, January 11, 1980, clipping in files of ACDP; Guillén interview.

24 "New Parochial School," *HC*, October 9, 1932, 9; "The Poor Will Have the Gospel Preached to Them," *MI*, January 1938, 16–17; Giles, *Changing Times*, 101.

25 Giles, *Changing Times*, 149; "Poor Will Have the Gospel," 16–17; Bob Giles, "Our Lady of Sorrows Parish," *TCH*, September 14, 1984, 28. The barrio of *El Crisol* took its name from the constant odor of creosote, a weathering agent used on railroad ties that was manufactured in a plant in the neighborhood; see Urbanovsky diary, May 1947, 306, CAT.

26 "Starving Kids Get Lift," *HC*, September 11, 1932, 14; ibid., October 9, 1932, 9.

27 "Their History," *HC*, January 16, 1950, 15; Giles, *Changing Times*, 98–99; handwritten ms., ca. 1950, St. Patrick School File, ACDP; last quote in SP *Codex*, 20.

28 Bishop C. E. Byrne to Rev. Walter Arnold, January 30, 1941, Provincial Records, AOMI; "Old Parish to Be Taken Over by Oblates," *HC*, February 6, 1941, 17; Mother M. Philothea to Rev. L. A. Ferrero, May 15, 1941, and Contract, September 28, 1943, both in SP *Codex*; Giles, *Changing Times*, 99.

29 SP *Codex*, 1943, 25–26.

30 Giles, *Changing Times*, 61.

31 "Poor Will Have the Gospel," 17; Urbanovsky diary, April 28–May 11, 1947, 304;

May 21–June 6, 1948, 121; October 1948, 166, CAT; "Bishop Blesses New Statue," *TCH* clipping, Our Lady of St. John (Houston) File, Parish Collection, CAT.

32 "Capsule History of Our Lady of St. John Church," and "Pertinent Data for Parish History," both in St. John File, ADGH; Urbanovsky diary, April 28–May 12, 1947, 304, CAT.

33 Rev. C. Conaty to bishop of Galveston Diocese, June 6, 1949, and Decree of Erection, June 28, 1957, both in Our Lady of St. John File, ADGH; Giles, *Changing Times*, 166.

34 Giles, *Changing Times*, 211; *TCH*, April 28, 1967.

35 See "St. Raphael Celebrates," commemorative in St. Raphael File, ADGH; Giles, *Changing Times*, 194–95; "Emphasizes Dignity," *TCH*, 11; and parish history form, St. Raphael File, ADGH.

36 Giles, *Changing Times*, 205; Urbanovsky diary, May 10–21 [ca. 1948], 118, CAT; Fr. Sylvester O'Toole to Bishop Morkovsky, April 26, 1966; and "St. Aphonsus Parish," *TCH*, June 17, 1966, clipping, both in St. Alphonsus File, ADGH.

37 Giles, *Changing Times*, 99; See also Feagin, *Free Enterprise City*, 257.

38 *FC*, April 1956, 146; Giles, *Changing Times*, 99; Father A. Goossens to bishop of Galveston Diocese, June 6, 1966, St. Patrick File, ADGH. See also letter to Monsignor Harris, April 27, 1964, St. Patrick File, ADGH; *TCH*, December 10, 1964, 10; and *TCH*, September 29, 1967, clipping in Parish Collection, CAT.

39 Giles, *Changing Times*, 99.

40 Ibid., 139, 149–50; De León, *Ethnicity in the Sunbelt*, 150–52.

41 Letter to bishop of Galveston-Houston Diocese, June 29, 1971, Immaculate Conception File, ADGH; De León, *Ethnicity in the Sunbelt*, 150.

42 Bishop John L. Morkovsky to Rev. John A. Hakey, March 13, 1967, Provincial Records, AOMI; Hakey to Rev. James Meagher, September 5, 1968, Immaculate Conception File, ADGH; see also Morkovsky to Meagher, March 19, 1969, Immaculate Conception File, ADGH.

43 Giles, *Changing Times*, 114, 133; "Houston Parish," *TCH*, April 24, 1970, 1; letter to Bishop John Morkovsky, August 28, 1970, Provincial Records, AOMI; quote in Zavala / Jiménez interview.

44 Traditionally, parishes have been defined by geographical boundaries, with all Catholics living within a specified area (e.g., a neighborhood) being members of that "territorial" parish. Membership in so-called national parishes (also known as "nationality" and "foreign-language" parishes) is based on language rather than place of residence. The Catholic Church historically has preferred

territorial parishes but has used nationality parishes to accommodate immigrants. See Harte, "Racial and National Parishes."

45 Olson, *Catholic Immigrants*, 101–67.

46 Dolan, *American Catholic Experience*, 295–303, 363–65; Shaw, *Catholic Parish as a Way-Station*.

47 Letter to Bishop Christopher Byrne, July 19, 1921, Provincial Records, AOMI.

48 Archbishop John J. Cantwell quoted in Sánchez, *Becoming Mexican American*, 159. See also Mario T. García, *Desert Immigrants*, 212–19; Richard A. García, *Rise of the Mexican American Middle Class*, 196–98; De León, *Ethnicity in the Sunbelt*, 28; Romo, *East Los Angeles*, 145–48; and George J. Sánchez, *Becoming Mexican American*, 156–61.

49 Valdez, *History of the Missionary Catechists*, 14. For a balanced discussion of the double-edged nature of Americanization and national parishes among Mexican Catholics in California, see Burns, "Mexican Catholic Community," 148–69.

50 In 1940 there were fifty-seven Mexican national parishes in the United States; eight years later there were forty-four; and by 1960 there were only twenty-two. See Olson, *Catholic Immigrants*, 147, 122, and Harte, "Racial and National Parishes," 162.

51 "Spanish Speaking Problems," *TC*, July 25, 1953, clipping in Nold File, Episcopal Collection, CAT.

52 "Memorandum of Visit of Provincial with Bishop of Galveston," ca. April 30, 1955, Provincial Records, AOMI.

53 Sylvester R. O'Toole to Bishop John Morkovsky, April 26, 1966, St. Alphonsus File, ADGH; "St. Alphonsus Parish," *TCH*, June 17, 1966, clipping in St. Alphonsus File, ADGH; Rev. Lawrence Peguero to Morkovsky, July 12, 1971, Our Lady of St. John File, ADGH.

54 O'Toole to Morkovsky, April 26, 1966; Peguero to Morkovsky, July 12, 1971.

55 Rev. B. A. Waggner to Miss Rickert, Chancery office, December 28, 1971, Our Lady of Guadalupe File, ADGH.

56 Bishop John L. Morkovsky to Oblate Provincial Reverend John A. Hakey, February 9, 1967, and Morkovsky to Hakey, February 24, 1967, both in Provincial Records, AOMI.

57 Morkovsky to Hakey, February 24, 1967, and Rev. M. [Maurice] Buckley to Morkovsky, August 2, 1967, both in St. Philip File, ADGH.

58 Rev. Buckley to Bishop Morkovsky, June 24, 1966, St. Stephen File, ADGH.

59 Bishop John L. Morkovsky to Rev. John A. Hakey, February 9, 1967, Provincial

Records, AOMI; Rev. M. Buckley to Bishop Morkovsky, June 24, 1966, St. Stephen File, ADGH. The story of the St. Stephen revolt is told below.

60 R. Laurence Moore, *Religious Outsiders*, 100.

61 "Spanish Speaking Problems."

62 Starting in the 1960s the Galveston-Houston Diocese began redesignating some of the city's national parishes as territorial ones. Hence Our Lady of St. John, which had been designated a national parish in 1957, was changed to territorial status in 1964; St. Patrick ceased to be a nationality parish in 1968, and plans to convert Immaculate Heart of Mary from a national to a territorial parish were discussed in 1969. See *TCH*, January 7, 1965, 8; Decree of Erection, June 18, 1968, St. Patrick File, ADGH; and Bishop Morkovsky to Rev. James Meagher, March 19, 1969, Immaculate Conception File, ADGH. On the knotty problem of changing the status of the Mexican parishes, see Father Nicholas [Tanaskovic] to Bishop Nold, June 5, 1952, Provincial Records, AOMI; and Oblate Provincial's letter to Bishop Nold, July 26, 1956, Our Lady of St. John File, ADGH.

Chapter Five

1 Villagómez October 25, 1990, interview; Zavala / Jiménez interview; "Capsule History of Our Lady of St. John Church," Our Lady of St. John File, ADGH.

2 "Mejicanos," flyer in OLG *Codex*.

3 OLG *Codex*, 6–7.

4 Villagómez October 25, 1990, interview; Zavala / Jiménez interview.

5 "The Poor Will Have the Gospel Preached to Them," *MI*, January 1938, 16–17.

6 Urbanovsky diary, April 28–May 12, 1947, 304–5, and May 21–June 6, 1948, 121–22, CAT; Urbanovsky interview; "Capsule History of Our Lady of St. John Church."

7 "Saint Raphael Celebrates," commemorative in St. Raphael File, ADGH.

8 Dolan, *American Catholic Experience*, 375; Hegarty, *Serving with Gladness*, 157–58. Hegarty (158) writes that the Society for the Propagation of the Faith gave the Galveston Diocese $249,000 between 1846 and 1901, "the largest sum contributed to any single diocese in the United States, just as the diocese was probably one of the poorest."

9 F. C. Kelley to Rev. N. A. Gallagher, August 19, 1912, Parish Collection, CAT; OLG *Codex*, 6, 7–8; "Appeal for Assistance," microfilm roll no. 11, Extension Society Records, ALUC.

10 "Appeal for Assistance," February 11, 1937, and Bishop W. J. Nold to Rev. Richard R. St. John, March 21, 1951, both in Diocesan Correspondence, Extension Society Records, ALUC; Rev. Joseph A. Cusack to Bishop John L. Morkovsky, April 7, 1966, St. Patrick File, ADGH; Cárdenas interview; see also Rev. E. B. Ledvina to Bishop Gallagher, October 17, 1912, and Ledvina to Gallagher, May 19, 1917, both in Gallagher File no. 5, Episcopal Collection, CAT.

11 "Gifts of the Catholic Church Extension Society to the Diocese of Galveston," Diocesan Chancery Collection, CAT; Dolan, *American Catholic Experience*, 375; ABCM *Reports*, 1940–55, ALUC.

12 Dolan, *American Catholic Experience*, 375.

13 Appeals for donations, Bishop N. A. Gallagher, January 9, 1912, and G. W. La Lumiere, railroad official, September 7, 1915, both in Immaculate Conception (Houston) File, AOMI; see also Pastoral Letter from Bishop Byrne, ca. 1924, Provincial Records, AOMI.

14 Valdez, *History of the Missionary Catechists*, 20, 36–39; OLG *Codex*, 6–8; Kelley, *Story of Extension*, 200; Sister M. Lucinda Schuler and Sister M. Rachel Moreno, "History of Our Lady of Guadalupe School," TMs, ACDP; letters of October 6, 1972, Scalan Foundation to Bishop Morkovsky and to sisters at Guadalupe School, Our Lady of Guadalupe File, ADGH.

15 Chancery Office Questionnaire, ca. 1929, Our Lady of Guadalupe File, Parish Collection, CAT; "Father Santos," *Houston Post*, April 23, 1949, clipping in Our Lady of Guadalupe File, ADGH; "*Desde el quinto barrio*," *TCH*, December 10, 1964, 10.

16 Jubilee program souvenir, 1935, Our Lady of Guadalupe File, ACDP.

17 "Father Santos," *Houston Post*, April 23, 1949, clipping in Our Lady of Guadalupe File, ADGH.

18 SP *Codex*, 29, 36.

19 Irene Rickert to Rev. B. A. Wagner, December 9, 1971, and Wagner to Rickert, December 28, 1971, both in Our Lady of Guadalupe File, ADGH.

20 Similar in socioeconomic makeup, the two parishes alternated between deficits and small surpluses of $1,000–$2,000 (typewritten document, January 30, 1971, St. Raphael File, ADGH; "Emphasizes Dignity," *TCH*, October 23, 1970, 11; Financial Report, 1969, St. Raphael File, ADGH; Financial Report, 1965, Our Lady of St. John File, ADGH).

21 Financial Report, 1971, Blessed Sacrament File, ADGH; Financial Report, 1965, Our Lady of Sorrows File, ADGH; Bishop John L. Morkovsky to Rev. John A. Hakey, February 9 and February 24, 1967, Provincial Records, AOMI; Financial Report, 1965, St. Patrick File, ADGH.

22 Bishop Byrne to Rev. Laboure, June 19, 1930, Provincial Records, AOMI; see any issue of *MI*.

23 Gonzales interview.

24 Ibid.; OLG *Boletín*, April 1928, 9–10; and July 1929, 10.

25 In the early 1950s, about 200 out of some 614 member families at St. Stephen used the envelope system. Census, 1953, St. Stephen File, ADGH. At St. Patrick, 425 out of some 1,500 families used the envelopes. St. Patrick Annual Parochial Report, 1960, File 8H64, AOMI; at Blessed Sacrament, 500 of 1,235 did so. Financial Report, 1971, Blessed Sacrament File, ADGH. See also Financial Report, 1965, Our Lady of Sorrows File, ADGH.

26 St. John Financial Report, 1965; St. Patrick Financial Report, 1965; Our Lady of Sorrows Financial Report, 1965; St. Raphael Financial Report, 1969; and Blessed Sacrament Financial Report, 1971, all in ADGH.

27 Parishioners sponsored the stained glass windows of the first Immaculate Heart Church, in 1926; the ones for the first Guadalupe Church were also paid for this way. See Zavala / Jiménez interview; OLG *Codex*, 6.

28 Immaculate Heart of Mary Church Commemorative Program, January 29, 1950, Villagómez Family Collection, HMRC. Apart from other contributions, the commemorative listed paid cash pledges from individuals and families totaling $8,255 in denominations of $25 (1); $50 (145); $60 (2); $80 (2); $100 (5); and $200 (1).

29 "Father Santos"; *FC*, March 1952, 116–17; parish bulletin, March 5, 1972, Our Lady of St. John File, ADGH; parish bulletin, June 6, 1971, St. Stephen File, ADGH; parish bulletin, May 30, 1971, St. Joseph–St. Stephen File, AGHD; Financial Report, 1965, Our Lady of St. John File, ADGH; Gonzales interview; Zavala / Jiménez interview.

30 OLG *Boletín*, April 1928, July 1929; *FC*, December 1944, 67–68; February 1946, 87–88; January 1950, 66; broadsides, January 23, 1938, and June 16, 1940, Rodríguez Family Collection, HMRC; parish bulletin, June 6, 1971, St. Stephen File, ADGH.

31 Villagómez October 25, 1990, interview; Gonzales interview; Zavala / Jiménez interview.

32 "Mexican Village," *HC*, December 13, 1935, 6; see also *HC*, November 30, 1935, 5; September 29, 1933, 18; November 27, 1935, 22; December 3, 1935, 2; April 20, 1940, 6A; April 26, 1940, 1D.

33 Zavala / Jiménez interview.

34 Ibid.; Gonzales interview.

35 Zavala / Jiménez interview.

36 This phrase is borrowed from León, "Born Again in East LA," 170.

37 Tarango, "Hispanic Woman," 57.

38 Although virtually nonexistent for Mexican Americans, food studies would seem a fertile field for historians interested in the study of ethnicity. A suggestive article is Brett Williams, "Why Migrant Women Feed Their Husbands Tamales." The word *tamalada* can refer either to the making of tamales or to a festive meal of tamales. Either way, the dish is often associated with religious celebration. A social worker's telling observation in 1930s Los Angeles reveals its ethnoreligious significance:

> On Christmas Eve in old Mexico it is customary among the families to hold a tamalada after the Midnight Mass. One family will make great preparation for such an occasion and will invite all its relations and perhaps one other family to be present at the festivities. . . . The tamaladas here [in Los Angeles] are not of that type. Instead of a private home, they are held in a rented dance hall. Everyone goes. There is not much order and a great deal of confusion. The girls sometimes smoke and drink, which would never be tolerated in Mexico. The older people consider this *a desecration of a sacred custom*. (Quoted in Sánchez, *Becoming Mexican American*, 167; emphasis added)

39 Gonzales interview.

40 Ibid.; clipping, SP *Codex*, 36. See also the parish queen photos in the Guillén Family Collection and Medellín Family Collection, HMRC. The *Family Circular*, the Sisters of Divine Providence newsletter, often mentioned the parish queen contests.

41 OLG *Codex* and SP *Codex*; FC, ACDP; see also *Día de la raza* flier, October 12, 1969, St. Stephen File, ADGH; and church bulletins, St. Joseph–St. Stephen Parish, May 30, 1971; St. Stephen Parish, June 6, 1971; and Our Lady of St. John Parish, March 5, 1972, all in ADGH. Local newspapers also frequently noted the *jamaicas*; see HC, September 29, 1933, 18; November 27, 1935, 22; November 30, 1935, 5; December 3, 1935, 2; December 13, 1935, 6; April 20, 1940, 6A; and April 26, 1940, 1D.

42 Financial Reports, Our Lady of St. John, 1965; Our Lady of Sorrows, 1965; St. Patrick, 1965; St. Raphael, 1969; and Blessed Sacrament, 1971, all in ADGH; OLG *Boletín*, July 1929, 8.

43 Our Lady of Guadalupe Band photo, 1930, Petra Guillén File, Mexican American Family and Photograph Collection, HMRC; Southern Pacific Lines Band photo, 1926, Gómez Family Collection, HMRC; Zavala / Jiménez interview.

44 Zavala / Jiménez interview.

45 Orsi, *Madonna of 115th Street*; Giles, *Changing Times*, 127–28.

46 Bishop John L. Morkovsky to Rev. John A. Hakey, September 19, 1966, Provincial Records, AOMI; "Surviving a Century of Storms," *TCH*, August 25, 1978, 6.

47 "Controversial Parish Here Split in Two," *HC*, July 20, 1973, sec. 3, 21; Father Emile J. Farge to Bishop Morkovsky, May 9, 1967, St. Stephen File, ADGH.

48 Father Emile J. Farge to Bishop Morkovsky, May 9, 1967, St. Stephen File, ADGH.

49 Petition from St. Stephen's parishioners to Bishop Morkovsky, ca. May 25, 1967; Resolution from St. Stephen Parish to Bishop Morkovsky, April 1971; and Resolution from St. Stephen Parish to Bishop Morkovsky, June 10, 1971, all in St. Stephen File, ADGH.

50 Chancellor Bernard J. Ganter to Mr. Joseph F. Montalbano, October 9, 1968, St. Stephen File, ADGH; "Angry Parishioners," *HC*, March 7, 1969, clipping in St. Stephen File, ADGH; "The Spirit of St. Joseph–St. Stephen," *TCH*, February 4, 1972, clipping in St. Stephen File, ADGH; "Surviving a Century of Storms."

51 "Angry Parishioners"; *El Sol*, May 23, 1969, 1; Memorandum, June 17, 1969, St. Stephen File, ADGH; *Noche Mexicana* advertisement, *TCH*, July 18, 1969, 11; *TCH*, August 1, 1969, 3; solicitation letter from Rev. P. F. Flores, August 12, 1969, copy in *TCH* Photograph Files (St. Joseph–St. Stephen), Chancery, ADGH; "Three Priests Compete," *TCH*, September 26, 1969, 3; *Día de la Raza* flier, October 12, 1969, St. Stephen File, ADGH.

52 Raymond Lomas to Bishop John L. Morkovsky, March 23, 1971, St. Stephen File, ADGH.

53 Ibid.

54 Resolution, April 1971, St. Stephen File, ADGH; "Dispute Surfaces in Joint Parish," *HC*, June 25, 1971, sec. 3, 7.

55 Resolution, April 1971, St. Stephen File, ADGH.

56 Resolution, June 10, 1971, St. Stephen File, ADGH.

57 "Dispute Surfaces."

58 As an example of how they were not taken seriously, the petitioners claimed that their priests did not believe they had met with the bishop but that the priests did listen to some nonparishioners who proposed an incredible scheme

to raise $400,000 within thirty-six hours for the proposed new church. See Resolution, June 10, 1971, and St. Joseph–St. Stephen Parish Council Meeting Report, May 16, 1971, St. Stephen File, ADGH.

59 St. Stephen's parishioners submitted documents they claimed proved that Sunday collections from the two churches were in fact being pooled, despite being told they were kept in separate accounts. See attachments to the Resolution, June 10, 1971, St. Stephen File, ADGH.

60 Resolution, June 10, 1971, St. Stephen File, ADGH.

61 Ibid.

62 St. Joseph–St. Stephen Parish Council Meeting Report, May 16, 1971, St. Stephen File, ADGH.

63 "Controversial Parish"; "The Spirit of St. Joseph–St. Stephen"; "Surviving a Century of Storms."

64 Copies of letters, Bishop John Morkovsky to Father Maurice Dho, May 24, 1973, Dho to Morkovsky, June 7, 1973, and Morkovsky to Dho, June 8, 1973, all in *TCH* Photograph Files (St. Joseph), Chancery, ADGH; "Surviving a Century of Storms."

65 Resolution, June 10, 1971, St. Stephen File, ADGH.

66 "Surviving a Century of Storms."

67 Ibid.; Resolution, June 10, 1971, St. Stephen File, ADGH.

68 "Surviving a Century of Storms."

69 On the concept of "use value" as applied to religious institutions, see Newman, "God and the Growth Machine." Newman (238) argues that, unlike the "exchange value" that property holds for entrepreneurs, congregants do not view their churches as commodities to be bought and sold. Instead, their "special relationship . . . with a place such as a church building [is] based on the use value of the place itself as well as the access it gives to other use values." I am indebted to my colleague Professor Kee Warner, of UC–Colorado Springs, for bringing this article to my attention.

70 Ibid., 238–39.

71 Reed-Danahay, "Talking about Resistance," 221–29.

72 Orsi, *Madonna of 115th Street*, 153.

Chapter Six

1 Privett, *U.S. Catholic Church*, 127; Valdez, *History of the Missionary Catechists*, 5–12, 19–20; Guillén interview.

2   Paul Decker, "Catholic Action and Social Action in the Oblate Southwest," *MI*, December 1949, 344; Villagómez November 9, 1990, interview.

3   Villagómez November 9, 1990, interview; Rev. Esteban de Anta, "Houston, Texas," *MI*, January 1930, 14.

4   Decker, "Catholic Action," 334; De Anta, "Houston, Texas," 14. This type of social action continued into the contemporary period. Sister Mary Rachel Moreno, C.D.P., a social worker who was principal of Our Lady of Guadalupe Parish School in 1965–66, tried to find jobs for parishioners through Houston employment agencies. She wanted them "to grow spiritually, intellectually [and] materially if possible." Letter to the author, July 11, 1990.

5   Valdez, *History of the Missionary Catechists*, 5–12, 19–20; *FC*, January 1916, 73; November 1916, 37; November 1934, 60; February 1935, 146–47; December 1937, 61; *HC*, September 11, 1932, 14.

6   Valdez, *History of the Missionary Catechists*, 8. Although Monsignor George T. Walsh is credited with starting the "Mexican Clinic" in 1924, Sr. Benitia's groundwork in the later 1910s most likely helped bring about the founding of this important health resource for Houston's Mexicans. For the clinic see "San Jose Clinic," typewritten manuscript, Mexican American Small Collections, Box 2, HMRC; see also De León, *Ethnicity in the Sunbelt*, 30.

7   Valdez, *History of the Missionary Catechists*, 5–12, 19–20; Guillén interview; *Today's Catholic* (San Antonio), June 20, 1980, clipping in Women Religious Orders Collection, CAT; quote in *TCH*, January 11, 1980, clipping in Catechists File, ACDP; see also Antonio Rodríguez, "In Tribute to Sister Benitia," *Southern Messenger*, June 23, 1938.

8   Bishop C. E. Byrne to Rev. A. C. Dusseau, January 28, 1938; Dusseau to Byrne, January 31, 1938; and Byrne to Dusseau, February 1, 1938, all in Provincial Records, AOMI; Mr. Toribio Cano, President of Diocesan Council, to Rev. Mother Philothea, May 16, 1938, Our Lady of Guadalupe File, ACDP; see also Valdez, *History of the Missionary Catechists*, 44–45.

9   Valdez, *History of the Missionary Catechists*, 36, 43; Privett, *U.S. Catholic Church*, 127.

10 Valdez, *History of the Missionary Catechists*, 43–45, quote on 44; Byrne to Dusseau, January 28, 1938; Dusseau to Byrne, January 31, 1938; Byrne to Dusseau, February 1, 1938, Provincial Records, AOMI.

11 "History of Our Lady of Guadalupe School," MS, ACDP; Cárdenas, *Meditaciones*.

12 Cárdenas interview; *FC*, January 1942, 114; December 1942, 69; *El Buen Vecino* (Houston), March 8, 1946, clipping in St. Patrick File, ADGH.

13 Cárdenas interview.

14 Sister Mary [Benitia] to Mr. Deden, S.P. Shops, February 7, 1934; and Sister M. Dolores to Daves Loan Office, December 2, 1927, Rodríguez Collection, HMRC; see also several other letters of this kind in ibid.

15 Rodríguez, "Tribute to Sister Benitia."

16 Coburn and Smith, "Creating Community and Identity," quote on 92. On the ideology of maternal feminism, see Gordon, "Putting Children First," and "Maternalism as a Paradigm." See also Coburn and Smith, *Spirited Lives*.

17 Martin McMurtrey, *Mariachi Bishop*, 35–38, 121, quote on 36. On Flores's historic stature, see David McLemore, "Beyond the Pulpit," *Dallas Morning News*, June 25, 2001, A1, A12.

18 Griffin, "Sisters of Divine Providence." See also Roberto R. Treviño, "Facing Jim Crow: Catholic Sisters and the 'Mexican Problem' in Texas," *Western Historical Quarterly* 34, no. 2 (Summer 2003): 139–64.

19 Decker, "Catholic Action," 345, 348; see also *New Catholic Encyclopedia*, 1967 ed., s.v. "Rerum Novarum," by J. Newman; and s.v., "Quadragesimo Anno," by R. J. Miller.

20 Appeal for donations, Bishop Nicholas A. Gallagher, January 9, 1912, Immaculate Conception (Houston) File, AOMI; Pastoral Letter from Bishop Byrne, ca. 1924, Provincial Records, AOMI; appeal for donations, G. W. La Lumiere, September 7, 1915, Provincial Records, AOMI.

21 Pastoral Letter from Bishop C. E. Byrne, April 15, 1942, Episcopal Collection, CAT.

22 See Richard A. García, *Rise of the Mexican American Middle Class*, ch. 2, ch. 5, esp. 167–73; Mario T. García, *Desert Immigrants*, 96–106; De León, *Ethnicity in the Sunbelt*, 17–18, 55; Zamora, *World of the Mexican Worker*, 49–50, 194.

23 *HC*, November 27, 1935, 22; November 30, 1935, 5; December 3, 1935, 2; December 13, 1935, 6; April 20, 1940, 6A; April 26, 1940, 1D.

24 *El Buen Vecino* (Houston), clipping in St. Patrick File, ADGH; Cárdenas interview; "Notes from Houston," *MI*, May 1931, 147; *FC*, April 1939, 130; April 1940, 173; March 1942, 158; December 1942, 69; Bishop Nold to Very Reverend Nicholas Tanaskovic, July 19, 1954, and Tanaskovic to Nold, July 27, 1954, Provincial Records, AOMI; "History of Our Lady of Guadalupe School."

25 Bishop Byrne to Rev. Theodore Laboure, May 21, 1932, Provincial Records, AOMI; Rev. A. Santos to Franklin Harbach, February 1, 1949, and Harbach to Santos, February 14, 1949, Harbach Papers, HMRC; Don Le Blanc, "Waterfront Priest," *MI*, March 1959, 16.

26 De León, *Ethnicity in the Sunbelt*, 105–10.

27 Bishop Byrne to Very Reverend Walter Arnold, June 11, 1943, Provincial Records, AOMI.

28 SP *Codex*, 1942, 24; *Houston Post*, April 23, 1949, clipping in Our Lady of Guadalupe File, ADGH; Le Blanc, "Waterfront Priest," 16–20; Bishop Wendelin Nold to Very Reverend Lawrence J. Seidel, July 9, 1957, Our Lady of St. John File, ADGH; see also letter to Bishop Byrne, April 24, 1942; Bishop Nold to Very Reverend Father Nicholas, May 21, 1956; and Seidel to Nold, August 9 and 13, 1957, all in Provincial Records, AOMI.

29 Letter to Bishop Byrne, April 24, 1942, Provincial Records, AOMI.

30 Bishop Nold to Father Nicholas, May 21, 1956, Provincial Records, AOMI.

31 Ibid. One proposal was to replace Father Santos at Our Lady of Sorrows Parish with Father Emmet Walsh, whose boys' club in Laredo was lauded by city officials there; see letter to Bishop Byrne, April 24, 1942, Provincial Records, AOMI.

32 *FC*, April 1957, 145; Urbanovsky diary, May 21–June 6, 1948, CAT.

33 *Houston Post*, April 23, 1949, clipping in Our Lady of Guadalupe File, ADGH.

34 The actual size of the Mexican American Protestant community at any given time is unclear, but the most often-cited figure until recently has been 5 to 10 percent. See Sánchez, *Becoming Mexican American*, 163 and 306 n. 51. A recent study funded by the Pew Charitable Trusts, "Hispanic Churches in American Public Life," found that "about 70 percent of the country's 35.4 million Hispanics are Roman Catholic, and 22 percent are Protestant." See Ted Parks, "Study Tallies Where Hispanics Worship, How They Vote," *Star-Telegram*, May 11, 2001, available from <http://www.star-telegram.com/new/doc/1047/1:FAITH20511101.html> (accessed May 17, 2001).

35 De León, *Ethnicity in the Sunbelt*, 28, 50–51, 57; Parish census, 1951, St. Patrick File, ADGH; "Census of St. Patrick Church 1953," typed ms., St. Patrick File, ADGH. For overviews of Mexican American Protestantism see Sylvest, "Hispanic American Protestantism," and Grebler et al., *Mexican American People*, 486–512. For samples of the abundant Catholic discussions about Protestant proselytization see Rev. F. Bormann, "Schools and the Children of the Missions," *Extension Magazine*, February 1916, 13; Rev. Gerard Mongeau, "A Chat with a Texas Missionary," *MI*, June 1926, 18–20; Mongeau, "Mexican Youth for Christ," *MI*, July 1934, 214–16; Frank A. Kilday, "The New Challenge," *MI*, January–February 1956, 14–18, 22; Jim Collison, "The Baptists," *MI*, October 1961, 23–25; and "Testigos de Jehova," *TCH*, December 19, 1969, 11. See also Gamio, *Mexican Immigrant*, 195–209.

36 De León, *Ethnicity in the Sunbelt*, 50–51.

37 María Cristina García, "Agents of Americanization," 122.

38 Bishop Byrne to Very Reverend Walter Arnold, April 15, 1942, Provincial Records, AOMI; De León, *Ethnicity in the Sunbelt*, 51.

39 Oblate Provincial Seidel to Bishop Nold, April 21 and June 16, 1958, Provincial Records, AOMI.

40 "Mejicanos" flier, OLG *Codex*; *HC*, February 22, 1912; see also *HC*, February 23, 1912, 27; and February 27, 1912, 10.

41 See José Hernández, *Mutual Aid for Survival*; for Houston see De León, *Ethnicity in the Sunbelt*, 31–33; on Oblates fostering the Liga de Protección Mexicana, see Carmen Tafolla, "Expansion of the Church," 234–35. Mutual aid societies had papal approval; see Decker, "Catholic Action," 344.

42 OLG *Codex*, 8; OLG *Boletín*, April 1928, Rodríguez Family Collection, HMRC.

43 De León, *Ethnicity in the Sunbelt*, 32 and 41 n. 36.

44 *FC*, November 1943, 36; March 1945, 144; March 1952, 116–17; *Houston Post*, 23 April 1949, clipping in Our Lady of Guadalupe File, ADGH.

45 "Christmas Came Early in Houston," *MI*, December 1955, 16. Father Sauvageau reported religious, social, and financial news to his parishioners via the local Spanish-language radio station, KLVL; see "Dial 1480 and the Rosary," *MI*, December 1954, 12–15.

46 "Christmas Came Early," 16, 18, 19.

47 "Rain and Relief," photo and caption, *HC*, July 7, 1954, 1A; "Flood Relief," photo and caption, in ibid., 8A.

48 Fr. Edward J. Murray, "A Parish That Licked the Loan Shark!" *MI*, June 1959, 2–3. See also García 1990 interview.

49 Murray, "Parish That Licked the Loan Shark," 5; Decker, "Catholic Action," 344.

50 Letter and pulpit announcement, April 28, 1960, Provincial Records, AOMI; for Tijerina's "little school of the 400" see Kreneck, *Mexican American Odyssey*, 198–203 and passim.

51 Bronder, *Social Justice and Church Authority*, 75.

52 ABCM *Reports*, 1939–40, 58, ALUC; Bishop Byrne to Very Reverend Walter Arnold, November 29, 1940; December 2, 1940; June 11, 1943, Provincial Records, AOMI.

53 Byrne to Arnold, June 11 and 16, 1943, Provincial Records, AOMI.

54 Very Reverend Nicholas Tanaskovic to Bishop Wendelin J. Nold, February 11, 1953; Nold to Tanaskovic, February 16, 1953; Archbishop Robert E. Lucey to

Nold, February 24, 1955; and Nold to Tanaskovic, February 28, 1955, all in Provincial Records, AOMI.

55 Bronder, *Social Justice and Church Authority*, 75–76; Sandoval, *On the Move*, 48. See also Walsh, "Work of the Catholic Bishops' Committee."

56 Letter to the author from Father William O'Connor, O.M.I., August 26, 1991. The same appeared to be true for Los Angeles and San Antonio; see Grebler et al., *Mexican American People*, 482–83 n. 56.

57 Father O'Connor to the author, August 26, 1991; De León, *Ethnicity in the Sunbelt*, 55.

58 Bronder, *Social Justice and Church Authority*, 75.

59 "Community Relations Unit Set Up," *TCH*, May 14, 1964, 2.

60 Ibid.

61 See the specific reference to "the rights and opportunities of our Negro brethern [*sic*]," in Pastoral Letter from the Bishops of the United States, August 25, 1963, Provincial Records, AOMI. Also note the absence of any references to Chicanos and the focus on black issues and speakers at a church-sponsored civil rights conference in Houston in 1966, in *TCH*, October 14, 1966, clipping in Diocesan Chancery Collection, CAT.

62 For background on Father Flores see McMurtrey, *Mariachi Bishop*.

63 O'Brien, "American Priest." See also Brown and McKeown, *Poor Belong to Us*.

64 O'Brien, "American Priest," 448.

65 For example, Dolan, "Religion and Social Change."

66 *TCH*, October 1, 1964, 2.

67 *TCH*, January 28, 1965, 9; May 27, 1965, 1, 10; July 29, 1965, 3; clipping, November 12, 1965, St. Stephen File, ADGH.

Chapter Seven

1 *Papel Chicano*, September 16, 1971.

2 Cox, "'New Breed'"; McNamara, "Social Action Priests."

3 Chávez quoted in Sandoval, *Fronteras*, 384.

4 *TCH*, February 11, 1965, 10. A Spanish immigrant, Crespo was well known for his civic involvement and business activities in the Mexican community since the 1930s; see Kreneck, *Mexican American Odyssey*, 67, 69, 71; and De León, *Ethnicity in the Sunbelt*, 74, 83. See also *TCH*, October 3, 1969, 1; September 18, 1970, 1, 11.

5 *TCH*, October 3, 1969, 1, 6. For similar sentiments, see Carrillo, "Sociological Failure."

6   *TCH*, October 13, 1972, 10; *HC*, February 19, 1970, 1, 4 (sec. 3).

7   See Document no. 43, Marta Cotera, "La Conferencia De Mujeres Por La Raza: Houston, Texas, 1971"; Document no. 44, Francisca Flores, "Conference of Mexican Women in Houston—Un Remolino [A Whirlwind]"; and Document no. 45, Anna NietoGomez and Elma Barrera, "Chicana Encounter," in Alma García, *Chicana Feminist Thought*, 155–64.

8   Editorial, *Compass*, October 1967, 4; October 1968, 10–11.

9   *Papel Chicano*, February 3, 1971, 9; February 29, 1972, 11.

10   "Listen, Christian," *Compass*, October 1968, 4. Some internet sources attribute slightly varying versions of this poem to Bob Rowland.

11   For studies and essays from the 1970s that focus on institutional racism and discrimination within the Catholic Church, see Hurtado, "Attitudinal Study"; Soto, "Chicano and the Church"; Carrillo, "Sociological Failure"; Juárez, "La Iglesia Católica"; and Isais-A., "Chicano and the American Catholic Church." More recent works include Mirandé, *Chicano Experience*, ch. 6, and Pulido, "Race Relations."

12   Eduardo N. López to Bishop John L. Morkovsky, ca. November 1970, Our Lady of Sorrows File, ADGH.

13   Ibid.

14   Ibid. While some parishioners at Our Lady of Sorrows fought to get other laity involved in social issues, the situation at St. Raphael's Parish in far southwest Houston was slightly different. There, a concerned priest complained he could not get working-class adults involved in the problems that afflicted their children—teen pregnancy, alcohol and drug abuse, and high school dropout rates. He explained, "Our people are workers, for the most part. They are not inclined to attend meetings. . . . The difficulty is that when the priest has most time for visiting the people, they just arn't [*sic*] at home." See typewritten manuscript, "St. Raphael's Church," January 30, 1971, St. Raphael File, AGHD.

15   For details of Flores's life see McMurtrey, *Mariachi Bishop*.

16   *TCH*, October 24, 1969, 1; June 30, 1972, 7.

17   McMurtrey, *Mariachi Bishop*, 55; Sandoval, *Fronteras*, 397–98; *TCH*, October 24, 1969, 1. See also Juan Romero, "Charism and Power."

18   Rev. Ralph Ruiz to Rev. L. C. Reyes, December 8, 1970, PADRES Collection, CAT.

19   Las Hermanas Proposal, Castillo Collection, HMRC; Sandoval, *Fronteras*, 405–7.

20   *Houston Post*, April 21, 1971, clipping in Joe Torres / Huelga Schools Collection, HMRC; "Qué Pasó Sheet," PADRES Collection, CAT. See also Basso, "Emerging 'Chicana' Sister."

21 Las Hermanas Conference Program, Joe Torres / Huelga Schools Collection, HMRC; *TCH*, November 26, 1971, 12; December 10, 1971, 1; *Papel Chicano*, October 28, 1971, 11; November 9, 1971, 2. For an in-depth study of the national organization see Medina, *Las Hermanas*.

22 Clipping, *Houston Post*, April 21, 1971, Joe Torres / Huelga Schools Collection, HMRC; "Spanish-speaking Sisters Unite," *TCH*, April 8, 1971.

23 Quotes from Quiñónez and Turner, *Transformation of American Catholic Sisters*, 72–73.

24 Pastoral Letter from the Bishops of the United States, August 25, 1963, Provincial Records, AOMI; clippings, *TCH*, October 14, 1966, June 23, 1967, and September 15, 1967, in Diocesan Chancery Collection, CAT.

25 Pastoral Letter from the Bishops; clipping, *TCH*, June 23, 1967, Diocesan Chancery Collection, CAT.

26 *TCH*, June 23, 1967, clipping in Diocesan Chancery Collection, CAT; Pastoral Letter from the Bishops.

27 For a fuller account see Rhinehart and Kreneck, "Minimum Wage March"; Joan Hart Cohen, "To See Christ in Our Brothers"; and Chandler, "Mexican American Protest Movement."

28 *TCH*, June 24, 1966, 1.

29 "La Marcha . . . Valley Farm Workers' 491-Mile March for Justice," in *Harris County PASO 5th Anniversary and Salute to Valley Farm Workers* (Houston: Harris County PASO, 1966), pamphlet in Mexican American Small Collections, HMRC.

30 *TCH*, July 1, 1966, 1, 6.

31 "La Marcha"; *HC*, July 5, 1966, 6.

32 "La Marcha"; *HC*, September 1, 1966, 19 (sec. 1), September 4, 1966, 10 (sec. 1); Chandler, "Mexican American Protest Movement," 244.

33 "La Marcha"; *HC*, September 5, 1966, 1, 18 (sec. 1), September 6, 1966, 1 (sec. 1).

34 *HC*, September 7, 1966, 13 (sec. 1), September 9, 1966, 11 (sec. 1); *TCH*, September 9, 1966, 1, 6.

35 Rhinehart and Kreneck, "Minimum Wage March," 39–44; Chandler, "Mexican American Protest Movement," 245; for similar assessments see De León, *Ethnicity in the Sunbelt*, 173–74; and Montejano, *Anglos and Mexicans*, 284–85.

36 Quoted in Rhinehart and Kreneck, "Minimum Wage March," 44.

37 Bishop P. F. Flores, "Mission and Vision, Mexican American Apostolate," typewritten manuscript (mimeographed), n.d. [ca. 1971], García Collection, HMRC.

38 *TCH*, December 5, 1969, 1; *HC*, April 8, 1970, 1 (sec. 4); clipping, *TCH*, February, 5, 1971, PADRES Collection, CAT; McMurtrey, *Mariachi Bishop*, 57–58.

39 *TCH*, October 24, 1969, 1.

40 *TCH*, October 1, 1964, 2; October 24, 1969, 1; October 2, 1970, 1; Flores, "Mission and Vision."

41 Flores became auxiliary bishop of San Antonio on May 5, 1970. Later that year, in December, a PADRES "action group" was initiated in Houston. See Sandoval, *On the Move*, 72, and "Qué Pasó Sheet."

42 Father Lawrence Peguero was PADRES diocesan director in Houston during the early 1970s, but his bootstraps philosophy contrasted dramatically with the outlook of more militant priests like Flores. While Flores attacked societal barriers, Peguero described himself as "a firm believer in the American system." A contemporary recalled that Houston PADRES was insignificant in the social arena and that Peguero was simply "not interested in social issues." Father Peguero believed that the function of the church was "strictly a moral one," that it was "not the function of a priest to be a leader in social work." Though at times he expressed support for some Chicano causes, Peguero's career and philosophy were summed up in the Franklinesque homilies he was fond of repeating: "We don't have any poor people in our neighborhood—only lazy ones" and "The only thing that has not been tried against poverty is work." See PADRES booklet (undated, ca. 1971), PADRES Collection, CAT; *Houston Post*, March 5, 1970 (Close-up sec.), clipping in Our Lady of St. John File, ADGH; *HC*, October 2, 1970, 5 (sec. 2); and McCarthy 1991 interview. See Sandoval, *Fronteras*, 401–2, for social activism of PADRES elsewhere; De León, *Ethnicity in the Sunbelt*, 206, briefly mentions PADRES emergency relief activities in Houston in the 1970s.

43 *National Catholic Reporter*, August 13, 1971, 1; résumé of Gloria Graciela Gallardo, Castillo Collection, HMRC.

44 De León, *Ethnicity in the Sunbelt*, 185–89; "MAEC preparing," *TCH*, August 6, 1971, 1. See also San Miguel, *Brown, Not White*. Leonel Castillo parlayed his high-profile activism into a successful run for the office of city controller and later served as the first Mexican American director of the Immigration and Naturalization Service in the Carter administration (Kreneck, *Del Pueblo*, 201–2).

45 *Papel Chicano*, September 26, 1970, 3, 5; October 24, 1970, 5; January 16, 1971, 7; February 20, 1971, 5; April 1, 1971; clipping, *Houston Post*, April 21, 1971, Joe Torres / Huelga Schools Collection, HMRC.

46 "San Jose Clinic," typewritten manuscript, Mexican American Small Collections, Box 2, HMRC; *TCH*, April 17, 1970, 12.

47 Much of the effort was carried out through the Bishop's Committee on the Inner City, the Council on Community Relations, and the Council of Catholic

Women. See Catholic Charities of the Diocese of Galveston-Houston 1967 Annual Report, Provincial Records, AOMI; Morkovsky memorandum to Monsignor Ganter, May 22, 1968, Blessed Sacrament File, ADGH; clipping, *TCH*, November 12, 1965, St. Stephen File, ADGH; clipping, *TCH*, June 19, 1970, Diocesan Chancery Collection, CAT; *TCH*, April 3, 1970, 6; May 3, 1970, 3; clipping, *TCH*, June 17, 1966, *TCH* Photograph Files (St. Stephen), ADGH; clippings, *TCH*, March 17 and 31, 1972, *TCH* Photograph Files (Immaculate Heart of Mary), ADGH; Bishop's Pastoral Letter, September 23, 1968, Provincial Records, AOMI; and clipping, *TCH*, December 5, 1969, Diocesan Chancery Collection, CAT.

48   *Houston Post*, November 13, 1965, clipping in Latin American Community Project (LAC) scrapbook; typewritten manuscript in LAC scrapbook; "Minister's Quarterly Report," Folder 2, Box 1; and "History, Structure and Purposes of the LACK Project," Box 2, Folder 1, all in VISTA Collection, HMRC. The LAC Project was also known as "LACK."

49   Flier in LAC scrapbook; LACK Project *Voice*, Box 1; and LACK Project Director's Report, Box 2, Folder 2, all in VISTA Coll., HMRC. An offshoot organization of LAC that involved some East End priests was The East End Mission (TEEM). See *TCH*, January 23, 1970, 12.

50   Oxford Place was managed by an "interfaith and interracial staff" led by director Lupe Maciel, a Baptist, and four Spanish- and non-Spanish-surnamed office personnel, two Catholics and two Baptists. See *TCH*, April 24, 1970, 2; and "Report of Self-Study Committee of Houston Metropolitan Ministries," undated, ca. August 1970, Organizations File, Castillo Collection, HMRC. The Galveston-Houston Diocese entered into two other ecumenical agreements to provide low-cost housing, Pleasantville Village in 1967 and Houston Home Ownership Corporation in 1969, though these were not exclusively aimed at Mexican Americans. Giles, *Changing Times*, 63.

51   *TCH*, April 3, 1970, 6.

52   LAC Project Director's Report, September 1967, Box 2, Folder 2, VISTA Collection, HMRC. On the national level, the hierarchy of the church in the United States formed the Campaign for Human Development in 1969 to empower the poor and attack root causes of inequality. See Evans, "Campaign for Human Development."

53   Bishop John L. Morkovsky to Rev. Antonio Gonzales, July 28, 1966, and Provincial John A. Hakey to Morkovsky, August 6, 1966, both in Provincial Records, AOMI.

54 *TCH*, July 15, 1966, 3.

55 Joan Hart Cohen, "To See Christ in Our Brothers," 24–25; McCarthy 1991 interview; quote in McCarthy 1972 interview. See also "Begin Aid Collections for Strikers," *TCH* clipping, June 24, 1966, and "Strikebreaking Aliens Decried by Texas Priest," *TCH* clipping, August 29, 1969, both in Bishop McCarthy Files, *TCH* Photograph Files, ADGH.

56 *TCH*, July 15, 1966, 3.

57 *TCH*, March 24, 1967, 3.

58 *Alamo Messenger* (San Antonio), February 7, 1969, clipping in Episcopal Collection, CAT; see also *TCH*, December 5, 1969, 1.

59 *HC*, August 20, 1967, 24 (sec. 1).

60 Bishop John L. Morkovsky to Rev. Antonio Gonzales, August 21, 1967, Provincial Records, AOMI.

61 *HC*, August 20, 1967, 24 (sec. 1).

62 Morkovsky to Gonzales, August 21, 1967.

63 Ibid.

64 Provincial John A. Hakey to Bishop John L. Morkovsky, February 13, 1968, Provincial Records, AOMI. In February 1968, Father Gonzales was reassigned to Houston. Back in the city, the priest renewed his political activities. His interest ranged from PASO and the Democratic Party to La Raza Unida Party, and eventually even the Republicans. In the opinion of a contemporary, Gonzales "lost touch with reality in the heady world of the Chicano movement" and was "used" by politicians. Within six months of his return to Houston, Gonzales was again in trouble with his bishop, and his association with the diocese was temporarily suspended while he explained reports of "irresponsible" behavior. This episode was apparently smoothed over, since within a week he was back at his post and communicating with the bishop regarding his latest political activity, a meeting with a representative of the incoming Nixon administration. Father Gonzales eventually left the priesthood. See Provincial John A. Hakey to Bishop John L. Morkovsky, February 13, 1968; Morkovsky to Gonzales, February 14, 1968; Morkovsky to Gonzales, November 27, 1968; and Gonzales to Morkovsky, December 5, 1968, all in Provincial Records, AOMI; *El Sol*, March 22, 1968; April 26, 1968; May 3, 1968; and McCarthy 1991 interview. Co-leader Rev. James Novarro similarly came under severe criticism. When newspaper pictures showed him carrying Father Gonzales's crucifix in a show of ecumenical solidarity in the priest's absence, many of his fellow Baptists were outraged; he eventually lost his pulpit because of his political activities. See Novarro interview.

65 Undated memorandum from Father Emile Farge (ca. August 1968), Organiza-
    tions File, Castillo Collection, HMRC.

66 Ibid. Farge described his job as social action director as one of "exposing people
    to people [through the Catholic Interracial Committee]," maintaining contact
    with grassroots organizations, and "political activities, especially pushing the
    good legislation, good political candidates." In the late 1960s, he led an effort to
    build an ecumenical social action coalition, the Joint Strategy and Action Com-
    mittee, which was "motivated by the common knowledge of the problem that
    many in our Greater Houston area are disenfranchised from real participation
    in the life of the city." He described the effort as "the only realistic ecumenical
    group working on the race-culture crises." See Farge letters and memoranda
    from 1968 to 1969 in Organizations File, Castillo Collection, HMRC.

67 Memorandum from Bishop Morkovsky to Father Farge, February 14, 1969,
    Organizations File, Castillo Collection, HMRC.

68 *Papel Chicano*, February 20, 1971, 2.

69 Ibid., September 16, 1971.

70 Ibid., August 22, 1970, 4; November 21, 1970, 2; January 16, 1971, 7; February 20,
    1971, 5; *TCH*, September 11, 1970, 8.

71 "Oxford Place, Another Well-Meaning Instant Slum," *Papel Chicano*, September
    16, 1971.

72 Ibid.

73 Houston Council on Human Relations, *Black / Mexican-American Project Report*,
    6.

74 Sandoval, "Organization of a Hispanic Church," 141–42; Bishop Flores quoted
    in *National Catholic Reporter*, July 7, 1972, 1, 2.

75 *TCH*, November 3, 1972. See also National Conference of Catholic Bishops,
    Hispanic Ministry, 8, 29; Sandoval, *On the Move*, 79–82.

76 Sandoval, *On the Move*, 74–79.

77 Ibid., 79–82; *National Catholic Reporter*, July 7, 1972, 2; *Compass*, October 1972, 4.

78 *Compass*, October 1972, 4; Bishop John L. Morkovsky to Rev. Robert J. McGrath,
    July 11, 1972, St. Patrick File, ADGH; Morkovsky to Rev. Edward F. Brauman,
    June 3, 1971, Immaculate Heart of Mary File, ADGH; photo, *TCH* Photograph
    Files (Immaculate Heart of Mary), ADGH.

79 Sandoval, *Fronteras*, 429.

80 *TCH*, October 20, 1972, 2; October 13, 1972, 10.

81 Sandoval, *On the Move*, 81; *TCH*, October 20, 1972, 2.

1 Ueda, *Postwar Immigrant America*, 44–57, 68–71; Shelton et al., *Houston*, 103–6; Néstor Rodríguez, "Hispanic and Asian Immigration Waves," 32–37.

2 Betty Guzmán, "The Hispanic Population: Census 2000 Brief," May 2001, <http://www.census.gov/population/www/cen2000/briefs.html> (accessed May 2, 2004).

3 De León, *Ethnicity in the Sunbelt*, 221, 233; Shelton et al., *Houston*, 96, 98; <http://www.census.gov/2002/ACS/Tabular/160> (accessed April 21, 2004); <http://www.census.gov/2002/ACS/Narrative/160> (accessed April 21, 2004).

4 De León, *Ethnicity in the Sunbelt*, 221–22, 239–40; Shelton et al., *Houston*, 109–10; <http://www.census.gov/2002/ACS/Narrative/160>.

5 For newspaper reports, see notes 6, 7, and 8 below; for examples of scholarly studies, see Matovina and Riebe-Estrella, ed., *Horizons of the Sacred*, and Jeanette Rodríguez, *Our Lady of Guadalupe*; also see "In the Hispanic Tradition, the Reverence of the Season Reigns," in *American Country Christmas, 1992*, ed. Patricia D. Wilson and Brenda W. Kolb (Birmingham, AL: Oxmoor House, n.d.), 72; and "Hidden Houston: The City You See on the Surface Is Not All the City There Is," interview of Petra Guillén by David Theis in *Cite: The Architecture and Design Review of Houston* 50 (Spring 2001): 24.

6 Guillén 2004 interview; Elena Vega, "Thousands Celebrate Virgin of Guadalupe," *HC*, December 18, 2003, <http://continuum.uta.edu> (accessed August 3, 2004).

7 Megan K. Stack, "A TREAT FOR BELIEVERS: Visitors Flock to See Ice Cream Stain Some Say Is Image of Virgin," *Dallas Morning News*, January 14, 2000, 29A, 30A; Richard Vara, "'Lady of the Light': Reflected Image Attracts Pilgrims to Houston Driveway," *HC*, August 4, 2001, <http://continuum.uta.edu> (accessed August 4, 2004).

8 Zelie Pollon, "HEALING PILGRIMAGE: Thousands Flock to Small Church Known for Its Restorative Powers," *Dallas Morning News*, April 23, 2000, 36A; Tara Dooley, "A Walk of Faith: Church Group Re-creates Jesus' Journey to Crucifixion," *HC*, April 18, 2003, <http://continuum.uta.edu> (accessed January 4, 2005); Richard Vara, "Beacon in the Barrio: WE'RE FAMILY SPIRIT BUILDS GROWTH AND A NEW CHAPEL AT LA DIVINA PROVIDENCIA IN PORT HOUSTON," *HC*, September 20, 2003, <http://continuum.uta.edu> (accessed August 4, 2004); Rhea Davis, "Church's Warm Greeting Stifling This Time of Year: Parishioners Are Trying to Raise Money for an Air Conditioner," *HC*, July 17, 2004, B1, B7; David Mc-

Lemore, "A Spirited Catholicism: Connecting to the Invisible World Includes Making Bargains with God," *Gazette Telegraph*, May 18, 1996, E1, E3; Richard Vara, "Hispanic-Catholic Tradition Runs Deep," *HC*, July 12, 1990, 19A; Mercedes Olivera, "Exhibit Shows Vast Ties to Virgin of Guadalupe," *Dallas Morning News*, November 27, 2004, 30; John Hillman, "Church to Celebrate All Souls Day with Spanish Service," *Arlington Morning News*, October 30, 1999, 1A, 5A; Joey Guerra, "Jessica's Big Day: Today's *Quinceañeras* Add Modern Flourish to an Old Tradition," *HC*, December 19, 2004, <http://continuum.uta.edu> (accessed January 3, 2005).

9 See Dávalos, "*La Quinceañera*," and Dávalos, " 'The Real Way of Praying': The Via Crucis, *Mexicano* Sacred Space, and the Architecture of Domination," in Matovina and Riebe-Estrella, ed., *Horizons of the Sacred*, 41–68.

10 Julie Salamon, "Celebrating Mexican Life in New York," *New York Times*, December 8, 2004, <http://www.nytimes.com/2004/12/08/arts/08mexc.html> (accessed December 8, 2004).

11 Luis D. León, " '*Soy una Curandera y soy una Católica*': The Poetics of a Mexican Healing Tradition," in Matovina and Riebe-Estrella, ed., *Horizons of the Sacred*, 95–118, quotes on 115. See also David McLemore, "Day of the Dead Becoming Increasingly Commercialized," *Dallas Morning News*, October 25, 1999, 17A, 20A.

12 Quoted in Salamon, "Celebrating Mexican Life in New York."

13 Sandoval, "Organization of a Hispanic Church," 142–43; Díaz-Stevens and Stevens-Arroyo, *Recognizing the Latino Resurgence*, 172–73.

14 Díaz-Stevens and Stevens-Arroyo, *Recognizing the Latino Resurgence*, 172–76; Sandoval, *On the Move*, 82–83; Poyo, " 'Integration Without Assimilation,' " 106.

15 Díaz-Stevens and Stevens-Arroyo, *Recognizing the Latino Resurgence*, 175.

16 Sandoval, "Organization of a Hispanic Church," 144.

17 Sandoval, *On the Move*, 82–83; Díaz-Stevens and Stevens-Arroyo, *Recognizing the Latino Resurgence*, 189–91.

18 Sandoval, "Organization of a Hispanic Church," 145.

19 Sandoval, *On the Move*, 83.

20 Secretariat for Hispanic Affairs, "Encuentro 2000," June 3, 2003, <http://www.usccb.org/hispanicaffairs/encuentro.htm> (accessed April 4, 2004); Araceli M. Cantero, "*Encuentro 2000 celebró la diversidad*," *La Voz Católica*, <http://www.vozcatolica.org/31/particip.htm> (accessed April 4, 2004); Agostino Bono, " 'Encuentro 2000' Gets Underway in Los Angeles," *Denver Catholic Register*, 12 July 2000, <http://www.archden.org/dcr/archive/20000712/2000071204wn

.htm> (accessed April 4, 2004); Pamela Schaeffer, "Catholics Show Their Diversity," *National Catholic Reporter*, 28 July 2000, <http://www.findarticles.com/cf—dls/m1141/35—36/63973888/print.jhtml> (accessed April 4, 2004).

21 Bono, "'Encuentro 2000' Gets Underway"; Schaeffer, "Catholics Show Their Diversity."

22 Stevens-Arroyo, "Emergence of a Social Identity," 13–15; Matovina, "Representation and the Reconstruction of Power," 226–27, quote on 226.

23 Stevens-Arroyo, "Emergence of a Social Identity," 115–17; Edmundo Rodríguez, "Hispanic Community," 225–27, quote on 227.

24 On Las Hermanas see the groundbreaking study Medina, *Las Hermanas*.

25 Matovina, "Representation and the Reconstruction of Power," 229–33.

26 Fiorenza interview; Guillén 2004 interview; Juan and Isidra Rodríguez interview; Julia Duin, "The Hispanic Exodus: Thousands Abandon Catholic Church for Other Faiths," *HC*, September 16, 1989, and Richard Vara, "The Spanish-Speaking Spirit: Growth among Hispanic Pentecostal Churches Continuing," *HC*, March 29, 1997, both at <http://continuum.uta.edu> (accessed August 4, 2004). Quote from the *New York Times* in Edwin H. Hernández, "Moving from the Cathedral to Storefront Churches," 216.

27 Edwin H. Hernández, "Moving from the Cathedral," 222; Díaz-Stevens and Stevens-Arroyo, *Recognizing the Latino Resurgence*, 35.

28 Díaz-Stevens and Stevens-Arroyo, *Recognizing the Latino Resurgence*, 190–91; Jay P. Dolan, *Hispanic Catholic Culture in the U.S.*, 449–50. Dolan sees the creation of a Latino church within the U.S. church as something that "far surpasses in scope and permanence" what large and well-established ethnic groups like Poles and Germans were able to achieve despite their prominence in U.S. Catholic history.

29 Fiorenza interview; Cecile Holmes White, "New Prelate to Serve Houston Diocese: A Bilingual, Bicultural Bishop," *HC*, January 30, 1993; Cecile Holmes White, "Catholics Plan Hispanic Outreach," *HC*, June 18, 1994; Richard Vara, "Se Habla Espanol: AUXILIARY CATHOLIC BISHOP SIGN OF GROWING HISPANIC INFLUENCE," *HC*, February 9, 2002; and Larry B. Stammer and Richard Vara, "U.S. Bishops Give More Attention to Hispanics," *HC*, November 16, 2002, all available at <http://continuum.uta.edu> (accessed August 4, 2004). See also Rossi and May, eds., *Recall, Rejoice, Renew*, 102–4.

30 Riebe-Estrella, "Strategies on the Left," 205, 215.

31 Díaz-Stevens and Stevens-Arroyo, *Recognizing the Latino Resurgence*, 202, 214–15.

32 Jim Morris, "TMO Gets More Clout with Age," *HC*, October 14, 1990, <http://

continuum.uta.edu> (accessed August 3, 2004); Betty L. Martin, "TMO Leaders Speak Up, Extract Officials' Plans," *HC*, March 18, 2004, <http://continuum.uta.edu> (accessed January 3, 2005). See also Kim Cobb, "East End Residents Oppose Plans to Build Trash Burner," *HC*, February 5, 1987, <http://continuum.uta.edu> (accessed August 4, 2004); Stephen Johnson, "TROUBLE WITHIN, TROUBLE WITHOUT: Cantinas Spill Violence and Noise into Surrounding Neighborhoods," *HC*, June 24, 1991; "Politicians Get Religion at Meeting: Church Leaders Seek Help on Social Issues," *HC*, May 7, 2001, <http://continuum.uta.edu> (accessed August 3, 2004); Fiorenza interview; and Guillén 2004 interview. On the history of TMO in Houston, see Mary Beth Rogers, *Cold Anger*, and Warren, *Dry Bones Rattling*, 61–65.

33   Betty L. Martin, "El Dorado Neighbors Want to Take Back Their Streets," *HC*, November 20, 2003, <http://continuum.uta.edu> (accessed August 3, 2004); Jo Ann Zúñiga, "James D. Steffes, 66, 'Unusually Dedicated'" (obituary), *HC*, September 26, 2001, <http://continuum.uta.edu> (accessed August 3, 2004); Guillén 2004 interview.

34   Díaz-Stevens and Stevens-Arroyo, *Recognizing the Latino Resurgence*, 205–10; Edwin H. Hernández, "Moving from the Cathedral," 232–34. See also Arlene M. Sánchez Walsh, *Latino Pentecostal Identity*.

35   Díaz-Stevens and Stevens-Arroyo, *Recognizing the Latino Resurgence*, 206–7.

36   Ibid., 209–10.

37   Ibid., 206.

38   Levitt, "Two Nations under God?" 157.

BIBLIOGRAPHY

ARCHIVAL AND MANUSCRIPT SOURCES

Austin, Texas
    Catholic Archives of Texas
        Diary of Father Frank Urbanovsky
        Diocesan Chancery Collection
        Episcopal Collection
        PADRES Collection
        Parish Collection
        Women Religious Orders Collection

Chicago, Illinois
    Archives of Loyola University of Chicago
        American Board of Catholic Missions *Reports*
        Catholic Church Extension Society Records

Houston, Texas
    Archives of the Diocese of Galveston-Houston
        Blessed Sacrament Parish Files
        Immaculate Conception Parish Files
        Our Lady of Guadalupe Parish Files
        Our Lady of St. John Parish Files
        Our Lady of Sorrows Parish Files
        St. Alphonsus Parish Files
        St. Joseph–St. Stephen Parish Files
        St. Patrick Parish Files
        St. Philip Parish Files
        St. Raphael Parish Files
        St. Stephen Parish Files
        Texas Catholic Herald Photograph Files

Houston Metropolitan Research Center, Houston Public Library
    Leonel Castillo Collection
    Hector García Collection
    Melesio Gómez Family Collection
    Petra Guillén Family Collection
    Franklin Harbach Papers
    Medellín Family Collection
    Mexican American Family and Photograph Collection
    Mexican American Small Collections
    Juan P. Rodríguez Family Collection
    Joe Torres / Huelga Schools Collection
    Ramón and Delfina Villagómez Family Collection
    VISTA Collection

San Antonio, Texas
    Archives of the Archdiocese of San Antonio
        Religious Congregations of Women Collections
    Archives of the Congregation of Divine Providence
        Catechists File
        Our Lady of Guadalupe Parish (Houston) File
        St. Patrick School (Houston) File
    Archives of the Oblates of Mary Immaculate
        Codex Historicus of Our Lady of Guadalupe Parish (Houston)
        Codex Historicus of St. Patrick Parish (Houston)
        Immaculate Conception Parish (Houston) File
        Immaculate Heart of Mary Parish (Houston) File
        Oblata File
        Provincial Records
        File 8H59

Government Documents

U.S. Bureau of the Census. *Thirteenth Census of the United States, 1910. Population.* Vol. 3. Washington, D.C.: Government Printing Office, 1913.

——. *Fourteenth Census of the United States, 1920. Population.* Vol. 3. Washington, D.C.: Government Printing Office, 1923.

——. *Fifteenth Census of the United States, 1930. Population.* Vol. 3, pt. 2. Washington, D.C.: Government Printing Office, 1932.

——. *Fifteenth Census of the United States, 1930. Special Report on Foreign-Born White Families . . . with an Appendix Giving Statistics for Mexican, Indian, Chinese, and Japanese Families.* Vol. 6, supplement. Washington, D.C.: Government Printing Office, 1933.

——. *Sixteenth Census of the United States, 1940. Population.* Vol. 2, pt. 6. Washington, D.C.: Government Printing Office, 1943.

——. *Seventeenth Census of the United States, 1950. Population.* Vol. 2, pt. 43. Washington, D.C.: Government Printing Office, 1952.

——. *Eighteenth Census of the United States, 1960. Census Tracts, Houston, Texas.* Final Report PHC(1)-63. Washington, D.C.: Government Printing Office, 1962.

——. *Nineteenth Census of the United States, 1970. Population.* Vol. 1, pt. 45, sec. 1. Washington, D.C.: Government Printing Office, 1973.

INTERVIEWS

The original tape recordings and notes of oral history interviews conducted by the author are held in the Houston Metropolitan Research Center, Houston, Texas.

Bello, Reverend E. Z. Interview by Ruth T. Bello, August 12, 1986, Houston, Texas. Tape recording. Ruth T. Bello Collection. Houston Metropolitan Research Center, Houston, Texas.

Cárdenas, Sister Mary Dolores. Interview by the author, April 17, 1990, San Antonio, Texas. Tape recording.

Fiorenza, Bishop Joseph A. Interview by the author, July 30, 2004, Houston, Texas. Tape recording.

García, Mrs. Esther. Director, Galveston-Houston Diocese Office of Hispanic Ministries. Interview by the author, November 14, 1990, Houston, Texas. Tape recording.

——. Interview by the author, June 3, 1992, Redwood City, California. Telephone interview.

Gonzales, Joe E., Raquel A. Gonzales, and anonymous participant. Interview by the author, December 16, 1990, Houston, Texas. Tape recording.

Guillén, Mrs. Petra R. Interview by the author, October 22, 1990, Houston, Texas. Tape recording.

——. Interview by the author, June 16, 1992, Redwood City, California. Telephone interview.

——. Interview by the author, July 29, 2004, Houston, Texas. Tape recording.

McCarthy, Bishop John E. Interview by the author, October 18, 1991, Austin, Texas. Tape recording.

——. Interview by Jan H. Cohen, March 10, 1972, Houston, Texas. OH 27, Texas Labor Archives, University of Texas at Arlington Special Collections Division.

Moreno, Sister Mary Rachel. Interview by the author, April 18, 1990, San Antonio, Texas. Typescript.

Novarro, Reverend James. Interview by Thomas H. Kreneck, December 13, 1984. Tape recording. Houston Metropolitan Research Center Oral History Collection, Houston, Texas.

Rodríguez, Sister Agnes Rita. Interview by Diana Torres. N.d. Mexican American Studies Oral History Collection, Our Lady of the Lake University, San Antonio, Texas.

Rodríguez, Juan and Isidra. Interview by the author, July 29, 2004, Houston, Texas. Tape recording.

Urbanovsky, Father Frank. Interview by Thomas H. Kreneck, 1979. Tape recording. Houston Metropolitan Research Center Oral History Collection, Houston, Texas.

Villagómez, Mary C. Interviews by the author, October 25 and November 9, 1990, Houston, Texas. Tape recording.

——. Interview by the author, June 3, 1992, Redwood City, California. Telephone interview.

Zavala, Mrs. Teresa Villagómez, and Mrs. Hope G. Jiménez. Interview by the author, December 12, 1990, Houston, Texas. Tape recording.

PERIODICALS

Compass, Houston, Texas, 1967–69, 1972.

Dallas Morning News, June 25, July 11, 2001.

El Puerto, Houston, Texas, 1959.

El Sol, Houston, Texas, 1968–72.

Extension Magazine (Catholic Church Extension Society), 1907–68 ca.

Family Circular (Sisters of Divine Providence newsletter), 1912–60.

Gazette Telegraph, Colorado Springs, Colorado, May 18, 1996.

Houston Chronicle, Houston, Texas, 1910–72.

La Gaceta Mexicana, Houston, Texas, April 15, June 1, 1928.

Mary Immaculate (Oblate Fathers' magazine), 1915–67.

National Catholic Reporter, Kansas City, Missouri, 1964–72.

Papel Chicano, Houston, Texas, 1970–72.

Southern Messenger, San Antonio, Texas, September 19, 1912, June 23, 1938, and November 2, 1950.

Star-Telegram, Fort Worth, Texas, May 11, 2001.

Books, Articles, Essays, and Pamphlets

Abramson, Harold J. *Ethnic Diversity in Catholic America.* New York: John Wiley & Sons, 1973.

Acuña, Rodolfo. *Occupied America: A History of Chicanos.* 3d ed. New York: Harper Collins, 1988.

Ahlstrom, Sidney E. *A Religious History of the American People.* New Haven, CT: Yale University Press, 1972.

Alba, Richard D. *Ethnic Identity: The Transformation of White America.* New Haven, CT: Yale University Press, 1990.

Alexander, June Granatir. "Religion and Ethnic Identity in a Slavic Community: Pittsburg's Slovak Catholics and Protestants." *Studi Emigrazione* 103 (September 1991): 423–41.

Allen, Ruth A. *East Texas Lumber Workers: An Economic and Social Picture, 1870–1950.* Austin: University of Texas Press, 1961.

Anderson, Karen. *Wartime Women: Sex Roles, Family Relations, and the Status of Women during World War II.* Westport, CT: Greenwood Press, 1981.

Armstrong, Reverend Walter W. *Room to Grow: A History of Houston Methodist Missions.* Houston, TX: privately printed, 1963.

Badillo, David A. "The Catholic Church and the Making of Mexican-American Parish Communities in the Midwest." In *Mexican Americans and the Catholic Church, 1900–1965,* edited by Jay P. Dolan and Gilberto M. Hinojosa, 235–308. Notre Dame, IN: University of Notre Dame Press, 1994.

Baer, Hans A., and Merrill Singer, *African-American Religion in the Twentieth Century: Varieties of Protest and Accommodation.* Knoxville: University of Tennessee Press, 1992.

Balderrama, Francisco E., and Raymond Rodríguez, *Decade of Betrayal: Mexican Repatriation in the 1930s.* Albuquerque: University of New Mexico Press, 1995.

Barton, Josef J. "Land, Labor, and Community in Nueces: Czech Farmers and Mexican Laborers in South Texas, 1880–1930." In *Ethnicity on the Great Plains,* edited by Frederick C. Luebke, 190–209. Lincoln: University of Nebraska Press, 1980.

Bass, Dorothy C., and Sandra Hughes Boyd. *Women in American Religious History: An Annotated Bibliography and Guide to Sources.* Boston: G. K. Hall, 1986.

Basso, Sister Teresita. "The Emerging 'Chicana' Sister." *Review for Religious* 30 (1971): 1019–28.

Bayard, Ralph. *Lone Star Vanguard: The Catholic Re-occupation of Texas, 1838–1848.* St. Louis: Vincentian Press, 1945.

Bean, Frank D., and Marta Tienda. "The Structuring of Hispanic Ethnicity: Theoretical and Historical Considerations." In *The Hispanic Population of the United States*, edited by Frank D. Bean and Marta Tienda, 7–35. New York: Sage, 1987.

Beeth, Howard, and Cary D. Wintz, eds. *Black Dixie: Afro-Texan History and Culture in Houston*. College Station: Texas A&M University Press, 1992.

Bogardus, Emory S. *The Mexican in the United States*. Los Angeles: University of Southern California Press, 1934; reprint, San Francisco: R & E Research Associates, 1970.

Bornstein, Daniel E. *The Bianchi of 1399: Popular Devotion in Late Medieval Italy*. Ithaca, NY: Cornell University Press, 1993.

Boyer, Paul, and Janet Wilson James, eds. *Women in American Religion*. Philadelphia: University of Pennsylvania Press, 1980.

Brackenridge, R. Douglas, and Francisco O. García-Treto, *Iglesia Presbiteriana: A History of Presbyterians and Mexican Americans in the Southwest*, 2nd ed. San Antonio, TX: Trinity University Press, 1987.

Bresette, Linna E. *Mexicans in the United States: A Report of a Brief Survey*. Washington, D.C.: National Catholic Welfare Conference, 1929.

Bronder, Saul E. *Social Justice and Church Authority: The Public Life of Archbishop Robert E. Lucey*. Philadelphia: Temple University Press, 1982.

Brown, Dorothy M., and Elizabeth McKeown. *The Poor Belong to Us: Catholic Charities and American Welfare*. Cambridge, MA: Harvard University Press, 1997.

Bullard, Robert D. *Invisible Houston: The Black Experience in Boom and Bust*. College Station: Texas A&M University Press, 1987.

Burns, Jeffrey M. "The Mexican American Catholic Community in California, 1850–1980." In *Religion and Society in the American West: Historical Essays*, edited by Carl Guarneri and David Álvarez, 255–73. Lantham, MD: University Press of America, 1987.

——. "The Mexican Catholic Community in California." In *Mexican Americans and the Catholic Church, 1900–1965*, edited by Jay P. Dolan and Gilberto M. Hinojosa, 129–233. Notre Dame, IN: University of Notre Dame Press, 1994.

Butler, Jon. "The Future of American Religious History: Prospectus, Agenda, Transatlantic Problematique." *William and Mary Quarterly* 42 (April 1985): 167–83.

——. "Historiographical Heresy: Catholicism as a Model for American Religious History." In *Belief in History: Innovative Approaches to European and American Religion*, edited by Thomas Kselman, 286–309. Notre Dame, IN: University of Notre Dame Press, 1991.

Camarillo, Albert. *Chicanos in a Changing Society: From Mexican Pueblos to American*

Barrios in Santa Barbara and Southern California, 1848–1930. Cambridge, MA: Harvard University Press, 1979.

Cárdenas, Sr. Mary Dolores. *Meditaciones.* San Antonio: Our Lady of the Lake Convent, 1976.

Cardoso, Lawrence A. *Mexican Emigration to the United States, 1897–1931.* Tucson: University of Arizona Press, 1980.

Carrillo, Alberto. "The Sociological Failure of the Catholic Church towards the Chicano." *Journal of Mexican American Studies* 1 (Winter 1971): 75–83.

Carroll, Michael P. *The Penitente Brotherhood: Patriarchy and Hispano-Catholicism in New Mexico.* Baltimore, MD: Johns Hopkins University Press, 2002.

Castañeda, Carlos E. "The Missionary Years in Texas." In *Centennial: The Story of the Development of the Kingdom of God on Earth in that Portion of the Vineyard Which for One Hundred Years Has Been the Diocese of Galveston,* by the Catholic Youth Organization Centennial Book Committee, 23–27. Houston, TX: Diocese of Galveston, 1947.

——. *Our Catholic Heritage in Texas.* 7 vols. Austin: Von Boeckmann-Jones, 1936–58.

Catholic Youth Organization Centennial Book Committee. *Centennial: The Story of the Development of the Kingdom of God on Earth in that Portion of the Vineyard Which for One Hundred Years Has Been the Diocese of Galveston.* Houston, TX: Diocese of Galveston, 1947.

Christian, William A., Jr. *Local Religion in Sixteenth-Century Spain.* Princeton, NJ: Princeton University Press, 1981.

Clark, Victor S. "Mexican Labor in the United States." *Bulletin of the Bureau of Labor* 17 (September 1908): 466–522. Reprinted in *Mexican Labor in the United States,* edited by Carlos E. Cortés. New York: Arno, 1974.

Coatsworth, John H. *Growth Against Development: The Economic Impact of Railroads in Porfirian Mexico.* Dekalb: Northern Illinois University Press, 1981.

Coburn, Carol K., and Martha Smith, C.S.J. "Creating Community and Identity: Exploring Religious and Gender Ideology in the Lives of American Women Religious, 1836–1920." *U.S. Catholic Historian* 14, no. 1 (Winter 1996): 91–108.

——. *Spirited Lives: How Nuns Shaped Catholic Culture and American Life, 1836–1920.* Chapel Hill: University of North Carolina Press, 1999.

Cohen, Gary B. "Ethnic Persistence and Change: Concepts and Models for Historical Research." *Social Science Quarterly* 65 (December 1984): 1029–42.

Collins, Donna Misner. *Ethnic Identification: The Greek Americans of Houston, Texas.* New York: AMS Press, 1991.

Connor, Seymour V. *Texas: A History.* Arlington Heights, IL: AHM Publishing, 1971.

Conzen, Kathleen Neils, et al. "The Invention of Ethnicity: A Perspective from the U.S.A." *Journal of American Ethnic History* 12 (Fall 1992): 3–41.

Cortés, Carlos E., ed. *Church Views of the Mexican American*. New York: Arno, 1974.

———. *Mexican Labor in the United States*. New York: Arno, 1974.

———. *Protestantism and Latinos in the United States*. New York: Arno, 1980.

Cox, Harvey G. "The 'New Breed' in American Churches: Sources of Social Activism in American Religion." *Daedalus* (Winter 1967): 135–50.

Crocker, Ruth Hutchinson. "Gary Mexicans and 'Christian Americanization': A Study in Cultural Conflict." In *Forging a Community: The Latino Experience in Northwest Indiana, 1919–1975*, edited by James B. Lane and Edward J. Escobar, 115–34. Chicago: Cattails Press, 1987.

Dávalos, Karen Mary. "*La Quinceañera*: Making Gender and Ethnic Identities." *Frontiers* 16, nos. 2 / 3 (1996): 101–27.

Davidson, Chandler. *Biracial Politics: Conflict and Coalition in the Metropolitan South*. Baton Rouge: Louisiana State University Press, 1972.

Davis, Natalie Zemon. "From 'Popular Religion' to Religious Cultures." In *Reformation Europe: A Guide to Research*, edited by Steven Ozment, 321–41. St. Louis: Center for Reformation Research, 1982.

———. "Some Tasks and Themes in the Study of Popular Religion." In *The Pursuit of Holiness in Late Medieval and Renaissance Religion*, edited by Charles Trinkaus and Heiko A. Oberman, 307–36. Leiden, Netherlands: E. J. Brill, 1974.

Deck, Allan Figueroa. *The Second Wave: Hispanic Ministry and the Evangelization of Cultures*. New York: Paulist Press, 1989.

———. "The Spirituality of United States Hispanics: An Introductory Essay." *U.S. Catholic Historian* 9 (Spring 1990): 137–46.

"Dedicated to Community Action." In *Harris County PASO 5th Anniversary and Salute to Valley Farm Workers*, unnumbered. Houston, TX: Harris County PASO, 1966.

De la Teja, Jesús F. *San Antonio de Béxar: A Community on New Spain's Northern Frontier*. Albuquerque: University of New Mexico Press, 1995.

De León, Arnoldo. *Ethnicity in the Sunbelt: A History of Mexican Americans in Houston*. Houston, TX: University of Houston, Mexican American Studies, 1989.

———. *Mexican Americans in Texas: A Brief History*. Arlington Heights, IL: Harlan Davidson, 1993.

———. *Racial Frontiers: Africans, Chinese, and Mexicans in Western America, 1848–1890*. Albuquerque: University of New Mexico Press, 2002.

———. *The Tejano Community, 1836–1900*. Albuquerque: University of New Mexico Press, 1982.

———. *They Called Them Greasers: Anglo Attitudes toward Mexicans in Texas, 1821–1900.* Austin: University of Texas Press, 1983.

Deutsch, Sarah. *No Separate Refuge: Culture, Class, and Gender on an Anglo-Hispanic Frontier in the American Southwest, 1880–1940.* New York: Oxford University Press, 1987.

Díaz-Stevens, Ana María. *Oxcart Catholicism on Fifth Avenue: The Impact of the Puerto Rican Migration upon the Archdiocese of New York.* Notre Dame, IN: University of Notre Dame Press, 1993.

Díaz-Stevens, Ana María, and Anthony M. Stevens-Arroyo. *Recognizing the Latino Resurgence in U.S. Religion: The Emmaus Paradigm.* Boulder, CO: Westview Press, 1998.

Diekemper, Barnabas C. "The Catholic Church in the Shadows: The Southwestern United States during the Mexican Period." *Journal of the West* 24 (1985): 46–53.

———. "French Clergy on the Texas Frontier, 1837–1907." *East Texas Historical Journal* 21 (Fall 1983): 29–38.

Dolan, Jay P. *The American Catholic Experience: A History from Colonial Times to the Present.* Garden City, NJ: Doubleday, 1985.

———. "The New Religious History." *Reviews in American History* 15 (September 1987): 449–54.

———. "The People as Well as the Prelates: A Social History of a Denomination." In *Reimagining Denominationalism: Interpretive Essays*, edited by Robert Bruce Mullin and Russell E. Richey, 43–57. New York: Oxford University Press, 1994.

———. "Religion and Social Change in the American Catholic Community." In *Altered Landscapes: Christianity in America, 1935–1985*, edited by David W. Lotz, 42–60. Grand Rapids, MI: Eerdmans, 1989.

———, ed. *The American Catholic Parish.* 2 vols. Mahwah, NJ: Paulist Press, 1987.

Dolan, Jay P., and Allan Figueroa Deck, eds. *Hispanic Catholic Culture in the U.S.: Issues and Concerns.* Notre Dame, IN: University of Notre Dame Press, 1994.

Dolan, Jay P., and Gilberto M. Hinojosa, eds. *Mexican Americans and the Catholic Church, 1900–1965.* Notre Dame, IN: University of Notre Dame Press, 1994.

Dolan, Jay P., and Jaime R. Vidal, eds. *Puerto Rican and Cuban Catholics in the U.S.: 1900–1965.* Notre Dame, IN: University of Notre Dame Press, 1994.

Doyon, Bernard. *The Cavalry of Christ on the Río Grande, 1849–1883.* Milwaukee: Bruce Press, 1956.

Dunn, Ethel, and Stephen P. Dunn. "Religion and Ethnicity: The Case of the American Molokans." *Ethnicity* 4 (1977): 370–79.

Elizondo, Rev. Virgilio P. *Galilean Journey: The Mexican-American Promise.* Maryknoll, NY: Orbis, 1983.

———. *Guadalupe: Mother of the New Creation*. Maryknoll, NY: Orbis Books, 1997.

———. *La Morenita: Evangelizer of the Americas*. San Antonio: Mexican American Cultural Center, 1980.

Erevia, Sr. Angela. *Quinceañera*. San Antonio: Mexican American Cultural Center, 1980.

Espín, Orlando O. "Popular Catholicism among Latinos." In *Hispanic Catholic Culture in the U.S.: Issues and Concerns*, edited by Jay P. Dolan and Allan Figueroa Deck, 308–59. Notre Dame, IN: University of Notre Dame Press, 1994.

Evans, Bernard F. "Campaign for Human Development: Church Involvement in Social Change." *Review of Religious Research* 20 (Summer 1979): 264–78.

Feagin, Joe R. *Free Enterprise City: Houston in Political-Economic Perspective*. New Brunswick, NJ: Rutgers University Press, 1988.

Fitzmorris, Sr. Mary Angela. *Four Decades of Catholicism in Texas, 1820–1860*. Washington, D.C.: Catholic University of America Press, 1926.

Flores, Richard R. *Los Pastores: History and Performance in the Mexican Shepherd's Play of South Texas*. Washington, D.C.: Smithsonian Institution Press, 1995.

Flores, Fr. Roberto, and Silvia Novo-Pena. *Interiores: Aspectos Seculares de la Religión*. Houston, TX: D. H. White, 1982.

Foley, Neil. "Becoming Hispanic: Mexican Americans and the Faustian Pact with Whiteness." In *New Directions in Mexican American Studies* (1997). Publications of the Center for Mexican American Studies. Austin: University of Texas Press, 1998.

———. *The White Scourge: Mexicans, Blacks, and Poor Whites in Texas Cotton Culture*. Berkeley: University of California Press, 1997.

Forbes, Jack D. "Race and Color in Mexican-American Problems." *Journal of Human Relations* 16 (1968): 55–68.

Galarza, Ernesto. *Merchants of Labor: The Mexican Bracero Story*. Santa Barbara, CA: McNally & Loftin, 1964.

———. *The Roman Catholic Church as a Factor in the Political and Social History of Mexico*. Sacramento, CA: Capital Press, 1928.

Gamio, Manuel. *The Mexican Immigrant: His Life Story*. Chicago: University of Chicago Press, 1931; reprinted as *The Life Story of the Mexican Immigrant*, New York: Dover Publications, 1971.

———. *Mexican Immigration to the United States*. Chicago: University of Chicago Press 1930; reprint, New York: Dover Publications, 1971.

García, Alma M., ed. *Chicana Feminist Thought: The Basic Historical Writings*. New York: Routledge, 1997.

García, Ignacio M. *Chicanismo: The Forging of a Militant Ethos among Mexican Americans*. Tucson: University of Arizona Press, 1997.

——. *United We Win: The Rise and Fall of La Raza Unida Party*. Tucson: University of Arizona, Mexican American Studies, 1989.

García, Juan Ramón. *Operation Wetback: The Mass Deportation of Mexican Undocumented Workers in 1954*. Westport, CT: Greenwood Press, 1980.

García, Juan R., and Ángel Cal. "El Círculo de Obreros Católicos 'San José,' 1925 to 1930." In *Forging a Community: The Latino Experience in Northwest Indiana, 1919–1975*, edited by James B. Lane and Edward J. Escobar, 95–114. Chicago: Cattails Press, 1987.

García, María Cristina. "Agents of Americanization: Rusk Settlement and the Houston Mexicano Community, 1907–1950." In *Mexican Americans in Texas History: Selected Essays*, edited by Emilio Zamora, Cynthia Orozco, and Rodolfo Rocha, 121–37. Austin: Texas State Historical Society, 2000.

García, Mario T. *Desert Immigrants: The Mexicans of El Paso, 1880–1920*. New Haven, CT: Yale University Press, 1981.

——. *Memories of Chicano History: The Life and Narrative of Bert Corona*. Berkeley and Los Angeles: University of California Press, 1994.

——. *Mexican Americans: Leadership, Ideology, and Identity*. New Haven, CT: Yale University Press, 1989.

García, Richard A. "The Mexican American Mind: A Product of the 1930s." In *History, Culture, and Society: Chicano Studies in the 1980s*, edited by Mario T. García and Francisco Lomelí, 67–93. Ypsilanti, MI: Bilingual Press, 1983.

——. *The Rise of the Mexican American Middle Class: San Antonio, 1929–1941*. College Station: Texas A&M University Press, 1991.

Genovese, Eugene D. *Roll, Jordan, Roll: The World the Slaves Made*. New York: Random House, 1972.

Gibson, Margaret A. *Accommodation Without Assimilation: Sikh Immigrants in an American High School*. Ithaca, NY: Cornell University Press, 1988.

Giles, Robert C. *Changing Times: The Story of the Diocese of Galveston Houston in Commemoration of Its Founding*. N.p.: Diocese of Galveston-Houston, [1972].

Gleason, Philip. "Immigrant Assimilation and the Crisis of Americanization." Chap. 3 in *Keeping the Faith: American Catholicism Past and Present*. Notre Dame, IN: University of Notre Dame Press, 1987.

Goizueta, Roberto S. *Caminemos con Jesús: Toward a Hispanic/Latino Theology of Accompaniment*. Maryknoll, NY: Orbis, 1995.

Gómez-Quiñones, Juan. *Chicano Politics: Reality and Promise, 1940–1990*. Albuquerque: University of New Mexico Press, 1990.

Goodman, Mary Ellen, et al. *The Mexican-American Population of Houston: A Survey of the Field, 1965–1970*. Houston, TX: Rice University Studies, 1971.

Gordon, Linda. "Putting Children First: Women, Maternalism, and Welfare in the Early Twentieth Century." In *U.S. History as Women's History: New Feminist Essays*, edited by Linda K. Kerber, Alice Kessler-Harris, and Kathryn Kish-Sklar, 63–86. Chapel Hill: University of North Carolina Press, 1995.

Gossett, Thomas F. *Race: The History of an Idea in America*. Dallas: Southern Methodist University Press, 1963.

Grebler, Leo, Joan W. Moore, and Ralph C. Guzmán. *The Mexican-American People: The Nation's Second Largest Minority*. New York: Free Press, 1970.

Griffin, Sister Janet, C.D.P. "Sisters of Divine Providence: Feminists in Ministry." Article on-line. Available from <http://www.cdptexas.org/reflections/Feminists—in—Ministry.html>. Accessed April 16, 2003.

Griswold del Castillo, Richard. *La Familia: Chicano Families in the Urban Southwest, 1848 to the Present*. Notre Dame, IN: University of Notre Dame, 1984.

Guarneri, Carl, and David Álvarez, eds. *Religion and Society in the American West: Historical Essays*. Lantham, MD: University Press of America, 1987.

Guerra, Roberto S., and Mary Ellen Goodman. *A Content Assessment of "El Sol," a Community Newspaper*. Houston, TX: Rice University Center for Research in Social Change and Economic Development, 1968.

Gutiérrez, David G. *Walls and Mirrors: Mexican Americans, Mexican Immigrants, and the Politics of Ethnicity*. Berkeley and Los Angeles: University of California Press, 1995.

Hackett, David G. "Sociology of Religion and American Religious History." *Journal for the Scientific Study of Religion* 27 (1988): 461–74.

Hall, David D., ed. *Lived Religion in America: Toward a History of Practice*. Princeton, NJ: Princeton University Press, 1997.

Halter, Marilyn. *Between Race and Ethnicity: Cape Verdean American Immigrants, 1860–1965*. Urbana: University of Illinois Press, 1993.

Harrington, Patricia. "Mother of Death, Mother of Rebirth: The Mexican Virgin of Guadalupe." *Journal of the American Academy of Religion* 56 (Spring 1988): 25–50.

Harte, Thomas J. "Racial and National Parishes in the United States." In *The Sociology of the Parish*, edited by C. J. Nuesse and Thomas J. Harte, 154–77. Milwaukee: Bruce, 1951.

Hegarty, Sr. Mary Loyola. *Serving with Gladness*. Milwaukee: Bruce, 1967.

Hernández, Edwin H. "Moving from the Cathedral to Storefront Churches: Under-standing Religious Growth and Decline among Latino Protestants." In *Protes-tantes / Protestants: Hispanic Christianity Within Mainline Traditions*, edited by David Maldonado Jr., 216–35. Nashville, TN: Abingdon, 1999.

Hernández, José A. *Mutual Aid for Survival: The Case of the Mexican American*. Mal-abar, FL: Krieger Publishing, 1983.

Herrera, Marina. "The Context and Development of Hispanic Ecclesial Leadership." In *Hispanic Catholic Culture in the U.S.: Issues and Concerns*, edited by Jay P. Dolan and Allan Figueroa Deck, 166–205. Notre Dame, IN: University of Notre Dame Press, 1994.

"Hidden Houston: The City You See on the Surface Is Not All the City There Is." Interview of Petra Guillén by David Theis. *Cite: The Architectural and Design Re-view of Houston* 50 (Spring 2001): 24.

Higham, John. "Current Trends in the Study of Ethnicity in the United States." *Jour-nal of American Ethnic History* 2 (Fall 1982): 5–15.

Hinojosa, Gilberto M. "The Enduring Hispanic Faith Communities: Spanish and Texas Church Historiography." *Journal of Texas Catholic History and Culture* 1 (March 1990): 20–41.

———. "Mexican-American Faith Communities in Texas and the Southwest." In *Mexican Americans and the Catholic Church, 1900–1965*, edited by Jay P. Dolan and Gilberto M. Hinojosa, 9–125. Notre Dame, IN: University of Notre Dame Press, 1994.

Hoffman, Abraham. *Unwanted Mexican Americans in the Great Depression*. Tucson: University of Arizona Press, 1974.

Hough, Richard L. "Religion and Pluralism among the Spanish-Speaking Groups of the Southwest." In *Politics and Society in the Southwest: Ethnicity and Chicano Plu-ralism*, edited by Z. Anthony Kruszewski, Richard L. Hough, and Jacob Ornstein-Galicia, 169–95. Boulder, CO: Westview Press, 1982.

Isais-A., Raoul E. "The Chicano and the American Catholic Church." *El Grito del Sol* 4 (Winter 1979): 9–24.

Isasi-Díaz, Ada María, and Yolanda Tarango. *Hispanic Women, Prophetic Voice in the Church*. San Francisco: Harper & Row, 1988.

Jordan, Terry G. "A Century and a Half of Ethnic Change in Texas, 1836–1986." *Southwestern Historical Quarterly* 89 (April 1986): 385–422.

———. "The 1887 Census of Texas' Hispanic Population." *Aztlán* 12 (Autumn 1981): 271–78.

Journal of the West 23 (January 1984). Special issue on religion.

Juárez, José Roberto. "La Iglesia Católica y el Chicano en Sud Texas, 1836–1911." *Aztlán* 4 (Fall 1974): 217–55.

———. "*Los Padres Rancheristas*: The 19th-Century Struggle for Mexican-American Catholicism in South Texas." In *Ranching in South Texas: A Symposium*, edited by Joe S. Graham, 15–43. Kingsville: Texas A&M University, 1994.

Kaplan, Barry J. "Houston, the Golden Buckle of the Southwest." In *Sunbelt Cities: Politics and Growth Since World War II*, edited by Richard A. Bernard and Bradley R. Rice, 196–212. Austin: University of Texas Press, 1983.

Kelley, Rev. Francis C. *The Story of Extension*. Chicago: Extension Press, 1922.

Kennelly, Karen, ed. *American Catholic Women: A Historical Exploration*. New York: Macmillan, 1989.

Keyes, Charles F. "The Dialectics of Ethnic Change." In *Ethnic Change*, edited by Charles F. Keyes, 4–30. Seattle: University of Washington Press, 1981.

Kiev, Ari. *Curanderismo: Mexican-American Folk Psychiatry*. New York: Free Press, 1968.

Kiser, George C., and Martha Woody Kiser, eds. *Mexican Workers in the United States: Historical and Political Perspectives*. Albuquerque: University of New Mexico Press, 1979.

Kreneck, Thomas H. *Del Pueblo: A Pictorial History of Houston's Hispanic Community*. Houston, TX: Houston International University, 1989.

———. "The Letter from Chapultepec." *Houston Review* 3 (Summer 1981): 268–71.

———. *Mexican American Odyssey: Felix Tijerina, Entrepreneur and Civic Leader, 1905–1965*. University of Houston Series in Mexican American Studies, no. 2. College Station: Texas A&M University Press, 2001.

Kselman, Thomas. Introduction to *Belief in History: Innovative Approaches to European and American Religion*, edited by Thomas Kselman, 1–15. Notre Dame, IN: University of Notre Dame Press, 1991.

———, ed. *Belief in History: Innovative Approaches to European and American Religion*. Notre Dame, IN: University of Notre Dame Press, 1991.

"La Marcha . . . Valley Farm Workers 491-Mile March for Justice." In *Harris County PASO 5th Anniversary and Salute to Valley Farm Workers*, unnumbered. Houston, TX: Harris County PASO, 1966.

Lane, James B., and Edward J. Escobar. *Forging a Community: The Latino Experience in Northwest Indiana, 1919–1975*. Chicago: Cattails Press, 1987.

Larkin, Emmet. "The Devotional Revolution in Ireland, 1850–75." *American Historical Review* 77 (June 1972): 625–52.

Lasswell, Mary. *John Henry Kirby, Prince of the Pines*. Austin: Encino, 1967.

León, Luís. "Born Again in East LA: The Congregation as Border Space." In *Gatherings in Diaspora: Religious Communities and the New Immigration*, edited by R. Stephen Warner and Judith G. Witner, 163–96. Philadelphia: Temple University Press, 1998.

Leonard, Karen. "Historical Constructions of Ethnicity: Research on Punjabi Immigrants in California." *Journal of American Ethnic History* 12 (Summer 1993): 3–26.

Levine, Lawrence W. *Black Culture and Black Consciousness: African American Folk Thought from Slavery to Freedom*. New York: Oxford University Press, 1977.

Levitt, Peggy. "Two Nations under God?: Latino Religious Life in the United States." In *Latinos: Re-making America*, edited by Marcelo M. Súarez-Orozco and Mariela M. Páez, 150–64. Los Angeles: University of California Press, 2002.

Lincoln, C. Eric, and Lawrence H. Mamiya, *The Black Church in the African American Experience*. Durham, NC: Duke University Press, 1990.

Liptak, Dolores Ann. *Immigrants and Their Church*. New York: Macmillan, 1989.

———. "Lost Hopes for Blacks and Hispanic Catholics." Chap. 11 in *Immigrants and Their Church*. New York: Macmillan, 1989.

Listening: Journal of Religion and Culture 19 (Fall 1984). Special issue on religion in the American West.

Lotz, David W. "A Changing Historiography: From Church History to Religious History." In *Altered Landscapes: Christianity in America, 1935–1985*, edited by David W. Lotz, 312–39. Grand Rapids, MI: Eerdmans, 1989.

Maas, Elaine H. *The Jews of Houston: An Ethnographic Study*. New York: AMS Press, 1989.

Manuel, Herschel T. "The Mexican Population of Texas." *Southwestern Social Science Quarterly* 15 (June 1934): 29–51.

Martínez, Oscar J. "On the Size of the Chicano Population: New Estimates, 1850–1900." *Aztlán* 6 (Spring 1975): 43–67.

Marty, Martin E. "The Editors' Bookshelf: American Religious History." *Journal of Religion* 62 (January 1982): 99–109.

———. "Ethnicity: The Skeleton of Religion in America." *Church History* 41 (1972): 5–21.

———. "Introduction: Religion in America, 1935–1985." In *Altered Landscapes: Christianity in America, 1935–1985*, edited by David W. Lotz, 1–16. Grand Rapids, MI: Eerdmans, 1989.

"Maternalism as a Paradigm." A symposium in *Journal of Women's History* 5, no. 2 (Fall 1993): 95–131.

Matovina, Timothy M. "Representation and the Reconstruction of Power: The Rise of PADRES and *Las Hermanas.*" In *What's Left? Liberal American Catholics*, edited by Mary Jo Weaver, 220–37. Bloomington: Indiana University Press, 1999.

———. *Tejano Religion and Ethnicity: San Antonio, 1821–1860.* Austin: University of Texas Press, 1995.

Matovina, Timothy, and Gerald E. Poyo, eds., *¡Presente!: U.S. Latino Catholics from Colonial Origins to the Present.* Maryknoll, NY: Orbis, 2000.

Matovina, Timothy, and Gary Riebe-Estrella, SVD, eds. *Horizons of the Sacred: Mexican Traditions in U.S. Catholicism.* Ithaca, NY: Cornell University Press, 2002.

Matthews, Fred H. *Quest for an American Sociology: Robert E. Park and the Chicago School.* Montreal: McGill-Queen's University Press, 1977.

Matusow, Allen J. *The Unraveling of America: A History of Liberalism in the 1960s.* New York: Harper & Row, 1984.

May, Henry F. "The Recovery of American Religious History." *American Historical Review* 80 (October 1964): 79–92.

Mazón, Mauricio. *The Zoot-Suit Riots: The Psychology of Symbolic Annihilation.* Austin: University of Texas Press, 1984.

McComb, David G. *Houston, the Bayou City.* Austin: University of Texas Press, 1969.

McCombs, Rev. Vernon M. *From Over the Border: A Study of the Mexicans in the United States.* New York: Council of Women for Home Missions, 1925.

McDannell, Colleen. "Catholic Domesticity, 1860–1960." In *American Catholic Women: A Historical Exploration*, edited by Karen Kennelly, 48–80. New York: Macmillan, 1989.

McMurtrey, Martin. *Mariachi Bishop: The Life Story of Patrick Flores.* San Antonio: Corona, 1987.

McNally, Michael J. *Catholicism in South Florida, 1868–1968.* Gainesville: University of Florida Press, 1982.

———. *Catholic Parish Life on Florida's West Coast, 1860–1968.* N.p.: Catholic Media Ministries, 1996.

McNamara, Patrick H. "Social Action Priests in the Mexican American Community." *Sociological Analysis* 29 (1968): 177–85.

McWilliams, Carey. *North from Mexico: The Spanish-Speaking People of the United States.* Philadelphia: J. B. Lippincott, 1949; reprint, Westport, CT: Greenwood Press, 1968.

Medina, Lara. *Las Hermanas: Chicana/Latina Religious-Political Activism in the U.S. Catholic Church.* Philadelphia: Temple University Press, 2004.

Meier, Matt S. "María Insurgente." *Historia Mexicana* 23 (1974): 466–82.

Meier, Matt S., and Feliciano Rivera. *The Chicanos: A History of Mexican Americans.* New York: Hill & Wang, 1972.

Melville, Margarita B. "Ethnicity: An Analysis of Its Dynamism and Variability Focusing on the Mexican / Anglo / Mexican American Interface." *American Ethnologist* 10 (1983): 272–89.

———. "Hispanics: Race, Class, or Ethnicity?" *Journal of Ethnic Studies* 16 (1988): 67–83.

Meyer, Jean A. *The Cristero Rebellion: The Mexican People Between Church and State, 1926–1929.* Cambridge: Cambridge University Press, 1976.

Mirandé, Alfredo. *The Chicano Experience: An Alternative Perspective.* Notre Dame, IN: University of Notre Dame Press, 1985.

Mirandé, Alfredo, and Evangelina Enríquez. *La Chicana: The Mexican-American Woman.* Chicago: University of Chicago Press, 1979.

Montejano, David. *Anglos and Mexicans in the Making of Texas, 1836–1986.* Austin: University of Texas Press, 1987.

Moore, James Talmadge. *Through Fire and Flood: The Catholic Church in Frontier Texas, 1836–1900.* College Station: Texas A&M University Press, 1992.

Moore, R. Laurence. *Religious Outsiders and the Making of Americans.* New York: Oxford University Press, 1986.

Morgan, Edward P. *The Sixties Experience: Hard Lessons About Modern America.* Philadelphia: Temple University Press, 1991.

Mosqueda, Lawrence J. *Chicanos, Catholicism, and Political Ideology.* New York: University Press of America, 1986.

Muir, Andrew Forest. "Railroads Come to Houston." *Southwestern Historical Quarterly* 64 (July 1960): 42–63.

Muñoz, Carlos, Jr. *Youth, Identity, Power: The Chicano Movement.* London: Verso, 1989.

National Catholic Welfare Conference. *The Spanish Speaking of the Southwest and West, Second Report.* Washington, D.C.: National Catholic Welfare Conference, n.d.

National Conference of Catholic Bishops. *Hispanic Ministry: Three Major Documents.* Washington, D.C.: United States Catholic Conference, 1995.

Neal, Marie Augusta. *From Nuns to Sisters: An Expanding Vocation.* Mystic, CT: Twenty-Third Publications, 1990.

Nelson-Cisneros, Victor B. "La clase trabajadora en tejas, 1920–1940." *Aztlán* (Summer 1975): 239–65.

Newman, Harvey K. "God and the Growth Machine." *Review of Religious Research* 32 (March 1991): 237–43.

New Mexico Historical Review 67 (October 1992). Issue on religion.

O'Brien, David J. "The American Priest and Social Action." In *The Catholic Priest in the United States: Historical Investigations,* edited by John Tracy Ellis, 423–69. Collegeville, MN: Saint John's University Press, 1971.

Olson, James S. *Catholic Immigrants in America.* Chicago: Nelson-Hall, 1987.

O'Neill, William L. *Coming Apart: An Informal History of America in the 1960s.* New York: New York Times Books, 1971.

Orsi, Robert A. " 'He Keeps Me Going': Women's Devotion to Saint Jude and the Dialectics of Gender in American Catholicism, 1929–1965." In *Belief in History: Innovative Approaches to European and American Religion,* edited by Thomas Kselman, 137–69. Notre Dame, IN: University of Notre Dame Press, 1991.

——. *The Madonna of 115th Street: Faith and Community in Italian Harlem, 1880–1950.* New Haven, CT: Yale University Press, 1985.

——. "The Religious Boundaries of an Inbetween People: Street *Feste* and the Problem of the Dark-Skinned Other in Italian Harlem, 1920–1990." *American Quarterly* 44 (September 1992): 313–47.

——. "What Did Women Think They Were Doing When They Prayed to Saint Jude?" *U.S. Catholic Historian* 8 (Winter / Spring 1989): 67–79.

Patrick, Anne E. "Women and Religion: A Survey of Significant Literature, 1965–1974." *Theological Studies* 36 (December 1975): 737–65.

Pérez, Arturo. *Popular Catholicism: A Hispanic Perspective.* Washington, D.C.: Pastoral Press, 1988.

Pérez, Lisandro. "Cuban Catholics in the United States." In *Puerto Rican and Cuban Catholics in the U.S., 1900–1965,* edited by Jay P. Dolan and Jaime R. Vidal, 145–208. Notre Dame, IN: University of Notre Dame Press, 1994.

Perrett, Geoffrey. *Days of Sadness, Years of Triumph: The American People, 1939–1945.* Madison: University of Wisconsin Press, 1985.

Pizaña, Reverend Alberto. "Hispanic Baptists in Houston." In *Hispanics in Houston and Harris County, 1519–1986,* edited by Dorothy F. Caram, Anthony G. Dworkin, and Néstor Rodríguez, 95–97. Houston, TX: privately printed, 1963.

Poyo, Gerald E. " 'Integration Without Assimilation': Cuban Catholics in Miami, 1960–1980." *U.S. Catholic Historian* 20 (Fall 2002): 91–109.

Poyo, Gerald E., and Gilberto M. Hinojosa. "Spanish Texas and Borderlands Historiography in Transition: Implications for United States History." *Journal of American History* 75 (September 1988): 393–416.

Privett, Stephen A. *The U.S. Catholic Church and Its Hispanic Members: The Pastoral Vision of Archbishop Robert E. Lucey.* San Antonio, TX: Trinity University Press, 1988.

Quiñónez, Lora Ann, and Mary Daniel Turner. *The Transformation of American Catholic Sisters*. Philadelphia: Temple University Press, 1992.

Raboteau, Albert J. "The Black Church: Continuity Within Change." In *Altered Landscapes: Christianity in America, 1935–1985*, edited by David W. Lotz, 77–91. Grand Rapids, MI: Eerdmans, 1989.

——. *Slave Religion: The "Invisible Institution" in the Antebellum South*. New York: Oxford University Press, 1978.

Redfern, Bernice. *Women of Color in the United States: A Guide to the Literature*. New York: Garland, 1988.

Reed, S. G. *A History of the Texas Railroads and Transportation Conditions under Spain and Mexico and the Republic and the State*. Houston, TX: St. Clair, 1941.

Reed-Danahay, Deborah. "Talking about Resistance: Ethnography and Theory in Rural France." *Anthropological Quarterly* 66 (4): 221–29.

Reisler, Mark. *By the Sweat of Their Brow*. Westport, CT: Greenwood Press, 1976.

Rhinehart, Marilyn D., and Thomas H. Kreneck. " 'In the Shadow of Uncertainty': Texas Mexicans and Repatriation in Houston During the Great Depression." *Houston Review* 10 (1988): 21–33.

——. "The Minimum Wage March of 1966: A Case Study in Mexican-American Politics, Labor, and Identity." *Houston Review* 11 (1989): 27–44.

Riebe-Estrella, Gary. "Strategies on the Left: Catholics and Race." In *What's Left? Liberal American Catholics*, edited by Mary Jo Weaver, 205–19. Bloomington: Indiana University Press, 1999.

Rivera, Julius. "Power and Symbol in the Chicano Movement." *Humanity and Society* (February 1978): 1–17.

Rodríguez, Edmundo, S.J. "The Hispanic Community and Church Movements: Schools of Leadership." In *Hispanic Catholic Culture in the U.S.: Issues and Concerns*, edited by Jay P. Dolan and Allan Figueroa Deck, 206–39. Notre Dame, IN: University of Notre Dame Press, 1994.

Rodríguez, Jeanette. *Our Lady of Guadalupe: Faith and Empowerment among Mexican American Women*. Austin: University of Texas Press, 1994.

Rodríguez, Néstor. "Hispanic and Asian Immigration Waves in Houston." In *Religion and the New Immigrants: Continuities and Adaptation in Immigrant Congregations*, edited by Helen Rose Ebaugh and Janet Saltzman Chafetz, 29–42. Walnut Creek, CA: AltaMira Press, 2000.

Rogers, Mary Beth. *Cold Anger: A Story of Faith and Power Politics*. Denton: University of North Texas, 1990.

Rogers, Sr. Mary Helen. "The Role of Our Lady of Guadalupe Parish in the Adjust-

ment of the Mexican Community to Life in the Indiana Harbor Area, 1940–
1951." In *Forging a Community: The Latino Experience in Northwest Indiana, 1919–
1975*, edited by James B. Lane and Edward J. Escobar, 187–200. Chicago: Cattails
Press, 1987.

Romano, Octavio. "Charismatic Medicine, Folk-Healing, and Folk-Sainthood."
American Anthropologist 67 (1965): 1151–73.

Romero, C. Gilbert. *Hispanic Devotional Piety: Tracing the Biblical Roots*. Maryknoll,
NY: Orbis Books, 1991.

Romero, Juan. "Charism and Power: An Essay on the History of PADRES." *U.S. Catholic Historian* 9 (Spring 1990): 147–63.

Romo, Ricardo. *East Los Angeles: History of a Barrio*. Austin: University of Texas
Press, 1983.

———. "Responses to Mexican Immigration, 1910–1930." *Aztlán* 6 (Summer 1975):
173–94.

Rosales, Francisco A. "Mexican-Americans in Houston: The Boomtown's Stepchild
Society." In *Invisible in Houston*, edited by Thomas H. Kreneck, 7–15. Houston,
TX: Houston Public Library, 1978.

———. "The Mexican Immigrant Experience in Chicago, Houston, and Tucson:
Comparisons and Contrasts." In *Houston: A Twentieth-Century Urban Frontier*, edited by Francisco A. Rosales and Barry J. Kaplan, 58–77. Port Washington, NY:
Associated Faculty Press, 1983.

———. "Shifting Self Perceptions and Ethnic Consciousness among Mexicans in
Houston, 1918–1946." *Aztlán* 16 (1987): 71–94.

Rossi, Reverend Frank H., and Lisa May, eds. *Recall, Rejoice, Renew: The Diocese of
Galveston-Houston, 1847–1997*. Dallas, Tex: Diocese of Galveston-Houston, [1997].

Royce, Anya Peterson, *Ethnic Identity*. Bloomington: University of Indiana Press,
1982.

Sánchez, George J. *Becoming Mexican American: Ethnicity, Culture, and Identity in Chicano Los Angeles, 1900–1945*. New York: Oxford University Press, 1993.

Sánchez, José M. *Anticlericalism: A Brief History*. Notre Dame, IN: University of
Notre Dame Press, 1972.

Sandoval, Moisés, ed. *Fronteras: A History of the Latin American Church in the USA
Since 1513*. San Antonio: Mexican American Cultural Center, 1983.

———. "Effects of World War II on the Hispanic People." In *Fronteras: A History of the
Latin American Church in the USA Since 1513*, edited by Moisés Sandoval, 341–76.
San Antonio: Mexican American Cultural Center, 1983.

———. *On the Move: A History of the Hispanic Church in the United States*. Maryknoll,
NY: Orbis Books, 1990.

———. "The Organization of a Hispanic Church." In *Hispanic Catholic Culture in the U.S.: Issues and Concerns*, edited by Jay P. Dolan and Allan Figueroa Deck, 131–65. Notre Dame, IN: University of Notre Dame Press, 1994.

San Miguel, Guadalupe, Jr. *Brown, Not White: School Integration and the Chicano Movement in Houston*. University of Houston Series in Mexican American Studies, no. 3. College Station: Texas A&M University Press, 2001.

———. *Let All of Them Take Heed: Mexican Americans and the Campaign for Educational Equality in Texas, 1910–1981*. Austin: University of Texas Press, 1987.

Saragoza, Alex M. "The Significance of Recent Chicano-Related Historical Writing: An Appraisal." *Ethnic Affairs* 1 (Fall 1987): 24–62.

Scott, George M. "A Resynthesis of the Primordial and Circumstantial Approaches to Ethnic Group Solidarity: Towards an Explanatory Model." *Ethnic and Racial Studies* 13 (April 1990): 147–71.

Scott, James C. *Weapons of the Weak: Everyday Forms of Peasant Resistance*. New Haven, CT: Yale University Press, 1985.

Shaw, Stephen J. *The Catholic Parish as a Way-Station of Ethnicity and Americanization: Chicago's Germans and Italians, 1903–1939*. Brooklyn, NY: Carlson, 1991.

Shelton, Beth Anne, et al., *Houston: Growth and Decline in a Sunbelt Boomtown*. Philadelphia: Temple University Press, 1989.

Sheridan, Thomas E. *Los Tucsonenses: The Mexican Community in Tucson, 1854–1941*. Tucson: University of Arizona Press, 1986.

Simon, Rev. Alphonse. *Pastoral Spanish*. 3d ed. San Antonio: Artes Gráficas, 1964.

Simons, Helen, and Roni Morales. "Churches, Chapels, and Shrines: Expressions of Hispanic Catholicism in Texas." In *Hispanic Texas: A Historical Guide*, edited by Helen Simons and Cathryn A. Hoyt, 107–18. Austin: University of Texas Press, 1992.

Sitton, Thad, and James H. Conrad. *Nameless Towns: Texas Sawmill Communities, 1880–1942*. Austin: University of Texas Press, 1998.

Smith, Timothy L. "Lay Initiatives in the Religious Life of American Immigrants, 1880–1950." In *Religion in American Life*, edited by John M. Mulder and John F. Wilson, 358–78. Englewood Cliffs, NJ: Prentice-Hall, 1978.

———. "Religion and Ethnicity in America." *American Historical Review* 83 (December 1978): 1155–85.

Sorrell, Richard S. "The *Survivance* of French Canadians in New England (1865–1930): History, Geography and Demography as Destiny." *Ethnic and Racial Studies* 4 (January 1981): 91–109.

Stagner, Stephen. "Epics, Science, and the Lost Frontier: Texas Historical Writing, 1836–1936." *Western Historical Quarterly* 12 (April 1981): 165–81.

Stevens-Arroyo, Anthony M. "The Emergence of a Social Identity among Latino Catholics: An Appraisal." In *Hispanic Catholic Culture in the U.S.: Issues and Concerns*, edited by Jay P. Dolan and Allan Figueroa Deck, 77–130. Notre Dame, IN: University of Notre Dame Press, 1994.

Stevens-Arroyo, Anthony M., and Gilbert R. Cadena, eds. *Old Masks, New Faces: Religion and Latino Identities*. New York: Bildner Center, 1994.

Stevens-Arroyo, Anthony M., and Ana María Díaz-Stevens, eds. *An Enduring Flame: Studies on Latino Popular Religiosity*. New York: Bildner Center, 1994.

Stevens-Arroyo, Anthony M., and Andrés I. Pérez y Mena, eds. *Enigmatic Powers: Syncretism with African and Indigenous Peoples' Religions among Latinos*. New York: Bildner Center, 1994.

Stewart, Kenneth L., and Arnoldo De León. *Not Room Enough: Mexicans, Anglos, and Socioeconomic Change in Texas, 1850–1900*. Albuquerque: University of New Mexico Press, 1993.

Stoddard, Ellwyn R. *Mexican Americans*. New York: Random House, 1973.

Stout, Harry S. "Ethnicity: The Vital Center of Religion in America." *Ethnicity* 2 (1975): 204–24.

Sweeney, Judith. "Chicana History: A Review of the Literature." In *Essays on La Mujer*, edited by Rosaura Sánchez and Rosa Martínez Cruz, 99–123. Los Angeles: University of California at Los Angeles Chicano Studies Center, 1977.

Sylvest, Edwin E., Jr. "Hispanic American Protestantism in the United States." In *Fronteras: A History of the Latin American Church in the USA Since 1513*, edited by Moisés Sandoval, 279–338. San Antonio: Mexican American Cultural Center, 1983.

Tafolla, Carmen. "The Church in Texas." In *Fronteras: A History of the Latin American Church in the USA Since 1513*, edited by Moisés Sandoval, 183–94. San Antonio: Mexican American Cultural Center, 1983.

——. "The Expansion of the Church in Texas." In *Fronteras: A History of the Latin American Church in the USA Since 1513*, edited by Moisés Sandoval, 225–37. San Antonio: Mexican American Cultural Center, 1983.

Takaki, Ronald. *Iron Cages: Race and Culture in Nineteenth-Century America*. New York: Knopf, 1979.

Tarango, Yolanda, C.C.V.I. "The Hispanic Woman and Her Role in the Church." *New Theology Review* 3 (November 1990): 56–61.

Taves, Ann. *The Household of Faith: Roman Catholic Devotions in Mid-Nineteenth-Century America*. Notre Dame, IN: University of Notre Dame, 1986.

Taylor, Paul S. *An American-Mexican Frontier: Nueces County, Texas*. Chapel Hill: University of North Carolina Press, 1934.

Taylor, William B. "The Virgin of Guadalupe in New Spain: An Inquiry into the Social History of Marian Devotion." *American Ethnologist* 14 (February 1987): 9–33.

Tentler, Leslie W. "On the Margins: The State of American Catholic History." *American Quarterly* 45 (March 1993): 104–27.

Thompson, Margaret Susan. "Women, Feminism, and the New Religious History: Catholic Sisters as a Case Study." In *Belief and Behavior: Essays in the New Religious History*, edited by Philip R. Vandermeer and Robert P. Swierenga, 136–63. New Brunswick, NJ: Rutgers University Press, 1991.

Tilly, Charles. "Transplanted Networks." In *Immigration Reconsidered: History, Sociology, and Politics*, edited by Virginia Yans-McLaughlin, 79–95. New York: Oxford University Press, 1990.

Torres, Olga Beatriz. *Memorias de mi viaje / Recollections of My Trip*. Trans. Juanita Luna-Lawhn. Albuquerque: University of New Mexico Press, 1994.

Treviño, Roberto R. "*Prensa y Patria*: The Spanish-Language Press and the Biculturation of the Tejano Middle Class, 1920–1940." *Western Historical Quarterly* 22 (November 1991): 451–72.

Trotter, Robert T., II, and Juan Antonio Chavira. *Curanderismo: Mexican-American Folk Healing*. Athens: University of Georgia Press, 1981.

Tweed, Thomas A. *Our Lady of the Exile: Diasporic Religion at a Cuban Catholic Shrine in Miami*. New York: Oxford University Press, 1997.

Ueda, Reed. *Postwar Immigrant America: A Social History*. Boston: Bedford St. Martin's Press, 1994.

Valdés, Dennis Nodín. *Al Norte: Agricultural Workers in the Great Lakes Region, 1917–1970*. Austin: University of Texas Press, 1991.

Valdez, Sr. Mary Paul. *The History of the Missionary Catechists of Divine Providence*. N.p.: Missionary Catechists of Divine Providence, 1978.

Vandermeer, Philip R., and Robert P. Swierenga. *Belief and Behavior: Essays in the New Religious History*. New Brunswick, NJ: Rutgers University Press, 1991.

———. "Introduction: Progress and Prospects in the New Religious History." In *Belief and Behavior: Essays in the New Religious History*, edited by Philip R. Vandermeer and Robert P. Swierenga, 1–14. New Brunswick, NJ: Rutgers University Press, 1991.

Vidal, Jaime R. "Citizens Yet Strangers: The Puerto Rican Experience." In *Puerto Rican and Cuban Catholics in the U.S., 1900–1965*, edited by Jay P. Dolan and Jaime R. Vidal, 9–143. Notre Dame, IN: University of Notre Dame Press, 1994.

Von de Mehden, Fred R., ed. *The Ethnic Groups of Houston*. Houston, TX: Rice University Studies, 1984.

Walsh, Arlene M. Sánchez. *Latino Pentecostal Identity: Evangelical Faith, Self, and Society.* New York: Columbia University Press, 2003.

Warren, Mark R. *Dry Bones Rattling: Community Building to Revitalize American Democracy.* Princeton, NJ: Princeton University Press, 2001.

Waters, Mary C. *Ethnic Options: Choosing Identities in America.* Berkeley and Los Angeles: University of California Press, 1990.

Waugh, Julia Nott. *The Silver Cradle.* Austin: University of Texas Press, 1955.

Weber, David J. *The Mexican Frontier, 1821–1846.* Albuquerque: University of New Mexico Press, 1982.

Weeks, O. Douglas. "The League of United Latin American Citizens: A Texas-Mexican Civic Organization." *Southwestern Political and Social Science Quarterly* 10 (December 1929): 257–78.

West, John O. *Mexican-American Folklore.* Little Rock, AR: August House, 1988.

White, Joseph M. "Historiography of Catholic Immigrants and Religion." *Immigration History Newsletter* 14 (1982): 5–11.

Williams, Brett. "Why Migrant Women Feed Their Husbands Tamales: Foodways as a Basis for a Revisionist View of Tejano Family Life." In *Ethnic and Regional Foodways in the United States: The Performance of Group Identity,* edited by Linda Keller Brown and Kay Mussell, 113–26. Knoxville: University of Tennessee Press, 1984.

Williams, Norma. *The Mexican American Family: Tradition and Change.* Dix Hill, NY: General Hall, 1990.

Williams, Peter W. *Popular Religion in America.* Englewood Cliffs, NJ: Prentice-Hall, 1980.

Wolf, Eric. "The Virgin of Guadalupe: A Mexican National Symbol." *Journal of American Folklore* 71 (1958): 34–39.

Woods, Sr. Frances J. *Mexican Ethnic Leadership in San Antonio, Texas.* Washington, D.C.: Catholic University of America Press, 1949.

Work Projects Administration. *Houston: A History and Guide.* Houston, TX: Anson Jones Press, 1942.

Wright, Robert E. "If It's Official, It Can't Be Popular? Reflections on Popular and Folk Religion." *Journal of Hispanic / Latino Theology* 1 (May 1994): 47–67.

Wuthnow, Robert, et al. "Sources of Personal Identity: Religion, Ethnicity, and the American Cultural Situation." *Religion and American Culture* 2 (Winter 1992): 1–22.

Zamora, Emilio. "The Failed Promise of Wartime Opportunity for Mexicans in the Texas Oil Industry." *Southwestern Historical Quarterly* 95 (January 1992): 323–50.

———. *The World of the Mexican Worker in Texas*. College Station: Texas A&M University Press, 1993.

Zikmund, Barbara Brown. "Women and the Churches." In *Altered Landscapes: Christianity in America, 1935–1985*, edited by David W. Lotz, 125–39. Grand Rapids, MI: Eerdmans, 1989.

Zinn, Maxine Baca. "Chicano Family Research: Conceptual Distortions and Alternative Directions." *Journal of Ethnic Studies* 7 (Fall 1979): 59–71.

DISSERTATIONS, THESES, REPORTS, AND UNPUBLISHED PAPERS

Chandler, Ray Charles. "The Mexican-American Protest Movement in Texas." Ph.D. diss., Tulane University, 1968.

Cohen, Joan Hart. "To See Christ in Our Brothers: The Role of the Texas Roman Catholic Church in the Río Grande Valley Farm Workers' Movement, 1966–1967." Master's thesis, University of Texas, Arlington, 1974.

Flores, Bishop P. F. "Mission and Vision, Mexican-American Apostolate." Typewritten manuscript [photocopy].

Houston Council on Human Relations. *The Black / Mexican-American Project Report*. Houston, TX: Houston Council on Human Relations, 1972.

Hurtado, Juan. "An Attitudinal Study of Social Distance Between the Mexican American and the Church." Ph.D. diss., United States International University, San Diego, 1975.

Medina, Lara. "Las Hermanas: Chicana / Latina Religious-Political Activism, 1971–1997." Ph.D. diss., Claremont Graduate University, 1998.

O'Loughlin, S. Raphael. "An Overview of the Basilian Fathers' Apostolate among the Spanish-Speaking." 1986. Typewritten manuscript [photocopy].

Pulido, Alberto L. "Race Relations Within the American Catholic Church: An Historical and Sociological Analysis of Mexican American Catholics." Ph.D. diss., University of Notre Dame, 1989.

Rodríguez, Jeanette. "The Impact of Our Lady of Guadalupe on the Psychosocial and Religious Development of Mexican-American Women." Ph.D. diss., Graduate Theological Union, 1990.

Schuler, Sr. M. Lucinda, and Sr. M. Rachel Moreno, comps. "History of Our Lady of Guadalupe School." Typewritten manuscript [photocopy].

Soto, Antonio R. "The Chicano and the Church in Northern California, 1848–1978: A Study of an Ethnic Minority Within the Roman Catholic Church." Ph.D. diss., University of California, Berkeley, 1978.

Treviño, Roberto R. *"La Fe*: Catholicism and Mexican Americans in Houston, 1911–1972." Ph.D. diss., Stanford University, 1993.

Turner, Kay Frances. "Mexican-American Women's Home Altars: The Art of Relationship." Ph.D. diss., University of Texas, Austin, 1990.

Tweed, Thomas A. "Diaspora Nationalism and Urban Landscape: Cuban Immigrants at a Catholic Shrine in Miami." Working Paper Series, no. 3. Cushwa Center for the Study of American Catholicism, University of Notre Dame, 1995.

Walsh, Br. Albeus. "The Work of the Catholic Bishops' Committee for the Spanish Speaking in the United States." Master's thesis, University of Texas, Austin, 1952.

Wright, Robert E. "Popular and Official Religiosity: A Theoretical Analysis and a Case Study of Laredo–Nuevo Laredo, 1755–1857." Ph.D. diss., Graduate Theological Union, 1992.

INDEX

by Bishop Lucey and BCSS, 172; seek church support, 177; supported by Catholic clergy, 192, 196–97, 199. *See also* Minimum Wage March

Feasts, 78; in pre-Tridentine Catholicism, 23; of Our Lady of Guadalupe, 44, 46–47; of St. James, 76; of St. John, 76

Federación de Sociedades Mexicanas y Latino Americanas (Federation of Mexican and Latin American Organizations), 164

Férnandez, Arturo, 41

Fiestas Patrias, 125

Fiorenza, Joseph A., 213

Fire of 1912, 129

First Communion, 64, 106–7

Flores, Patricio, 40, 161, 194; first Mexican American bishop, 51; and Mariachi Mass, 61; on importance of Baptism to Mexican Catholics, 62; and *cursillos*, 72, 235 (n. 90); and St. Joseph–St. Stephen controversy, 144, 146; and local Committee for the Spanish-Speaking, 172–74, 182; and first *encuentro*, 202

Foley, Neil, 83

Foreign-language parishes. *See* National parishes

Forrest Hill (subdivision), 86

Fund-raising. *See* Parishes: fund-raising for

Gallagher, Nicholas A., 85, 104, 105, 107, 161

Gallardo, Gloria, 40, 101, 183, 193, 202

Gangs. *See* Juvenile delinquency

García, Angie, 3, 4

García, Dominic, 112

García, Esther, 60, 64, 65, 77

García, María Cristina, 166

Garza, Adolfo, 47

Garza, Eloisa, 55

Gender, 7, 10; and inequality of women, 52, 55, 57; and empowered domesticity versus the María paradox, 57–59; and participation in parish organizations, 68–69; and *cursillos*, 73; and nun-priest disputes, 158; and oppression of women, 178–79. *See also* Catholic sisters: and maternal feminism; Home altars; *Quinceañeras*; *Tamaladas*

GI generation, 73

Gómez, José, 111

Gonzales, Antonio, 187, 196, 197–99, 266 (n. 64). *See also* Minimum Wage March

Gonzales, Aurora, 141

Gonzales, Joe, 60

Gonzales, Rodolfo "Corky," 38

González, Henry B., 177

Grape boycott, 192

Great Depression, 34–35, 109, 127, 163

Guadalupana Society. *See* Our Lady of Guadalupe Society

Guatemala, 207

Guillén, Petra, 28, 31, 49, 53, 56, 111, 157, 208

Gutiérrez, José Ángel, 38

Gutiérrez, William, 178

Hamilton, Agnes, 133

Head Start Program, 174

Hennessy, Thomas, 103